UFO

CHARLES E. SELLIER

WITH JOE MEIER

CB

CONTEMPORARY BOOKS

Library of Congress Cataloging-in-Publication Data

Sellier, Charles E.
    UFO / Charles Sellier and Joe Meier.
       p.   cm.
    Includes index.
    ISBN 0-8092-3137-9 (cloth), 0-8092-2946-3 (paper)
      1. Unidentified flying objects—Sightings and encounters.
2. Life on other planets.   3. Human-alien encounters.
I. Meier, Joe.   II. Title.
TL789.S325   1997
001.942—dc21   97-401

                              CIP

The Operation Majestic 12 briefing document appears courtesy of
Stanton T. Friedman.

Interior design by Mary Ballachino

Published by Contemporary Books
An imprint of NTC/Contemporary Publishing Company
4255 West Touhy Avenue, Lincolnwood (Chicago), Illinois 60646-1975 U.S.A.
Printed in the United States of America
International Standard Book Number: 0-8092-3137-9 (cloth)
                                  0-8092-2946-3 (paper)

17   16   15   14   13   12   11   10   9   8   7   6   5   4   3   2   1

CONTENTS

PREFACE

In over twenty years as a writer, researcher, and filmmaker, I have made an important discovery that I have come to accept as one of life's absolutes—*Truth has a life of its own.*

No matter where it is hidden, how deeply it is buried, how it is dismantled or covered with ridicule, at some point and usually in some unexpected way the truth will emerge.

My experience with this concept began when, as a young and ambitious writer, I undertook a study of the assassination of Abraham Lincoln. With hundreds of books in print covering every aspect of this great man's life and death, could there be anything left to say? But certain anomalies in the story engaged my interest. These were off-beat tales about the assassination that were not part of the public record but that, nevertheless, kept cropping up ever since that fateful night at Ford's Theatre. These stories suggested that maybe the assassination didn't happen the way the history books said it did or that people other than John Wilkes Booth might have been involved.

No one in official circles paid much attention. The stories were widely and officially discredited; but over the years they refused to go away. Slowly, almost inevitably, I came to the conclusion that all of them deserved a closer look.

When I started my research in 1972, I discovered, to my total amazement, that the U.S. government still had documents, photographs, and pertinent testimony marked, *"Classified."* It had been well over a century since the assassination and a U.S. citizen still could not find out what actually happened to one of our greatest presidents.

What I had thought would be a project of a few months

turned into three years of research. Despite the fact that five generations had come and gone, I was forced to sue the government under the Freedom of Information Act, in order to get access to important documents and photographs.

Finally *The Lincoln Conspiracy* was published. The result, in addition to enormous personal satisfaction, was an honorary degree from Lincoln Memorial University. It was awarded, the university officials said, for my efforts in "uncovering the true story of the events surrounding Lincoln's death." It was a story quite different from the chronicle of events given to the public at the time of the assassination and maintained as "fact" up to the book's publication.

For over a hundred years the government had kept the truth "classified." The implications of that blew my mind. Why? How many other truths has the government swept under this convenient and all-encompassing rug?

My company went on to other projects, and from time to time our research uncovered the concept of extraterrestrial visitations in some highly unlikely places—the captain's log of Christopher Columbus, for example, that spoke of strange lights in the night sky. Certain paleolithic cave paintings discovered in Italy and France look for all the world like a modern astronaut, complete with a space suit and helmet. In every instance we found that there were "officials" or "scholars" ready to block access to "classified" information or, failing that, discredit any suggestion that an extraterrestrial connection had any validity. I quickly realized that the whole business of unidentified flying objects, UFOs, to use the modern shorthand, was getting the same treatment I had encountered with the Lincoln project.

There was a difference, however. When it came to UFOs and extraterrestrials, the opposition and obfuscation were much more intense. Having worked with Erich Von Däniken on his amazingly popular *Chariots of the Gods*, I was stunned by the wide diversity and intensity of his critics, even in the face of almost universal public interest in his work.

The book, and later a motion picture of the same name, purported to show a visual link between certain archaeological artifacts and well-known stories of extraterrestrial visitors to Earth. In some cases the correlation was to events in our own space program. Von Däniken was the first author to couch the subject in scientific terms, an accomplishment that I found personally compelling but which seemed to enrage the scientific community. I concluded that the difference had to do with the fact that we were not dealing with a long-dead president, but rather with events that were going on around us every day—events that could and perhaps already have begun to reshape our lives.

So far, in spite of a concerted effort by not only the U.S. government, but other governments worldwide to discredit the whole notion of unidentified flying objects; in spite of the ridicule heaped on anyone who even hints they may have seen something remotely resembling a UFO; in spite of official debunkings and even threats, people still step out of the shadows of their own fear to tell their amazing stories. Sometimes these stories are funny, sometimes they are filled with terror, and sometimes they are told in an average, run-of-the-mill, "guess what happened to me," sort of way. Whatever their nature, they continue to pour forth.

If anything, the controversy surrounding UFOs is becoming more heated. Some eyewitnesses are now confirming that the real threat has involved our own military who would show up at a site, take possession of all the evidence, and threaten anyone who talked about what they had seen. (The Roswell and Kecksburg incidents are important examples.) Yet even as reports of these threats are circulated, more people come forward with tales of seeing not only the craft, but various types of aliens as well. We're not entirely sure why people are so willing to tell their stories now. They may feel there is safety in numbers, or perhaps they have less fear of being ridiculed as more voices join the chorus of those who claim to have been part of these extraordinary events. One eyewitness to the events at Roswell, for example, saw a story about captured aliens in a supermarket tabloid. He was a former U.S. Army Air Corps pilot who had kept his silence for forty years, but now he picked up the paper and handed it to his wife. "If they're printing it in the paper," he said, "I guess it's all right to tell you. It's all true. I'm the pilot who flew the wreckage to Wright Field."

Whatever the reason for this upsurge of reports, it is undeniably taking place. We have become a society less tolerant of government secrecy and intimidation and more tolerant of those who have the courage to speak out.

It is this atmosphere of growing controversy, heated debate, new and more elaborate stories about UFOs and their occupants, and the consistent, almost cavalier way the government and media tended to dismiss the matter that made me decide to do a more detailed study of the phenomenon.

As a result, four years ago I and several of my colleagues began a quiet but intensive research program into the subject of UFOs. We wanted to examine every angle, every facet of the controversy. Rather than focus on a single subject, such as "abductions" or "crop circles," we determined to try to incorporate the entire landscape. We hoped that by examining everything, we could detect any consistencies or inconsistencies that might escape a more narrow view. One thing we discovered very quickly was that the discussion was now being conducted in a much larger arena.

Recently a symposium was organized to examine in detail stories of people who claimed they were abducted by alien beings and taken aboard some strange aircraft from another world. Ten years ago, maybe even five, all of these stories were being dismissed with a sneer, or at the very least with good-natured derision. But this symposium was held at the prestigious Massachusetts Institute of Technology and hosted by Pulitzer Prize–winning author, Dr. John Mack. We were left with the unmistakable impression that the thousands of stories about unidentified flying objects, their occupants, and their activities are no longer being relegated to the realms of supermarket tabloids and cult magazines.

For reasons that will become clear, this subject has held a fascination for me. As we put the project in motion, the only thing I was sure of was that the truth, the real truth, had yet to surface. Somewhere there was a thread that with a tiny pull would start the process of unraveling decades, perhaps even centuries of fear, half-truths, and outright lies.

Let me assure you, there is no lack of material. During the course of our investigation, we have pored over thousands of documents, interviewed hundreds of witnesses, consulted the most widely respected experts, examined a mountain of photographs, and talked one on one with dozens of citizens who are convinced, beyond any shadow of a doubt, that they have seen, touched, or been in the presence of spacecraft and/or aliens from another world. It has been a mammoth undertaking, but I believe this book will provide ample vindication for the effort.

In any event, like the stories surrounding the assassination of Abraham Lincoln, these tales, if tales they are, show no signs of going away. Despite government efforts to suppress them, the number of reported sightings is growing in almost geometric proportions. New eyewitnesses are found, seemingly on a daily basis. Government scientists and former military officers are now willing to speak candidly about their own involvement in what they flatly call elaborate government cover-ups. Some of these reports amount to deathbed confessions. From every state in the union and from people all over the globe, new information is challenging our assumptions and requiring us to ask, what is it about the UFO phenomenon that is so compelling? Why are we still hearing about aliens and flying saucers? Significantly, the questions are being asked by serious scientists and many in the mainstream press as well.

Can these questions be ignored? And if we do ignore them, are we doing so at our own peril?

It is possible to ignore a smoldering volcano so long as it is just smoldering, but once it erupts, it invariably gets your undivided attention. Often those who have turned a deaf ear to the distant rumblings are the first to be swallowed up.

The analogy is not that far-fetched. Indeed, as we will see, one of the reasons given for government secrecy in the matter of aliens and UFOs is the fear that a general acceptance of the notion of "travelers from outer space" will disrupt, perhaps irrevocably destroy, the institutions that hold our societies together.

Will a sudden eruption of truth end life as we know it on our planet? Or is it possible that the scriptures have it right: ". . . the truth will make you free"?

You will, of course, come to your own conclusions about these issues. But one thing we're sure of: this book will bring you closer to the heart of the controversy than you have ever been. It will put you in the room with white-gowned pathologists examining what may be an extraterrestrial life-form. It will let you leaf through a "Cosmic–Top Secret" government report and read tales of ancient astronauts told in the clay tablets of the library of Ninevah. You will travel to the surface of the planet Mars and beyond, and stand next to a 6,000-year-old astronomer who *knew* that the Earth was the seventh planet, counting from the outer rim of our solar system. You will unfold maps of ancient origin that show details of our planet that could not be verified until the modern age of flight, and you will stand in the grand gallery of what may be the world's largest astronomical observatory. We will probe deeper into the vastness of the cosmos and look closer at some of the most controversial accounts of aliens and UFOs than has ever been attempted before.

Whether you come to this discussion as a skeptic or a believer is irrelevant. Your current viewpoint is bound to change in some significant way. New information requires new thinking, and you are about to come face to face with some of the world's most perplexing and long-held secrets.

UFO

CHAPTER 1

SHADOWS IN SPACE

>> For nearly fifty years the secrecy appa-
ratus within the United States
government has kept from the public
UFO and alien-encounter information.

Dr. Brian O'Leary, astronaut

I t was early autumn 1995 when the call came. It must have been a complete surprise to the former military photographer now in his eighties, living in quiet seclusion somewhere in the United States. The caller was looking for film of Elvis Presley.

Ray Santilli, a documentary film producer from London, was putting together a project about rock and roll artists in the military during the '50s. He had collected the names of six former military photographers and was calling each one systematically. We imagine the conversation went something like this:

"Hello, my name is Ray Santilli. I produce documentaries, and your name was given to me as a possible source of army footage from the late forties and early fifties."

"Mr. San-tilli is it?"

"Yes, that's correct. I'm looking specifically for any footage you might have of Elvis Presley or any other rock and roll artists that were in the U.S. Army."

"Yes, I think I may have something like that." He paused and added, "I uh . . . I also filmed other things."

The photographer seemed hesitant to talk, but something in his voice suggested that maybe he didn't want the conversation to end. Santilli, always on the lookout for unique footage of any kind, decided to play a hunch.

"I see. What sort of things did you shoot?"

"I . . . uh . . . I participated in some . . . in several rather unique events."

"During the war, you mean, or after the war?"

"Well, both actually, but it's the uh . . . I mean, after the war I shot some stuff I think maybe you might like to see."

To Santilli it was beginning to sound like this photographer was caught between a rock and a hard place. He obviously had some film he wanted somebody to look at, but for some reason he wasn't sure he should release it. Santilli decided to find out something about the subject matter.

"How long after the war was this film taken?"

"Oh, a couple of years—1947, actually."

Nineteen forty-seven? There was nothing of any real significance going on in 1947 that Santilli was aware of. But something in this man's voice riveted his attention.

"Can you tell me a bit more? How much footage do you have?"

"I'm not sure. At least four rolls, maybe as many as seven or eight." There was a long pause. "I understand if you're not interested."

"No, no. I'm very interested." A short time later Santilli was knocking on the photographer's door.

In fact, Santilli has never made it entirely clear just how he first made contact with the photographer. Based on the events that followed (which we will explore more fully in

Chapter 6), we assume their first conversation was on the telephone. In any case, that initial contact left him curious, perhaps even exhilarated, at the prospect of seeing what the old man had. Something very exciting (he didn't know quite what) was almost within his grasp.

Ray Santilli, documentary producer from London, England, was about to discover the awesome power of the proverbial Pandora's box. By opening that first can of film, he created a firestorm of controversy that blazed across the Internet and aroused the passions of such widely diverse groups as historians, pathologists, forensic scientists, several other movie producers, and UFO experts and researchers around the globe.

According to Santilli, the photographer (whose anonymity Santilli agreed to protect) gave him several small canisters of 16mm film taken as part of a military investigation following the reported crash of an unidentified flying object. The footage was shot in and around Roswell, New Mexico, and, most significantly, at Carswell Air Force Base near Fort Worth, Texas. The latter was, the photographer said, the actual footage he had personally taken of the autopsy of one of the aliens who died in the Roswell crash.[1]

Why had he waited so long to bring it to light? Why now? According to Santilli, who is the only one we know of who has spoken directly to the photographer, it began as a simple oversight and turned into ordinary forgetfulness.

During his time in the service, the photographer said, the person shooting the film also did most of the processing. The photographer had taken many more rolls of film than those still in his possession, but these few had needed some special processing. He had tossed them into a box, intending to take care of it later.

---

[1] *Alien Autopsy: Fact or Fiction?* Vidmark Entertainment, Robert Kiviat, executive producer, 1995.

But life in the army is not always conducive to well-laid plans. A number of years passed before he remembered the small canisters tucked away in a cardboard box in his basement. He got the film out, looked at it, and thought maybe he should try and turn it over to the military. Only by now the government had taken a very firm stand: nothing had crashed at Roswell, New Mexico, in 1947 except a weather balloon. Officially, at least, the issue had been put to rest, and nobody, he reasoned, walks into a cave and kicks a sleeping bear. The film went back into the cardboard box and stayed there for another thirty years.

As to the question of why he chose this particular moment to make the film public, we can only guess. He has insisted on remaining anonymous, so it can't be that he wanted recognition or publicity. Perhaps he detected a mood in the country that suggested people might be more receptive today than in years past, and he wanted to get the matter off his mind. Or maybe he just ran across them the day Santilli called. Only he knows for sure, and so far he isn't talking.

One thing was certain, however. If the film Santilli now had in his possession could be authenticated, he knew it would be the story of the century. But could it be? Nearly fifty years had elapsed since the events on the film had taken place. Was it even *possible* to prove the film was what the photographer claimed it to be? Santilli's solution was simple. Once he obtained the film, he made it available to any expert who had an interest in proving or *disproving* its authenticity. Rather than try to prove the film real or false to the world, the producer would let the world prove it to their own satisfaction.

Already modern filmmakers are at odds with one another over whether this film is a hoax. Veteran military photographers familiar with the equipment of the '40s and '50s claim the camera and film used are entirely consistent with what they had to work with in that era. Experts from

Kodak, the manufacturer of the film, have checked it carefully and have come to the conclusion that the film bears the authentic markings of 16mm celluloid produced during that period.

One expert concludes that if the film is authentic, it should be hailed as a record of one of the most important events in history. If it is not, the "alien autopsy" deserves to be applauded as one of the best and most elaborate hoaxes of all time.

In succeeding chapters we will place before you the testimony of witnesses, investigators, film experts and pathologists. We will examine the U.S. government's position relative to this film, which has become one of the most heated debates in the annals of UFO investigation. And we will talk to those, still living, who were in Roswell, New Mexico, in 1947. Some of them claim they can verify the existence of alien bodies at the crash site. Others claim they not only saw but actually handled the debris. And there are some who actually participated in or had knowledge of what is perhaps the most successful cover-up of all time.

The government, of course, still insists the UFO crash never happened. By the time you finish this book, you will have the information necessary to make up your own mind.

But the puzzle of Roswell is just one of the events, past and present, that we will be examining in the light of new and surprising discoveries that have emerged in recent months, even, in some cases, within recent days.

Many people will remember the unprecedented attempt at cooperation between United States and Soviet space scientists at the very height of the Cold War. Both nations had been trying desperately to reach the planet Mars. A number of attempts by both sides had ended in total failure. There was even talk of a "Galactic Ghoul" guarding the red planet from earthly intrusion. Finally, NASA and its Soviet counterparts broke the ice in the Cold War and set up a joint program to put an unmanned probe (actually two probes,

Phobos 1 and *Phobos 2*) on the planet's surface. *Phobos 1* tripped off into outer space, never to be heard from again; but *Phobos 2* seemed to be on the verge of success. Its sensors and transmitters were working perfectly as it descended toward the frigid crust of the planet. Suddenly, both the American and Soviet scientists monitoring the descent saw an enormous dark shadow come into view on their screens. With amazing speed, it overtook the small probe, and in the blink of an eye, *Phobos 2* fell silent.

At this point the thaw in the Cold War iced up once again. Perhaps the Russians thought the failure was our fault. Maybe we thought it was theirs. Whatever the reasons, neither side was willing to share their theories of why *Phobos 2* had suddenly, inexplicably stopped transmitting data. The "Galactic Ghoul" aside, it does seem odd that so many American and Soviet Mars missions have ended in failure. The "Red Planet" has left space scientists around the globe red-faced time and time again. In any case it's a good bet that the scientific guessing game over what happened to *Phobos 2* will continue.

There was speculation, believed to have come from a Russian source, that the Phobos moon of Mars, thought by many astronomers to be hollow, might actually be artificially made. Was it this "moon" that overtook and destroyed the *Phobos* probe? NASA ignored the discussion, maintaining then, as they do now, that they have no interest in UFOs.

There is, of course, more to the story. You will have the opportunity to examine the most recent documents and photographs from the NASA archives and even some recently released Russian documents. It could be that we still have much to learn from our nearest planetary neighbor.

The Soviet space program, like ours, included highly sophisticated spy satellites. For years the Soviets have had one or more of these devices parked in orbit over the United States. Our government is aware of this and has made adjustments accordingly. For instance, ICBMs have always been buried deep underground, as have several major military installations. The expense of "hardening," or surrounding these facilities in concrete, was enormous but, under the circumstances, probably unavoidable.

Then came the event that took the whole world by surprise. The once impenetrable and immutable Soviet Union split apart, not slowly through painful social and economic change, but virtually overnight in one, giant political crash. Among other things, U.S. scientists learned that the Soviet government had made an impressive study of the UFO phenomenon. The Soviets also believed that the U.S. government was deeply involved in an investigation of its own. If, for example, the U.S. Army Air Corps really believed the crash at Roswell involved a weather balloon, we soon learned that the Soviets did not. Nor did they hesitate to suggest, in official communiqués, that the object could be an alien craft of some sort.

And there was yet another surprise in store for U.S government officials. Residents of Las Vegas, Nevada, tuned in the evening news one night on the local CBS affiliate and saw a mysteriously cloaked individual telling them that the U.S. military not only had alien space craft in their possession, they were actually trying to make them fly. Furthermore, all of this work was taking place just a hundred miles or so to the north at a super-secret base called Area 51.

The source of this information was a man who claimed to be a physicist assigned to work on the propulsion system of these craft. It was his job to try and "back engineer" them; in other words, to find out how the craft worked.

Special lighting kept his features concealed in darkness, and his voice was electronically altered. For eight straight nights, the man, who called himself "Dennis," submitted to questioning from one of the Las Vegas area's leading TV reporters, a man named George Knapp.

The series of special reports touched off a storm of controversy across the country. The Pentagon vigorously, even angrily, denounced the matter as pure hogwash. There was no such place as Area 51. Nevertheless, the Air Force set about acquiring 80,000 acres of public land surrounding an ancient sink known as Groom Lake, in the desert wastes of Nevada. The obvious reason was to prevent thousands of UFO enthusiasts from climbing the surrounding mountains and looking down on the complex. Why shouldn't people want to see for themselves? After all, U.S. citizens were footing the bill for whatever was out there, and "Dennis" had said "real" flying saucers were being operated in the area.

All such reports were roundly ridiculed, but official scorn just seemed to add fuel to the fire. "What was going on in the desert wasteland so close to Las Vegas?" the public wanted to know.

"Nothing," the government replied with finality.

Then came the most recent surprise. A widow, whose husband had worked at this nonexistent base and had died under mysterious circumstances, decided to sue the government for her husband's wrongful death. She alleged that her husband had been required to handle environmentally hazardous material. Not so, replied the Pentagon. The federal court, in a twist worthy of O'Henry, ruled the suit could not proceed unless the official name of the installation was entered into the record. Because the place doesn't exist officially, the legal action has been effectively halted.

Ah, but there's more. Both the Justice Department and the Environmental Protection Agency (EPA) have taken an interest in these proceedings. As this book goes to press, both agencies are considering petitioning the military attaché at the Russian Embassy for . . . you guessed it . . . Soviet satellite photographs of the Area 51 complex. Apparently what U.S. citizens are not allowed to know has been common knowledge in Moscow for years. The EPA contends the photographs will prove once and for all that a highly sophisticated military complex does, in fact, exist in the vast wasteland of the Nevada desert.

George Knapp traveled to Russia not long ago and has seen some of these photographs firsthand. He will share them with you later in this book. In fact, we'll be discussing his involvement with the Area 51 controversy from the very beginning right up to the present. We will also introduce you to the man who called himself "Dennis" and give you information (including his real name) that will help you decide whether his allegations are true.

We'll also give you the frank and sometimes astonishing views of certain Russian officials who participated in the Soviet UFO investigations. For the first time ever, you'll be able to evaluate the involvement of nations other than our own who have maintained a great interest in this ever-growing phenomenon of UFOs.

On the other hand, there may be more here than you care to know. One of the nation's leading "think tanks" has suggested that the general population of the world simply could not deal with the reality that a more advanced civilization from another world exists. You'll meet people who believe this is the reason for the U.S. government's obsession with secrecy.

Perhaps that's a notion worth considering. Could it be that, in spite of our desire to explore space, there is some primal fear of simply admitting someone or *something* besides ourselves exists in the universe? That this knowledge will destroy our dearly held belief system? Is it possible to face the reality of intelligent life from other worlds and still maintain our social, intellectual, and political equilibrium? It may surprise you to know that some of the world's most powerful policy makers are convinced that we cannot.

By the time you complete this book, however, those are questions you should be able to answer, at least to your own satisfaction.

A number of other events have also taken on new significance in recent months that tend to fuel old arguments about extraterrestrial visitors contacting Earth. We'll be presenting the very latest findings on this debate. For example, serious scholars and scientists have speculated about the possibility of life on Mars for hundreds of years. The combined attempt by the U.S. and Soviet space agencies in the 1960s was partially designed to address that issue. Now the question being asked is, has NASA discovered proof of ancient inhabitants on Mars? NASA scientists insist they have *not*, but other scientists who have access to the same data make a strong case for the opposing view. These scientists, by the way, are not backing down in the face of official attempts to discredit their findings. We will speak with them, examine their data, look carefully at the views and arguments on the other side, and present the very latest information for your evaluation.

There is another question of recent origin. Do any of the discoveries on Mars have anything to do with ancient mysteries here on earth? At first glance you would think that there is nothing left to say about the Great Pyramid of Giza in Egypt. The ancient Greek historian Herodotus supposedly settled the matter some 2,500 years ago. He stated that the pyramid was built as the tomb for the Egyptian Pharaoh Khufu. Furthermore, even though the pyramid was already ancient by the time Herodotus visited Egypt, he claimed to know precisely how it was built and stated flatly that its construction took twenty years.

Unfortunately, no mummy was ever found in the Great Pyramid, nor in any other pyramid for that matter. As to the twenty-year time frame, modern construction engineers tell us that in order to meet that requirement, the ancient Egyptians would have had to position one of the gigantic limestone blocks that make up its structure every two minutes, twenty-four hours a day, seven days a week for twenty years. That's something that could not be accomplished even today. How, then, was it built? More to the point, why?

Details of official NASA photographs of Mars suggest the answer may lie somewhere in the ancient Sumerian texts discovered in the ruins of the library of Ninevah. As unlikely as it seems, *Voyager's* race through the solar system and the stunning data being sent back to Earth, may provide proof that the Sumerians were looking at the Great Pyramid thousands of years before the Egyptians even came on the scene. What's more, several credible geologists and archaeologists have recently presented evidence that the Great Pyramid may be 6,000 to 10,000 years older than it was previously thought to be. To the surprise of many, and the chagrin of some, when all of these diverse sources of information, new and old, are brought together, they seem to support one another in startling ways.

Interestingly enough, the Sphinx—the very symbol of silence—may also be contributing to the discussion. The weathering patterns on this giant monument are beginning to speak volumes to both geologists and archaeologists about the age of the structures on the Giza plateau.

Could the pyramids have had some other purpose than burial, a purpose related to extraterrestrials visiting a prehistoric earth? We'll give you a whole new world of possibilities to help you decide.

One of the real difficulties in putting together a book of this kind is overcoming the wall of secrecy and suspicion that has been thrown up around some of the more controversial issues. I am more than just passingly familiar with this particular aspect of the work. In 1979 I began work on a UFO book entitled *Hangar 18*, purported to be the final resting place of the "flying saucers" that crashed near Roswell in 1947. The research was yielding some very interesting information. My company, a subsidiary of Schick Electric Corporation, decided that upon completion of the book we would produce a documentary film based on my findings. Once the decision was made, it seemed prudent to announce that the film was in the works as part of the promotion for the book. Almost immediately my staff and I began receiving calls from people and organizations completely unfamiliar to us. We were asked questions like, what was the scope of the project? What information would we be presenting? Then we discovered that no less than the Department of Defense (Office of Motion Pictures) in Los Angeles was making a concerted effort to obtain a copy of the script—not through my office, mind you, but through the actors and employees involved in the film. Some of our suppliers even reported that they had been asked for a copy of the working script.

Rather than guess what the officials' objective might be, we called them. The official response was that they just wanted to "help." Would we need any of their equipment? Did we want to use any of their people as technical advisors? We assured them we did not. That was not the end of the matter.

Shortly after our conversation with the Defense Department personnel, I began to hear rumors that highly placed government officials were speaking with officers of the parent company that owned Schick. A few weeks later, I was summoned to a board meeting and informed that I could not produce the show as scripted. If we continued with the film, it would have to be done as a fictional drama, *not* a documentary. The pertinent facts and events that we had uncovered were removed from the final script. Now, at long last, we will be able to present that information. You will have the opportunity to take a close-up look not only at the full range of the available data we had at the time, but at the most recent details as well.

We also will show you evidence that this policy of official government secrecy goes back at least as far as the Truman administration. During World War II, both Allied and Axis pilots told stories about the mysterious "foo fighters." These were craft that would pull up alongside military aircraft, follow them for some distance, and then disappear. Our pilots were carefully debriefed on this subject and told not to speak to the press. At first, Allied military officials feared that the Germans had developed aircraft that could literally fly circles around ours. But why didn't they ever take any aggressive action? Following the war it was discovered that German pilots had told the same stories, which their government also kept secret, presumably for the same reasons.

Some researchers suggest that President Truman, on the strength of the Roswell incident in 1947, may have established a top-level group of scientists to monitor and investigate any reports of UFO sightings. The code name for the group was "Majestic," and it consisted of twelve members. Government shorthand being what it is, the name of the group was quickly shortened to MJ–12. The group ostensibly operated under the cloak of deepest secrecy for many years before it was disbanded.

But was it really disbanded? We will interview some researchers who believe the group is still going strong, perhaps stronger than ever before. According to unofficial sources, the new name or designation for this super-secret policy group is PI–40. Does that mean the group has gotten bigger and perhaps more pervasive? Can it be fairly implied from the existing documents and witnesses that some government agency, by whatever name, has for decades set policy and determined all actions taken in regard to UFOs or extraterrestrial anomalies? You will have the opportunity to judge for yourselves.

For the past fifty years, questions like these have been asked only by serious UFO investigators or the more demanding skeptics. There is some indication now that at least a few *officials* are willing to start asking questions of their own. The wraps, if not the wheels, might be coming off of government efforts to keep the public insulated from the UFO phenomenon. Congressman Steven Schiff (D) of New Mexico has requested from the General Accounting Office a complete investigation of the 1947 Roswell crash in New Mexico and of what many say is an ongoing government "cover-up" of the incident. We will share with you what his inquiry has uncovered so far.

A similar request from Senator Diane Feinstein (D) of California has yielded a large cache of documents that refer explicitly to the "MJ–12" committee. You will have an opportunity to view some of those papers.

In 1994, Dr. Brian O'Leary, a former astronaut, was speaking to the International Forum on New Science. Among other things he said:

> For nearly fifty years the secrecy apparatus within the United States government has kept from the public UFO and alien-encounter information. Those who have investigated this hydra-headed beast believe that the 'Cosmic Watergate' of UFOs, aliens, mind control, genetic engineering, free energy, antigravity propulsion, and other secrets will make Watergate or Irangate look like kindergarten exercises. [2]

Even President Clinton is said to be dissatisfied with his own CIA briefings on the subject. Although bringing up the subject of UFOs to the president when he was running for reelection may not have been too productive, the issue may now surface anyway. There are those who believe, unequivocally, that the government policy of secrecy has compromised constitutional guarantees. We'll find out who these people are, examine their views, and see if we can discover what they and perhaps all of us can do about the situation.

Victor Marchetti, former special assistant to the director of the CIA, has given us a glimpse into the government paranoia that has created this smothering blanket of secrecy.

According to Marchetti there are three principal reasons for the "UFO cover-up."

1. "[It is necessary] to maintain a workable stability among the nations of the world . . . the national oli-

---

[2] Richard J. Boylan, *CONCEPTS* (September/October 1995), p. 50.

garchic establishments, even civilization as we now know it, could collapse into anarchy.

2. "The military and intelligence communities must preserve their exclusive access to the wealth of technology possessed by (extraterrestrial) visitors.

3. "Governments, [admitting] that there are beings from outer space . . . with mentalities and technological capabilities obviously far superior to ours, could, once fully perceived by the average person, erode the foundations of the Earth's traditional power structure."[3]

Mr. Marchetti probably felt that he had the best interests of all of us in mind when he formulated those thoughts. But in the final analysis, isn't it just another way of saying that "they," whomever "they" happen to be at any given moment, should be permitted to decide what's best for all of us? Increasingly, however, the citizens of the world seem to be telling their leaders that they feel perfectly capable of deciding such issues for themselves. Besides, if the technology and culture of these visitors is so far ahead of ours, why wouldn't we want to get to know them better?

The second item in Marchetti's explanation does raise some interesting questions. It implies that the military and intelligence communities already have and "must maintain their exclusive access to" alien technology. Could that be interpreted to mean that there really was an alien crash at Roswell and perhaps other places? Does the use of the plural when referring to "communities" suggest that other governments around the world also have captured alien technology? If they don't know what that technology is, how do they know there is a "wealth" of it? Is it possible that our government and other world governments have already made peaceful contact with extraterrestrials and know what's in store for us?

3 Ibid., p. 49.

There's another possibility, one that's been around for a couple of decades but is only now gaining support. This theory, based on written texts of ancient origin, holds that the extraterrestrials are really our benefactors. They have, from time to time, brought us knowledge and otherwise nurtured our existence in the universe. From a scientific point of view, this idea offers some fascinating possibilities that the careful reader will find difficult to dismiss.

In the following chapters, we will open the newest windows of information to give you the clearest possible view of what is currently known, what is conjecture, and what is somebody's SWAG (sophisticated wild ass guess). The distinctions will not always be what you expect them to be. You might even find them a little bit frightening. But that's the risk one takes when seeking to discover the truth. In this regard, we will, to employ an old cliché, leave no stone unturned. Our approach has been that everything, no matter how outlandish it appears on the surface, deserves *serious* consideration. You will have an opportunity to review documents, see the latest physical evidence, and find out what the most active investigations have produced. You will be attending the most recent conferences and conventions with us; and you will be participating in conversations, discussions, and sometimes disagreements with former military officers, government officials, and people who describe themselves as UFOlogists, witnesses, and observers.

Unlike other books that tend to define and deal with only one aspect of the UFO phenomenon, this work embraces a broad universe of thought relative to each of the different areas of our UFO investigation. If UFOs are here, we would like to know where they come from. If there is any way to find out, we will pursue it.

Perhaps the most difficult task will be to try and determine if our extraterrestrial visitors have some purpose in visiting earth. In the next chapter, we will get a firsthand look at a monumental study conducted to investigate that very issue.

At the moment, however, we are like children in the dark, frightened by sights and sounds that we only dimly perceive. Our intention in the following chapters is to illuminate all of the unlit corners of the controversy so that we may look to the stars with clarity . . . unobstructed by fleeting shadows in space.

CHAPTER 2

THE SHAPE OF THINGS TO COME

>> **It is very likely the most single important issue of our time and very likely the most important issue of the human race.**

**Master Sergeant Robert O. Dean,
Supreme Headquarters Allied Powers, Europe**

When orders came reassigning him to Paris, France, in 1963, Master Sergeant Robert O. Dean was delighted. In spite of his youth he was already closing in on twenty-five years in the military, and this was the kind of assignment that made it all worthwhile. For one thing he could bring his wife and children with him. There was a good chance his children could complete their high school requirements in Paris.

When Dean arrived in Paris, he was assigned immediately to Supreme Headquarters Allied Powers of Europe (SHAPE), a sprawling complex located at Raquencourt, just outside of Paris. SHAPE was the military arm of NATO (North Atlantic Treaty Organization), formed after World War II to counter the Soviet Union's bloc of nations, known as the

Warsaw Pact. SHAPE was under the command of General Lyman Lemnitzer. His second in command, though both men carried the same rank of five-star general, was Air Marshall Sir Thomas Pike of the British Royal Air Force. These men were the "front-line" commanders in a cold war that constantly threatened to turn hot. Their thumbs, so to speak, hovered closest to the nuclear button.

Master Sergeant Robert O. Dean knew these facts so he was not surprised that when he reported for duty, he was given a "Cosmic–Top Secret" clearance. It was and is the highest clearance NATO can grant military personnel. Once his clearance was confirmed, he was assigned to the NATO War Room, the planning and strategy room for the Supreme Headquarters Operation Center, or SHOC. It was in this room that Master Sergeant Dean would discover just how close the world was to a nuclear holocaust. He would also learn how several false alarms involving UFOs had brought NATO and the Warsaw Pact nations of the Soviet bloc to the brink of war on more than one occasion.

Those cushy military assignments, while much sought after, always come with a price. In this case the price was twenty-four-hour-a-day operation, seven days a week. There was not a moment, day or night, that SHOC was not manned and ready to go into action. Although it is largely true that the master sergeants do run the day-to-day military operations, not even a ranking sergeant major can get out of some things. This meant that Sergeant Dean would have to take his place in the weekend and overnight rotation schedules.

He quickly settled into the new routine. Then something happened that shook him deeply and changed his life forever. The singular event took place in the pre-dawn hours one morning in 1963. Things had been quiet for several days. No one had spotted any planes flying in or out of anyone's protected air space, and the 2400:00 to 0800:00 detail was a crashing bore. About 4 A.M. the sergeant's head began to droop on his chest. The black coffee was no longer working, and the only noises breaking the silence were the occasional clatter of the teletype machine and a slight rustle of the newspaper that the lieutenant in another corner of the room was reading.

Suddenly Dean was jolted awake by a loud thud on the desk in front of him. Startled, he looked up to see a large, red report on his desk and his captain standing beside him.

"Glance through this," the captain said, indicating the report. "That'll keep you awake."

Sergeant Dean nodded, "Thank you, sir."

He stood up to get the blood circulating in his legs again, picked up his cup, and walked over to the coffee machine. As he turned back to his desk, the cup of coffee stopped halfway to his lips. For the first time he focused on the report the captain had dropped on his desk. It was at least eight inches thick and looked absolutely pristine. That thing can't have been opened more than twice since it was put together, he thought, and I'll bet there's a good reason.

Dean slid back into his chair to take a closer look at the report cover. "*Cosmic–Top Secret*" jumped out at him. Underneath in slightly smaller letters it read "An Assessment," and below that, in brackets, "[An Evaluation of a Possible Military Threat to Allied Forces in Europe.]"

The sergeant looked for the captain, who had gone back to his desk. Dean wanted to make certain this was something he really should be reading. He discovered that the captain was watching him with an almost amused expression.

"Go ahead, read it," the Captain said. "Let me know what you think."

From that moment on, the sergeant's life would never be the same.

As he began poring over the documents contained in the "Assessment" everything and everybody else faded away. All thoughts of sleep vanished, and he began to wonder if he would ever sleep again. By his own account, he felt as if he were caught in a waking nightmare, and before long he realized that his handkerchief was soaked from wiping the sweat from his brow.

Over the next weeks and months Dean was able to get through the entire document, reading and rereading some of its most salient points. The study that formed the basis of the "Assessment" was initiated in 1961 in response to several "brinksmanship" encounters with the Soviets and the Warsaw Pact countries. On these occasions one side or the other would spot groups of objects, flying at high rates of speed, that appeared on their radar. Obviously under intelligent control, these craft would fly across the borders that were supposed to be protected. Each side, of course, thought they belonged to the other side. Anxious thumbs poised above red buttons were often held in check only at the last moment.

These objects, according to the report, would fly at high altitudes and at high rates of speed in close formation. At some point they would turn north of the English Channel and disappear off NATO radar screens somewhere over the Norwegian Sea. The Soviets, convinced they belonged to us, warned of retaliation for these "blatant over-flights." NATO, on the other hand, was just as certain they belonged to the Soviets and warned them not to get cute in European territory. Then someone took a look at what these craft were doing and pointed out to their various commanders that the technology being demonstrated repeatedly in these over-flights was far beyond anything possessed by either NATO or the Soviet bloc.

Air Marshall Sir Thomas Pike, Deputy Supreme Allied Commander in Europe, decided it was time to initiate a study of these aerial phenomena. He directed the study personally, but it is almost certain that he had the full backing of his immediate superior, General Lemnitzer.

Over the next three years Dean would delve into the "Assessment," which contained testimony, interviews, photographs, and in-depth studies by historians, theologians, atmospheric physicists, astronomers, astrophysicists, sociologists, and psychologists. He would learn that these objects were flying over the Soviet Union, Central Europe, and NATO military installations at will—a frightening prospect that neither London nor the United States was willing to acknowledge openly.

The study covered all the areas included in the NATO theater of operations, from Norway south through Turkey and Greece.[1] Only fifteen copies of the "Assessment" were ever produced. Washington and London provided no information for the study because everything given to NATO at the time went directly to Moscow via an enormous French spy ring known as TOPAZ.[2] The ring was later broken up, and it was discovered that a number of French ministers were involved. Whether the discovery of the spy ring had anything to do with the decision, we're not sure. The French government chose this moment to insist SHAPE headquarters be moved from France. As it turned out, one of Dean's last assignments in NATO was to help move SHAPE headquarters to Casteau, near Brussels in Belgium, where it is located to this day.

Master Sergeant Robert O. Dean left the military shortly thereafter with twenty-seven years of service to his country. However, it was not the retirement he had envisioned. For the past thirty years he has devoted his life to making the world aware of what he truly believes are the "facts" about extraterrestrial visitors to Earth.

Why? Why would a man who had majored in ancient history, psychology, and philosophy at Indiana University and completed extensive studies in archaeology and theology want to fly in the face of a skeptical world and incur the wrath of the military he had served so long and so valiantly?

The answer, of course, is the "Assessment."

---

[1] *MUFON Symposium Proceedings* (Seguin, TX: Mutual UFO Network, 1994).
[2] Leon Uris, *TOPAZ* (New York: McGraw-Hill, 1967).

"I read that thing," he told us, "and I've never been quite the same. The old, hard-nosed, crewcut, pragmatic professional soldier realized for the first time that all of this was not science fiction, it wasn't fantasy, it was real. It has launched me on a thirty-year study which I'm still involved with, trying to put together what it really means."

According to Dean, the conclusions of the "Assessment" were "pretty impressive." Those conclusions were:

1. The planet Earth has been the subject of an extensive, massive, and very thorough survey by *several* extraterrestrial civilizations.
2. "They" demonstrated extremely advanced technology, possibly a thousand years or more beyond us.
3. There was a *process* or *plan* of some kind unfolding, as the study demonstrated. One-on-one contact at first, then two or more aliens meeting with us, then several, then "they" would show themselves and their ships to a few dozen people. After that, they would make flyovers, then landings, then they would even seem to pose for photographs.
4. Evidence indicated that this has been going on for several millennia.
5. There did not appear to be a major military threat involved. If "they" were hostile, we could do absolutely nothing about it.[3]

But what could Robert Dean have seen in that study that so thoroughly convinced him it was not "science fiction" and that the conclusions were valid?

According to a paper he delivered at the MUFON (Mutual UFO Network)[4] proceedings near Austin, Texas, in 1994, a conference which we attended, there were photographs of crash retrievals, little bodies, and some limited analysis of

---

[3] MUFON *Symposium Proceedings* (Seguin, TX: Mutual UFO Network, 1994).

"plasti-metals" that military experts didn't seem able to decipher in 1964.

Dean also tells us that, according to the SHAPE "Assessment," humans, or human-looking, aliens had been photographed outside of their ships. They had made contact with farmers, fishermen, and one Italian airman. There were also a number of crash sites identified in the "Assessment," but there were no reports indicating human-looking aliens ever crashed. The only bodies ever recovered from any of the crashes were of the "little grays,"[5] small aliens with grayish skin.

Dean spent literally hundreds of hours reading the "Assessment." During the years he was assigned to SHAPE headquarters, there were many days when he would simply retrieve the document and settle in for an uninterrupted session of reading. According to Dean, the "Assessment" included, among other things, a report of the retrieval of a crashed ninety-foot disk with alien bodies near Bremen, Germany. There was also a report of a Turkish Air Force plane that was being tracked on radar in 1963 when an unidentified craft began following it and "swallowed it up." Search and rescue missions never found a trace of the plane or crew. There were reports of the abduction of humans by alien craft and how the physical characteristics of some of the members of the different civilizations visiting us caused alarm at the Pentagon.[6] Dean said, "I read that thing [and] it launched me . . . on what I call a synthesis, trying to make sense out of what I've learned, trying to put together what it really means. And I have found it to be probably the single most important issue that I have ever been involved with."

Dean is an accomplished public speaker and has spoken

---

[4] *MUFON* is a loosely knit organization of UFO investigators with chapters throughout the U.S. and a number of other countries, which share UFO information for their mutual benefit.

[5] Ibid.

[6] Ibid.

several times at the University of Arizona and is in high demand on local TV stations in Tucson as well as at UFO conferences and symposiums around the world. Usually beginning his story in a quietly engaging manner, he fairly shakes with passion when he warms to the subject. "I must be honest with you," he says, his finger jabbing the air in front of him for emphasis, "and tell you the subject itself, the ramifications of it, the implications of it, are so vast that it is very likely the most single important issue of our time and very likely the most important issue of the human race. And I say that purposely because I'm so convinced that this subject needs to be brought out, the cover-up has got to be removed [so] that the people of this country and the people on this planet can be read into this thing, because eventually it's going to affect the lives of every man, woman, and child on the planet."[7]

Even though he is retired, Dean realizes he is breaking his oath of secrecy under the National Security Act by revealing the contents of a top-secret document that became available to him while he carried a top-secret clearance. So far the government has seemed disinclined to prosecute or even make an issue of it. He also realizes that he is the only one talking about it. That does not deter him in the least.

"It's crucial," he says, "that people start to pay attention, and it's crucial that the government starts to tell us the truth. I'll be frank," Dean continued, "I'm so concerned about the cover-up and the lies because I have seen, and many of my fellow retirees and some of my friends [still] on active duty are convinced, that the lies and the cover-up have literally threatened our constitutional process. That's why I'm involved . . . why I'm speaking out."[8]

Having interviewed Robert Dean in person and having heard him make his impassioned presentation to a number of

---

[7] Robert O. Dean, taped interview, Sun International Pictures, 1995.
[8] Ibid.

groups over the past several years, I find it hard to imagine anyone who really listens to what he has to say not taking him seriously, or at the very least, not believing that *he* takes all of this very seriously. Why then, one wonders, hasn't someone in the government made some effort to keep him quiet? That would seem to be a prudent course for the government to take if for no other reason than the fact the document he refers to was, and still is, classified "Cosmic–Top Secret." At a UFO conference in November 1995, Dean reported that a friend, still on active duty at SHAPE headquarters, confirmed the "Assessment" is still there and still carries the same high-level classification.

The SHAPE "Assessment" concludes that Earth is being visited by several different forms of intelligent life. According to Dean, "Whoever these intelligences were, they repeatedly demonstrated technology so far beyond anything we had that if they were hostile or malevolent it would have probably been over a long time ago."

Although Dean is not a scientist, he was reading the conclusions of a number of scientists in the report. Those conclusions suggest that Earth has been visited by four separate types of intelligent beings, at least one of which appeared to be completely human. This species, Dean recounts with a broad grin, was the one that "bothered the generals and admirals the most. The idea that one of these advanced intelligences could sit next to you on a plane or in a theater and you would never know . . . bothered them a lot."

The "Assessment" findings, again according to Dean, also speculated about life beyond our own solar system. "They concluded that from what they could determine . . . we were apparently dealing with not only interplanetary [intelligences], we were dealing with interstellar and very likely we were dealing with intergalactic intelligences."

In the immensity of a universe whose infinite structure in terms of both space and time is far beyond our powers of comprehension, who is to say that these other worlds could not have been supporting life far longer than the six thousand years of Earth's written history? That is, after all, barely a tick of the universal clock.

But if the men who prepared the SHAPE "Assessment" report are correct, the question of whether humans are supreme or even alone in the universe is at best superfluous. Science, philosophy, and religion notwithstanding, the aliens, according to the "Assessment," are already here. It is in this arena of discussion that the former master sergeant is perhaps most passionate.

"In the thirty years of research that I've done since my exposure to the "Assessment," he told us, "I've concluded that the human race, literally the entire planet, has had an ongoing, intimate relationship with advanced intelligence . . . from the beginning of our history and even beyond. There is overwhelming evidence that some of those advanced intelligences have had a hand in our being here. Now *that* reality in itself is literally dynamite to [the] world paradigm, as it were. You might say that our world as we have known it will come to an end. Now I don't mean the planet's going to explode, but I mean that our worldview of ourselves, our species, the human race, is going to have to go through such a drastic change [that] we're going to have to eliminate all of the old savagery . . . and we're going to have to begin to think of ourselves as human beings—one people, one species, one race from one, small planet.

"I've concluded that an invitation is being extended, that a door is literally being opened, inviting us to come out. That these advanced intelligences, our kinfolk, our family, are saying: 'hey guys, it's time to grow up.' It's time to walk away from the bloody, savage past—all the religious differences, all of the ethnic differences . . . and I think that's what the twenty-first century is offering us."

Until Robert Dean broke his oath of secrecy, these NATO findings were, presumably, the exclusive property of the leaders of the NATO nations. But the SHAPE "Assessment" is not the only study of this type to have been commissioned by the military.

Nearly fifty years ago, September 23, 1947, to be exact, Lt. General Nathan F. Twining wrote a letter to the office of the commanding general of the Army Air Corps. The letter was in the form of a report on the unusual assignment he had been given in the wake of the UFO phenomena that had come to the Air Corps' attention over the summer. In the letter Twining told Brigadier General George Schulgen that "The phenomenon reported is something real and not visionary or fictitious."[9] Twining described these "flying disks" as metallic in appearance, round, soundless in all but a few cases, and remarkably maneuverable. "It is recommended," Twining wrote, "that . . . Headquarters, Army Air Forces issue a directive assigning a priority, security classification, and code name for a detailed study of this matter."

Three months later the recommendation was approved, and "Project Sign" was born. It carried a 2A restricted classification (1A was the highest) and was to be set up under the Air Materiel Command at Wright Field (now Wright-Patterson Air Force Base), in Dayton, Ohio. From the very beginning the military and, presumably, the civilian authority to whom they reported believed secrecy to be essential. Even the name was classified although it was popularly known as "Project Saucer."[10]

The Project Sign group began their work in January 1948 with an investigation of the death of Kentucky Air National Guard captain, Thomas F. Mantell, Jr. Mantell died when his P–51 fighter plane crashed after pursuing what Mantell described as a UFO. The group's first explanation, that Mantell had been chasing the planet Venus, was not well received. In 1952 the Air Force reinvestigated the

---

[9] *The UFO Encyclopedia*, vol. 2 (Detroit: Omnigraphics, 1992), p. 282.
[10] Ibid.

incident. This time their conclusion was that the captain had really been in pursuit of a Skyhook balloon.

In fairness to those investigators who prepared the summaries for Project Sign, it should be pointed out that their research and analysis procedures improved with time and experience. It is also fair to say that the work of the investigators didn't always get past their superiors. In July 1948, for example, at precisely 2:45 A.M., a rocket-shaped object with two rows of square "windows" streaked past a commercial DC–3 at an altitude of 5,000 feet. The crew and at least one passenger reported seeing it clearly and even described flames shooting from the rear of the craft. An hour earlier a ground maintenance crewman at Robins Air Force Base in Georgia had reported seeing a similar object. Further investigation turned up reports of a rocket with two rows of windows being seen over The Hague in the Netherlands on July 20. As it turned out this was just one of a number of reports of "ghost rockets" seen over northern Europe in the preceding months.[11]

A top-secret "estimate of the situation" was prepared and sent up the chain of command. No copy of that estimate has ever surfaced. However, one officer, Captain Edward J. Ruppelt, saw it later and said it recounted the DC–3 encounter and other reports by credible observers and declared that the evidence pointed to interplanetary visitation. When the "Estimate" got to Air Force Chief of Staff General Hoyt S. Vandenberg, however, he rejected it on the grounds that it had not proven its case.[12]

By December 1948, Project Sign had been renamed Project Grudge. Captain Ruppelt, who would later be called to head up yet another government investigation that would be called Project Blue Book, declared the "dark ages" of UFO investigation had begun.

[11]   Ibid., p. 283.
[12]   Ibid.

Up to this point investigators in Project Sign had been more or less equally divided between those who accepted the possibility of alien intervention and those who believed everything could be explained in more prosaic terms. Following General Vandenberg's rejection of the "Estimate," the character of the group began to change. UFO believers simply went out of favor. Still, as late as February 1949, a Project Sign report refused to reject UFOs outright. It acknowledged that a full 20 percent of the cases the group had examined were unexplainable.[13] The report did not indicate how many sightings, in terms of actual numbers, that 20 percent might represent.

It is interesting to note the almost studied smugness with which the skeptics and detractors make their case. The comments of Dr. J. Allen Hynek, in "debunking" the DC–3 incident, are illustrative. The "sheer improbability of the facts as stated" suggested to Hynek that the pilots were clearly mistaken. "The object *must have been* [emphasis mine] an extraordinary meteor."[14] The clear implication here is that the pilots (and presumably the passenger) couldn't possibly have seen what they said they saw.

It is these "official" explanations such as those that suggest experienced military pilots get killed chasing the planet Venus or the seemingly arbitrary method of substituting an "expert supposition" in place of the actual eyewitness accounts that drives Robert Dean up the wall.

"Some of their explanations," he bristles, "are more outrageous than the report itself. They think we're all stupid."

Citizens in the Eastern bloc countries, of course, didn't have that problem. Nothing was ever explained to them.

Although it is safe to assume that neither the Soviet Union nor any of the Warsaw Pact nations were privy to a copy of either the "Estimate" or the SHAPE "Assessment," it

[13] Ibid.
[14] Ibid.

would be a mistake to conclude they weren't involved in investigations of their own. Only a mere decade ago, everything that went on behind the "Iron Curtain" was a "riddle wrapped in an enigma," as Winston Churchill so aptly put it. Today, in one of the most ironic twists of political fate, it is Russia that is opening up their files on UFO studies.

In a broadcast aired on The Learning Channel in March 1996, Colonel Boris Sakiloff (sic), former head of a Soviet Defense Ministry investigation into UFOs, described in explicit detail the event that triggered what may be the world's most extensive UFO investigation to date.

On September 20, 1977, at about 4 A.M., according to Sakiloff, a large, glowing object was observed over the town of Petrozaavodsk on the Russian–Finnish border. About 170 people observed this incident. They were mostly military and border guards who watched as the object rained beams of light down onto the town. The object was clearly seen for some fifteen minutes before it moved off toward the Finnish border.

Through an interpreter Sakiloff said, " . . . after having read the report, I found that a large group of military men had witnessed the event about 700 kilometers away from Petrozaavodsk. When they tried to report it using their usual field communications . . . they had telephones and cable lines, radio and short wave . . . none of them worked. After the incident, which had lasted several hours over Petrozaavodsk, and a little shorter period of time over the border areas, all communications were suddenly restored."

Unable to explain either the object or the disruption of communications, the Soviets did something completely unprecedented. The Soviet military and the Soviet scientists began a cooperative state-funded research project. According to the broadcast, this action gave the proposed investigation a potential observer force of some six million troops.

Colonel Sakiloff remembered the scope of the undertaking as being even larger, with more than just the military involved. "[It was a] huge number, an experiment that will never be repeated. It lasted ten years, and the whole of the Soviet Union was involved. One sixth of the globe. And the number of potential observers was over ten million."

What little information did leak out was chalked up by the West's intelligence community as "disinformation" designed to mask some sort of secret missile launch. But Colonel Sakiloff's (sic) live, on-camera interview left no doubt that an actual UFO event had triggered probably the world's most extensive UFO research project.

One of the results of that study has been an ongoing, state-funded organization in Moscow that is actively investigating new propulsion systems based on UFO reports. Dr. Anatoly Akimoff, director of this group, was also featured in a live interview.

"What we are trying to do," he said, "is go beyond the normal investigative boundaries. If we believe and *we certainly have good reason to do so* [emphasis mine] that UFOs exist as a real phenomenon, then, naturally, the question arises whether our contemporary science can come to some understanding of them."[15]

Wouldn't it be reasonable to ask NATO to offer to trade a copy of the SHAPE "Assessment" to the Russians for a copy of the findings of their study? Even given the astonishing openness of the current Russian government, it doesn't appear that such an exchange will happen any time soon.

What of other major world powers? Are there other investigations that have been undertaken or are still ongoing? It is difficult to be sure but from time to time we do discover a few UFO clues.

Similar to UFO investigations in the United States, Great Britain's investigations seem to be blanketed by secrecy. However, according to the same broadcast on the Learning Channel, the British Ministry of Defense has a special

---

[15] *U.F.O.*, The Learning Channel, March 6, 1996.

department that deals exclusively with UFO sightings. Over the past thirty years some eight thousand reports have been processed by this department. About 5 percent, or nearly 400, of these sightings are still unidentified. A spokesman for the Ministry of Defense is quick to point out, however, that just because a sighting can't be explained today doesn't mean it might not be explained tomorrow. That comment would seem to suggest the British do have an ongoing UFO investigative effort in place at the highest levels of government.

One of the incidents the British are still trying to explain took place in December of 1980 at the Woodbridge British–American Air Force Base near Suffolk, England. The activity of this base was highly secret, probably because it held one of NATO's largest stockpiles of nuclear weapons. Security procedures were rigidly enforced and anything even remotely out of the ordinary was investigated.

According to the report, "in the early hours of December 28, two teams of base security officers left the east gate to investigate strange lights in the forest."[16] The deputy base commander, Lt. Colonel Halt, headed up one of the teams. In the other team was a young enlisted man named Larry Warren. The colonel, in strict adherence to security procedures, carried a recording device with him and tape-recorded a description of everything he encountered. Warren claims he saw still photographers and motion picture and video cameramen at the scene as well, though no photographs or video of the strange events that took place have ever surfaced.

Essentially the incident as recorded by the deputy base commander and reported by Warren involved a bright light, easily seen in the forest by both teams. In addition Warren claims his team encountered a strange circular mist in the center of a large open field near the forest. After watching the "object" on the ground for some time Warren says, "a

---

[16] Ibid.

red ball of light moved in. I thought it was an A–10 [coming into] Woodbridge, [which was] behind me about a mile. It came in over that far stand of trees, stopped over the circular, fog-like object on the ground, [and] dispersed in an explosion of color that was soundless, heatless, and what happened was a transformation, somehow, of this mist to a structured object. It was about thirty feet at the base, twenty feet in height, [with] a bank of blue lights at the base of it, and mother-of-pearl or rainbow effect all over . . . it was very difficult to look directly at."[17]

Some ran, Warren said, while he and some others just stayed glued to the spot. In the meantime, Colonel Halt and his team were making their way through the forest toward the light. The audiotape the colonel made is difficult to understand without augmentation, but certain key words can be picked out. "We're about 150 to 200 yards from the site . . . there's no doubt about it . . . this is strange."[18]

Apparently, military personnel were not the only ones to see some strange objects flitting about. People living near the air base also reported lights of some kind diving down into the forest and coming up again nowhere near the runway to the airfield.

All of this notwithstanding, the official reaction was reminiscent of the reports of the Roswell, New Mexico, crash some thirty-five years earlier and half a world away. A strict security shutdown was put into effect and alternative explanations and outright denials followed quickly on the heels of the initial eyewitness reports. Even though the British Ministry of Defense has authenticated Lt. Colonel Halt's report as genuine, it was not released until three years after the incident and then only because of pressure from Warren and others. Officially the explanation of the incident was that the lights were the beam from a lighthouse several

---

[17] Ibid.
[18] Ibid.

miles away, or a bright star of some kind, or some other "natural" occurrence.

Official pronouncements aside, at least one high-ranking government official isn't altogether convinced the Defense Ministry's position is viable. Lord Peter Hill Norton, Admiral of the Fleet and the former chief of the defense staff, questioned their findings. In a taped interview, Lord Norton said:

> It seems to me that something physical took place. I have no doubt that something landed at this U.S. Air Force Base, and I have no doubt that it got the people concerned, the U.S. Air Force people, and the commanding general at the base into a very considerable state. My view is that the Ministry of Defense, who were repeatedly questioned about this, not only by me but by other people, have doggedly stuck to their normal line, which is that nothing which is of defense interest took place on that occasion. My position about this has always been quite clear, and I have said this both in public and on the television and on the radio. . . . Either large numbers of people, including the commanding general at Bentwaters, were hallucinating, and for an American Air Force nuclear base this is extremely dangerous, or what they say happened, did happen. And in either of those circumstances, there can only be one answer and that is that it was of extreme defense interest to the United Kingdom. I have never had a satisfactory rebuttal of that view.[19]

It seems self-evident that various governments, their agencies, and military establishments have a history of investigating UFOs. But how long has this business of UFO sightings been going on? Is it a relatively modern phenome-

[19] Ibid.

non, or as the SHAPE "Assessment" concludes, has it been a part of world history for "several millennia"?

In fact, a number of UFO experts, Robert Dean among them, believe Earth has been visited by extraterrestrials since the beginning of its history. Some researchers even present startling evidence that suggests extraterrestrials are the very reason we exist.

Are these views invested with any scientific credibility? Is there any reliable way to track such events through the historical record? We'll seek the answers to those questions in the next chapter.

CHAPTER 3

A HISTORICAL PERSPECTIVE

>> Nine bright, saucer-like objects flying at "incredible speed" at 10,000 feet altitude were reported here today.

East Oregonian, Pendleton, Oregon, June 25, 1947

A young man was traveling from his hometown to a far away city in his father's homeland. He was in search of a bride. It was a long journey, and when darkness fell, he decided to rest. He lay down in a field and went to sleep. But in the middle of the night, he was awakened by strange noises and bright lights. He awoke to see something hovering above him in the air. There was an open doorway and steps or a ladder leading down to the ground. Men were going up and down the ladder, and he could see a form in the doorway, silhouetted against the brilliant light. The young man heard someone speak to him as if in a dream. The next morning whatever he had seen was gone. He left the place, terrified, but vowed to do whatever he was told to do from that moment on.

The young man's name was Jacob, and this frightening incident in his life can be found in the twenty-eighth chapter of Genesis in the Bible.

There are a number of UFO investigators who firmly believe that the Bible, particularly the Old Testament, is a treasure trove of UFO stories. But even if that's true, it would still be of relatively recent origin in the overall history of extraterrestrial events.

According to the *Final Report to the Fund for UFO Research* prepared by Dr. Louis Winkler and subtitled "Analysis of UFO-Like Data Before 1947," the record goes back to somewhere around 50,000 B.C. The "Analysis" begins with a reference to an alien figure discovered near Lake Titicaca in South America. It is the representation of a female with a cone-shaped head, huge ears, and four webbed fingers per hand, landing in a spaceship.[1]

Images in paleolithic cave paintings discovered in France and Spain, suggest UFO-like objects. According to archaeologists these paintings were created sometime between 30,000 and 10,000 B.C.[2]

Erich Von Däniken, author of *Chariots of the Gods*, has suggested that stone plates with spiral grooves discovered in Baian Kara Ula, Sino-Tibet, give an account of aliens landing there that were unable to take off again. These artifacts date back as far as 10,000 B.C. Von Däniken and others also suggest that the very existence of megaliths such as Cheop's Pyramid and the great terrace near Baalbek, dating back to 3000 B.C., are evidence that an alien technology was on the Earth at least that long ago.[3]

How seriously should we take these observations? According to Dr. Winkler, "The history of societies before

---

[1] Louis Winkler, "Final Report to the Fund for UFO Research" (University Park: PA), Mar. 1982–Feb. 1984.

[2] Ibid.

[3] Ibid.

the first millennium B.C. is at best sketchy and discontinuous," which would lead us to believe that the conclusions drawn from these discoveries are not necessarily trustworthy. Dr. Winkler goes on to say, however, that "four entries in [this catalog] . . . offer information concerning aliens and craft with astounding detail. These entries are as conspicuously more detailed, compared to any other archeological evidence of the period, as they are unsubstantiated."

Although impossible to verify, such archaeological clues do tend to support the view that extraterrestrials have been visiting Earth for thousands of years. But what of the "written" record? Many, probably most, of the Judeo-Christian world will reject out of hand the notion that the story of Jacob's ladder or Ezekiel's fiery wheel are records of the biblical prophets' encounters with UFOs. That being the case, are there any other written records as old, or even older than the biblical writings purport to be?

The astute reader may have noticed, and perhaps wondered, at the reference in the preceding chapter to the "six thousand years of Earth's *written* history." That was not an error or misprint. Modern archaeology has identified written texts dating back to what was at one time thought to be the "prehistoric" civilization of Sumer. The discovery of the library of Ninevah, the ancient capital of Assyria, in the mid-twentieth century established that not only did this ancient Near-Eastern society have a written language, they had a highly sophisticated social system and science as well. All of this existed a full 2,000 years before Abraham began his journey from Ur of the Chaldees.

Because there is no evidence of an evolutionary, pre-Sumerian culture, the colossal question left by this discovery is how did their culture develop? The findings seem to suggest the society appeared, full-blown as it were, and not only flourished at the confluence of the Tigris and Euphrates rivers, but created a language, religion, code of morality, and system of commerce that we still borrow from today. That the society existed in rather splendid isolation is no longer a question, but does all that have anything to do with aliens from another world?

The most scholarly answer to that question is found in the work and the writings of Dr. Zechariah Sitchin. Dr. Sitchin was born in Russia and raised in Palestine, where he acquired a profound knowledge of modern and ancient Hebrew, along with other Semitic and European languages. He is also a leading authority on the Old Testament and on the history of Near-Eastern archaeology.

In this particular instance, however, it is his ability to read the ancient Sumerian texts and translate them into understandable language that intrigues us. His scholarship is strengthened by his knowledge of biblical texts and his willingness to make straightforward, sometimes startling comparisons. Interestingly enough, far from creating conflict, Dr. Sitchin's writings suggest a direct correlation between the Sumerian tablets and certain biblical accounts.

According to Dr. Sitchin, three corresponding stories mark the beginning of history's written record; the biblical story of the Nefilim, the "giants" of the book of Genesis, who lost their place in heaven by consorting with earthly females; the Egyptian tradition, recorded by Herodotus, which tells a tale of demigods, offspring of the "Neterus'" intercourse with human females, who ruled the land before the time of the pharaohs; and the Sumerian text that tells of the "Anunnaki," or "those who from Heaven to Earth came," and who likewise consorted with earthly women. The similarity between the three traditions is unmistakable. The translation of the Sumerian term "Anunnaki," incidentally, provides an interesting coincidence of language. The translation "those who from Heaven to Earth came" is amazingly similar to the literal translation of the biblical word "Nefilim," which according to Dr. Sitchin is, "those who came or fell down to Earth."

All of that is interesting, but how does it translate into a history of extraterrestrial visitations to Earth? The answer is in the translation of the thousands of cuneiform tablets discovered in the ancient library of Ninevah.

The story told by the ancient Sumerian texts begins some 450,000 years ago on a planet called Nibiru, the home of the Anunnaki. This huge world, according to Dr. Sitchin's book, *The 12th Planet*, swings through our solar system every 3,600 years in a great elliptical orbit. Nibiru, so the Sumerians tell us, was in need of gold, not for its decorative value but to use in some sort of shield above their planet to avert a devastating ecological disaster. During one of their sojourns in our solar system, the Anunnaki sent an expedition to Earth to mine the precious metal. They splashed down at the head of what is now the Persian Gulf, waded ashore, and established a settlement, which they named ERIDU, meaning "Home in the Faraway." According to Dr. Sitchin, this ". . . is the source of the name by which we call the planet, Erde, in the Indo-European languages."[4]

The Anunnaki set about dividing the Earth among themselves. They established four regions, three of which were allotted to humanity. The fourth zone, Dr. Sitchin tells us, ". . . was declared a 'sacred' region. It was the Sinai peninsula, and it was here that the Anunnaki established their post-diluvial spaceport. The Sumerians called the area Tilmun, literally, 'Land of the Missiles.' The pyramids of Giza were built by the Anunnaki to serve as beacons for the landing corridor; Jerusalem was the new Mission Control Center."[5]

Some of us may find all of this a little hard to believe, but apparently ancient people didn't have such difficulties. The Sumerian texts tell of certain humans that were taken aboard the spaceships. A famous Sumerian king went to "The Landing Place" and saw a rocket ship rising. It is all

[4] *MUFON Symposium Proceedings* (Seguin, TX: Mutual UFO Network, 1991), p. 22.
[5] Ibid., p. 23.

described in considerable detail in the Sumerian writings. Scholars translating the story call it, *The Epic of Gilgamesh*.

As we might suspect, most scholars quickly relegate these tales to the realms of ancient myth. Fascinating, sometimes even beautifully poetic, but myth just the same. There is nothing the texts reveal that can be corroborated by modern scientific effort.

Or is there?

In August 1977, NASA launched the Voyager probes out into the solar system. They were to travel to Jupiter, Saturn, and beyond. Indeed, the Voyager missions have been one of NASA's most spectacular successes.

Voyager 2 reached Uranus in 1986 and sent back the first photos and close-up data on that planet. In August 1989, twelve years after being launched, *Voyager 2* swept by Neptune. The photos and data were breathtaking. For the first time, Earth scientists could compare actual, close-up photographs of the two planets. Imagine their chagrin when they realized Zechariah Sitchin, in an article written months before the Neptune encounter, had described the qualities of both Neptune and Uranus almost to perfection. Both planets, he wrote, "will be found to be twin-like in many respects, blue-green in color, with various patches, watery . . ."[6]

"I knew all that," Dr. Sitchin said, "because the Sumerians had known all that 6,000 years ago. In my book, *The 12th Planet* [written a year before *Voyager 1* and *Voyager 2* were launched] I quote Sumerian descriptions of all the planets, and they were right regarding each and every one of them."[7]

There is another curiosity in the Sumerian text. Modern astronomy, as we all know, situates Earth as the third planet from the sun. The Sumerians, however, referred to Earth as

[6] Ibid.
[7] Ibid., p. 21.

the *seventh* planet. If they were getting such good information from their other-world tutors, how could they have made such a mistake?

In his book,[8] Dr. Sitchin points out that the Sumerians had it right. Earth *is* the seventh planet if you count from the outer rim of the solar system *toward* the sun. But that only deepens the mystery. Uranus and Neptune were not discovered until the nineteenth century, and Pluto was unknown prior to 1930. If the Sumerians knew 6,000 years ago that this was an eleven-planet solar system and Earth was number seven, where did they get the information?

The answer, according to Dr. Sitchin, is found in the extensive writings of the sixth millennium B.C.! We should point out that this is not another "lost civilization" where scientists are required to make broad extrapolations from a minimal amount of data. There are thousands of tablets inscribed with the strange, wedge-shaped writing archaeologists call "cuneiform." The Sumerians, in fact, invented the concept of the rotary press. Their craftsmen could engrave, in reverse, drawings upon small cylinders made of hard or semi-precious stones. Sitchin tells us that when these were rolled on wet clay a "positive" image became permanently imprinted.[9] Tens of thousands of these cylinder seals have been unearthed, providing an extensive record of Sumerian life in the far distant past.

The cylinder seals, writings, and archaeological evidence combine to paint a portrait of a civilization of large cities, high-rise temples and palaces, courts of justice (a thousand years before the code of Hammurabi), commerce, irrigation, metallurgy, mathematics, medicine, and an astounding understanding of astronomy and the cosmos.[10]

---

[8] Zechariah Sitchin, *The Twelfth Planet* (New York: Avon Books, 1978).
[9] MUFON *Symposium Proceedings* (Seguin, TX: Mutual UFO Network, 1991), p. 19.
[10] Ibid.

Dr. Sitchin is aware that most modern archaeologists place the Sumerian writings in the realm of "myth." Many scholars also put the Old Testament in that category. But in his four books, which he calls, *The Earth Chronicles*, Sitchin dares to ask *what if*? What if these are not just stories concocted out of whole cloth? What if they are actual records of real events?

Almost as if they were trying to give us an answer to the puzzle, the Sumerian texts repeatedly state that all they know of science, language, architecture, religion, morality, law, and astronomy was taught to them by the Anunnaki. Could it be these same interplanetary travelers are still returning to check up on us today?

Neil Freer,[11] in an article entitled, "In Tune with Our True History," borrows from the Sitchin chronicles in advancing his own solution to the enigma of the origins of mankind. Freer tells us:

> [A] new paradigm is now emerging. It can be summed up simply: we are homo-erectus-Nefilimus, a genetically engineered species with a dual genetic origin, a bicameral mind and hence a dual consciousness.
>
> This corrects and includes both the creationist and evolutionary models and presents us with the key to the next plateau of racial maturity.[12]

Freer goes on to suggest that the only reason this is not common knowledge is, "Because it contradicts the official Judeo-Christian ethos that has formed Western culture."

That allegation may be true, but we are indebted to the monks, priests, and astronomers of the ancient world for keeping a record of events that would otherwise have been

---

[11] Neil Freer is a writer, researcher, and lecturer. He authored *Breaking the Godspell*, which was published by Falcon Press.

[12] Neil Freer, UFOs and Religion, UFO, 5(2), p. 31.

lost during subsequent ages of fear and superstition. They were, for the most part, the only ones who could write.

A similar situation has occurred throughout human history. The astronomer/priests of ancient Egypt and Mesopotamia, for example, were avid record keepers when it came to celestial events. The ancient Chinese kept extensive records that provide almost continuous coverage of astronomical events from the first century B.C.

There are detailed Mayan records as well, kept by a priesthood that believed, as did most enlightened astronomers of that era, that signs in the heavens had great portent for what might happen in their lives and in the world generally.[13]

The monastic writers of the Middle Ages recorded the history of their era. Such "chronicles" also list events in an orderly timeline. Their references to strange sights in the sky frequently can be found side by side with entries detailing the conquests of various kings.[14]

Whatever their origins, the simple fact is that there is no shortage of records defining strange and exotic events in the sky. Here is just a small sample.

Rome, 91 B.C.: "About sunrise a ball of fire flashed forth from the northern heavens with a great noise in the sky."

England, A.D. 555: "There was seen the appearance of lances in the northwest quarter of the heavens."

France, December, A.D. 584: "A great beacon traversed the heavens, lighting up the land far and wide some time before the day dawned."

Japan, A.D. 637: "A great star floated from east to west, and there was a noise like that of thunder."

England, A.D. 1171: "A great dragon . . . flew through

---

[13] Thomas E. Bullard, The emergence of a phenomenon: Anomalous aerial phenomenon before 1800, *The UFO Encyclopedia*, vol. 2 (Detroit: Omnigraphics, 1992), p. 53.

[14] Ibid.

the air not far from the ground, and in his flight raised a great fire in the air which burnt a house to ashes, with all that was about it."

France, January 13, 1537: "A star of wonderful greatness was seen in the element, which by little and little spreading into the air took the form of a whitish circle, whereof afterward through a great violence of the wind, flames were rained down upon the earth and did burn only those things which otherwise are not commonly consumed with devouring flames . . ."

Annam (Vietnam), May 22, 1618: In the early evening "a star moved swiftly westward, like a roll of cloth."[15]

Suffice it to say, the history of the world is replete with descriptions of strange and wonderful sights and events occurring in the skies. Many of them were undoubtedly natural phenomena, inexplicable to people of the time except in mystic terms. But are we so different? Couldn't the same thing easily be said of our reaction to similar reports in the modern era?

At this point it might be well to attempt to define the "modern era," at least as far as UFO excitement is concerned. It is probably impossible to pin down a specific year or even decade when the current commotion began, because almost any year or event selected will appear to be arbitrary. There was, however, one defining moment that might serve as a useful benchmark. The event itself was of little consequence, but it did prove that given even the smallest amount of information, the public, worldwide, was enormously fascinated with the idea of extraterrestrial visitors.

On June 24, 1947, a pilot by the name of Kenneth Arnold, on a flight out of Seattle, Washington, to Yakima, decided to make a slight detour toward Mt. Rainier. A C–46 Marine transport had crashed, and he wanted to see if he could help spot the downed airplane. Suddenly he was star-

[15] Ibid.

tled by a brilliant flash of light. Like any good pilot he began an immediate inspection of everything in the cockpit and in the sky around him. The day was sunny and cloudless, with the horizon easily visible in all directions. It took only a moment to spot them. Arnold saw nine circular craft, flying in echelon, or "V", formation, clearly visible against the backdrop of the mountains. Occasionally, one craft would dip slightly, its highly polished surface reflecting the sun like a giant mirror. It was this flash of reflected sunlight that illuminated his cockpit and caught his attention.

Arnold watched with unbelieving eyes as the craft raced along at incredible speeds. Setting the second hand on his watch, he began a count as the craft flashed between Rainier and a peak just south of it. They covered the fifty-mile distance in a minute and forty-two seconds. A quick calculation told him they were flying at speeds in excess of 1,700 miles an hour. What was even more astonishing was their amazing maneuverability. They darted around the smaller peaks, flipping from side to side in unison, with only slight changes in formation.

Arnold estimated their size to be as wide as the two furthest engines of a DC–4. He watched as they disappeared over the last high peak of Mt. Adams. He glanced at his watch and realized he had been watching them for about two and a half minutes. At one point he was probably within twenty-three miles of them.

Arnold forgot about the C–46 and flew on to Yakima. He told a helicopter pilot about his experience, but the pilot dismissed the whole thing as "a flight of guided missiles from Moses Lake." Arnold was not convinced. He flew on to Pendleton, not knowing that someone at Yakima had radioed ahead with the message that the pilot of the Callair, who would soon be arriving, had seen some strange craft.

By the time he touched down, a large crowd, already there to attend an air show, began to crowd around his plane. Some shouted questions at him, but they soon drifted away. The consensus of the crowd was basically in agreement with the helicopter pilot in Yakima—Arnold had seen guided missiles. That explanation seemed to satisfy everyone but Arnold himself.

The next morning Arnold, now more convinced than ever that he had seen something truly unique, went to the offices of the *East Oregonian*, Pendleton's only newspaper. A reporter named Bill Bequette, impressed with Arnold's intelligence and obvious sincerity, decided to do a small story. Among other things, Arnold told him the movement of the objects had reminded him of a flat rock bouncing up and down as it skipped across the water. That turned into the following story:

> PENDLETON, Ore., June 25 (AP)—Nine bright, saucer-like objects flying at 'incredible speed' at 10,000 feet altitude were reported here today by Kenneth Arnold, Boise, Idaho, pilot who said he could not hazard a guess as to what they were.[16]

The age of the "flying saucer" was born.

Just weeks later the world would be stunned by reports, published with the sanction of the military, that a "flying saucer" had crashed in Roswell, New Mexico, and was in the hands of the United States Army Air Corps. We will devote an entire chapter to this particular event, one of the most famous in the annals of UFO investigation. Suffice it to say here that within twenty-four hours the "official" report was changed from "flying saucer" to "weather balloon," which is the government line to this day.

But the cat was out of the proverbial bag. Even though the Army moved quickly to quash the story of the Roswell crash, the miracle of electronics had already carried it world-

---

[16] Jerome Clark, *The UFO Encyclopedia*, vol. 2 (Detroit: Omnigraphics, 1992), p. 217.

wide. People were convinced that not only did the U.S. government have some sort of spacecraft in hand, rumors persisted that several occupants had been found as well. These rumors were all denied, of course, and the subject was dropped, at least officially. The media coverage of these two events, however, had brought the whole subject of UFOs out of the closet and into the glaring light of a bright, new media-saturated day.

The next event to get extensive media coverage occurred in 1952. A man named George Adamski told of seeing a spacecraft hovering near his home. He not only described it, he photographed it and claimed the occupants of the craft were in touch with him. Eventually, he said, a meeting took place between himself and aliens from another world. He described how that first meeting came about.

"Suddenly, as though a veil was removed from my mind," Adamski wrote, "the feeling of caution left me so completely that I was no longer aware of my friends or whether they were observing me as they had been told to do. By this time [the alien and I] were quite close. He took four steps toward me, bringing us within arm's length of each other.

"Now for the first time I fully realized that I was in the presence of a man from space—*a human being from another world!*"[17]

From that time until his death George Adamski would remain in the center of controversy. His writings as well as his photographs were roundly denounced as fake and nothing more than attempts to profit from a gullible public. To this day UFOlogists are likely to quarrel over the validity of the Adamski stories and photographs.

In 1964 the subject of UFOs took a more sinister turn with the reported abduction of Betty and Barney Hill. They were, they said, taken aboard a spacecraft, punctured, poked, and otherwise examined before being released; their

[17] Roy Stemman, *Visitors from Outer Space* (London: Aldus Books, Ltd), 1979.

memory had been erased but they were seemingly none the worse for wear. It was only under hypnosis that they recalled their brief time aboard the ship. Betty remembered being shown a "Star Map" and was told it was the star system from which the ship had come. Remember that star map. It will take on new significance in a later chapter.

Since the Betty and Barney Hill abduction, literally hundreds of other such stories have been reported. Even Hollywood has gotten into the act. Producer/director Steven Spielberg has made two mega-hits dealing with the extraterrestrial theme: *Close Encounters of the Third Kind* and *ET*. Both attracted massive audiences the world over.

By 1964 the government had been bombarded with so many reports of UFOs they established Project Blue Book, which was actually the public incarnation of Project Sign and Project Grudge, the government's earlier and more clandestine efforts to investigate UFO sightings. Unlike its predecessors, both of which were highly classified, Project Blue Book was well publicized. It was, however, still under the direction of the Air Force. The group's mandate, also well publicized, was to "thoroughly investigate" all reports of UFOs. During its twenty-year history, covering thousands upon thousands of incidents, not one was ever confirmed by the Air Force as being of extraterrestrial origin. We'll have a good deal more to say about that in a later chapter as well.

From the cone-headed, web-handed female landing in a spaceship near Lake Titicaca some 50,000 years ago, to the cave paintings of beings in space suits believed to have been created in 10,000 B.C., to Sitchin's Anunnaki/Nefilim of the sixth millennium B.C., right up to last week's newspaper, it is clear that there has never been a time in human history when there wasn't an awareness of some kind of extraterrestrial, or at the very least, unexplainable astronomical activity.

There is, of course, one vast difference between then and now. Today we live in a world filled with cameras and

VCRs. Satellites have photographed virtually every square inch of the globe, and we have a worldwide communications system that can send pictures and reports to millions of people at the speed of light. There is also a voracious media eager to exploit controversy of any kind.

And there is no lack of controversy surrounding UFOs. The issue can appear even on local television. Imagine coming home to dinner and turning on the TV to get the latest news. Instead, you see someone who claims to be a physicist telling an interviewer that not only are flying saucers real, but he works on them every day trying to figure out what makes them go.

What is this, you wonder. A commercial for a new science fiction movie?

Read on.

CHAPTER 4

AREA 51

> >> **Because of the nature of the programs that are there, it has extremely severe security measures.**
>
> **George Knapp, television reporter**

I t may come as a surprise to many of you to learn that roughly 85 percent of Nevada is under the control of some agency or other of the U.S. government. A fairly good-size chunk is known as the Nevada Test Site, so named for the atomic bomb tests conducted there for over forty years. Within the confines of the Test Site is an area known as the Nellis Range, part of the sprawling Nellis Air Force Base headquartered in North Las Vegas. Tucked away in the northern reaches of the Nellis Range is a small piece of real estate unofficially referred to as "Area 51."

To give you a better idea of what all this means in terms of ground miles and to pinpoint the location of the place we'll be talking about in this chapter, we need to refer you to your favorite map of the western United States. Preferably a

U.S. Geological Survey (USGS) map, but some of the more detailed road maps will do.

First, locate the border between Utah and Nevada, then focus your attention on the very southwest corner of Utah. You should see a town called St. George. Now locate a point approximately 125 miles due west of St. George, Utah. That point should be approximately 120 miles north of Las Vegas, Nevada. You'll notice that nothing is there except a vast, empty stretch of desert. If you're using a USGS map, the point you have selected should be near a spot labeled "Groom Lake." Named for a body of water that disappeared hundreds of thousands of years ago, Groom Lake is one of the land sinks that was left when the huge, inland sea called Lake Bonneville began to recede sometime in the prehistoric past. Your map won't show it, but Groom Lake falls within the confines of the Nellis Range. That means there are at least three layers of government administration (not counting local authorities) guarding access to this particular chunk of sagebrush and gravel.

A few miles farther south of Groom Lake lies another, similar piece of terrain called Papoose Lake. No other official designation appears on any map that we have been able to find for either area. Unofficially, however, this inhospitable and unimpressive piece of desert has many names, the most famous being "Area 51." No one knows what that means, but the name is believed to have come from an old military map of the Nevada Test Site. This particular spot, for some reason or another, carried that designation. If you ask the Air Force, no such place exists, and the map that might have shown it has long since vanished.

But the area surrounding Groom Lake and Papoose Lake has many other names as well: "Dreamland," "The Box," "The Skunk Works," and "S–4," the operational name for the complex said to be located near Papoose Lake. Although all of these names have their own origin and history, none of them is acknowledged by any authority.

"Dreamland" and "The Skunk Works" are names affectionately applied by employees of both the government and Lockheed, the huge corporation that is supposed to have designed the complex for the development of super-secret, off-budget projects such as the U–2 spy plane, the SR–71 Blackbird, and the now famous "Stealth" fighter-bomber. Although it can be argued that the design of each of these craft and perhaps the original construction took place elsewhere, there seems to be little doubt that all of them were put through their final flight tests at Area 51.[1]

Among other things, the complex boasts the world's longest runway (recently extended to 27,000 feet), which leads some experts to believe another new, top-secret project is under way. An unexplained line item in a Pentagon budget, labeled only, "Aurora,"[2] has given rise to speculation that the Air Force is developing an "aircraft carrier" in the sky—a "mothership" of sorts from which smaller, faster aircraft could be launched and retrieved.[3] Others believe it could be another spy plane capable of Mach 5 to Mach 8 speeds. The military, of course, vigorously denies the existence not only of either project but of the base as well. The denial is interesting as the name "The Box" is most commonly used by military and commercial pilots who are forbidden to fly over the area. The name refers to the roughly square dimensions of a region in the sky above the area that pilots must go around, no matter what the circumstances.

Extraordinary measures have also been taken by the government to keep this area hidden from observers on the ground. In the 1980s the Air Force was granted jurisdiction over 80,000 acres of federal land, an entire mountain range

---

[1] Stuart F. Brown, Searching for the Secrets of Groom Lake, *Popular Science* (March 1994) pp. 53–59.

[2] The Secrets of Area 51: A collection of literature on black budget aircraft, *Aviation Week & Space Technology* (October 1, 1990) pp. 20–23.

[3] Stuart F. Brown, Searching for the Secrets of Groom Lake, *Popular Science* (March 1994) pp. 84, 85.

surrounding Area 51. More recently, according to an article published in the *Salt Lake Tribune* in September 1993, Air Force Secretary Sheila Whitenow requested control over nearly 4,000 additional acres of publicly owned land in the Nellis Range complex.[4] Most investigators believe this was yet another attempt to seal off the Area 51 complex from public view.

The area, by all accounts, is hidden from congressional view as well. During the course of my research for this book, I happened to run into the former U.S. Senator from Utah, Jake Garn. I have known Jake for many years, but I was unaware that he had spent considerable time on the Senate Military Appropriations Committee. It was a chance meeting and in the course of telling him about the project I was working on, I asked him, "What can you tell me about Area 51?" His reply: "Never heard of it."

For a brief moment in 1995 it looked as though the public would, at long last, learn the "official" name of the place. This came about partly because outraged members of the House and of Senate Military Appropriations Committees were trying to find out where all their money was going. The subject of Area 51 also came up as a simple point of law in a civil suit. If the secret had come out, we would probably have had the Russians to thank.

In February 1995 *Newsweek* published a story in their "Environment" section entitled, "It Dares Not Speak Its Name." According to the article, the widow of a former government employee who had worked at the super-secret facility, and five other current and former employees filed a lawsuit against the Air Force. In the suit, they claimed that they had evidence the Air Force denied the workers protective clothing when they were asked to burn plastics and chemicals that were thrown into an open pit and doused

[4] Joshua B. Good, No peeking from peak: Air Force wants to seize mountain to protect secret base, *Salt Lake Tribune* (October 17, 1993) p. A-1.

with jet fuel. Their attorney, a professor at George Washington University Law School, claims the widow's husband was found to have high levels of dioxins and furans in his body, toxins produced when plastic is burned.

Proving that exposure to toxic fumes and chemicals may have contributed to the death of one man and the illness suffered by the others is, according to the authors of the news article, a tough job for any lawyer. But that wasn't the main problem. The real difficulty was that while the government finally admitted that an "operating location" existed in the area, they refused to reveal its name. The suit could not proceed without the "officially recognized name" of the facility where the men had worked. The request for the name, according to a government brief, was "vague, overbroad, and unreasonably burdensome."

Meanwhile, the attorney for the plaintiffs made plans to call the military attaché at the Russian Embassy as a witness. Russian spy satellites, it seems, have been flying over "The Box" and taking pictures for years. Some of these photos have already been published in this country. Our citizens aren't permitted to know what is apparently common knowledge to the Russian high command.

Enter the Justice Department and the Environmental Protection Agency (EPA). With or without a name, they launched an investigation into hazardous waste violations at Area 51. "Of course," the authors reminded us, "if the Pentagon blocks the suit by refusing to release the name of the site, the validity of the charges won't matter."[5]

Who could have predicted such an amazing turn of events? Imagine the Justice Department and the EPA preparing a case against the Air Force over violations at an installation the Pentagon insists doesn't exist. Now imagine lawyers poring over dozens of photographs taken by Soviet

---

[5] Bruce Shenitz and Sharon Begley, It Does Not Speak Its Name, *Newsweek*, February 10, 1995, p. 55.

spy satellites in order to prove their case. It's not unlike the district attorney preparing a case against the police and asking the criminals for pictures to prove there was a crime.

Unfortunately, the Justice Department and EPA efforts came to naught. We still won't find out what the official name of the base is, at least not for a while. As this book was being written, word reached us that a federal judge had tossed the case out of court. The Pentagon, alas, does not have to reveal the name of the "operating location."

But what does all this have to do with UFOs? In the final analysis, the United States, like other nations, probably should have some place that is more or less secret, where the government and military can research and develop new, exotic weapons of war. Area 51, by whatever name, is probably as good a place as any in the country. Up to this point, at least, it seems to have served that purpose well and for a long period of time. How do we know? Simple deduction, mostly, with a little bit of help from a Russian surface-to-air missile.

In 1958, Americans didn't know about the U–2 spy plane until the Soviets shot one out of the sky over Russia in the 1960s. Subsequent investigation into the incident revealed that the United States had been flying this particular aircraft for at least ten years before that. The U–2 was also revealed to be a product of the infamous "Skunk Works," aka "Area 51." That means that some group has been operating successfully and secretly from Area 51 for nearly four decades, perhaps longer.[6]

We talked to former Lt. Colonel Wendelle C. Stevens, United States Air Force, Ret., to try and discover if anyone outside the confines of the base really knows what kind of work is being done there.

"We should all remember," Colonel Stevens told us,

---

[6] George Knapp, taped interview, Salt Lake City, 1995.

"that [not only was] the U–2 spy plane . . . flying out of Area 51 for years, the same is true of the Blackbird SR–71 and the Stealth Fighter. They were all flying for many years before we heard about them."

A good argument can be made that such a facility was not only desirable but even essential during the Cold War. But why now? The Soviet threat has largely disappeared. The United States stands as the preeminent superpower in the world. Humanity seems to be making at least some progress toward a more peaceful global community. The destruction of the Berlin Wall has become a symbol of international movement toward a more open, productive world society. Why, then, with barriers coming down all around us—with even the old Soviet Union opening doors that have been closed for decades—why is the wall of secrecy becoming higher and more impenetrable around Area 51?

Many believe the answer can be found in the enigmatic designation, "S–4," and a man named Bob Lazar who claims to have worked there.

In a series of highly publicized interviews, broadcast by a local Nevada TV station, Robert Lazar told reporters that between 1988 and 1989 he was employed as a research specialist at a hidden base near Papoose Lake, even more secret than the Groom Lake installation. Lazar said:

> When I went to work I was flown from McCarran Airport in Las Vegas to Area 51. From Area 51, I was bused to an even more highly secured facility located about fifteen miles south of Area 51 called S–4. S–4 is situated at the base of the Papoose Mountains by the Papoose dry lake bed. The installation is built into the mountain, and the nine hangar doors are angled at about sixty degrees. These doors are covered with a sand-textured coating to blend in with the side of the mountain and the desert floor.

Not only did I read briefings, and not only was I taught the theories of these technologies, but they were demonstrated for me, and I know they are true and accurate.[7]

According to Bob Lazar, it was in this hidden base that he worked on disk-shaped flying craft that were based on a technology given to us, either voluntarily or involuntarily, by beings from another planet.

Lazar went on to claim that there are several fully working flying disks at the S–4 facility, but only one on which he personally worked. "Because of its sleek appearance," he said, "I nicknamed it the 'sport model.' The sport model is about sixteen feet tall and forty feet in diameter. The center level of this disk also houses the control consoles and seats, both of which were too small and too low to the floor to be functional for adult human beings."[8]

If the story Lazar tells is true, then this design is no mere fantasy, but a reality that puts us well along the road to proving that Earth has been visited by intelligent beings from another planet.

Could the U.S. government actually have one or more UFOs in their possession? Is it possible they could keep such a secret from the public and the press?

A few years ago a man by the name of Glenn Campbell moved to Rachel, Nevada, the postage-stamp–size town nearest the boundaries of Area 51. These boundaries, by the way, are patrolled by unmarked helicopters and ground vehicles, whose occupants let visitors know, in no uncertain terms, that the signs "Deadly Force Authorized" mean what they say.

Rachel, Nevada, boasts one black mailbox, the property of a rancher who leases the Bureau of Land Managment (BLM) land in the area, and a combination motel, saloon, and

---

[7] UFO Diaries, Area 51. Sun International Pictures, Salt Lake City, 1995.
[8] Ibid.

restaurant affectionately called "The Little A'le'inn." This edifice, the heart and soul of Rachel, has become the unofficial headquarters for the Area 51 Research Center, whose director and sole, full-time employee is Glenn Campbell.

In 1993 Campbell published "An Area 51 Viewers' Guide" to take advantage of, or perhaps to assist, the influx of visitors who have found their way into the desert ever since the Lazar story broke.

"Since [Lazar's] claims were first publicized, many people have come here looking for flying saucers and think they have seen them," Campbell writes. "Lazar and the black mailbox have been featured on national and international television. The area now attracts bus tours, conferences, believers, skeptics, and charlatans."[9]

Area 51, whatever its role in the past, does not seem to be much of a secret in the present.

"Until the early 1980s," Campbell tells us, "it was actually possible to drive up to the Groom dry lake bed and look across and see the base in the distance. It was a secret base, but an open secret. In the mid-1980s the military seized an entire mountain range, the Groom Mountains, to keep Soviet spies from looking down on the base. At that point the base became nonexistent. It disappeared from USGS maps, and ever since then the government has refused to refer to the base in any manner or form."

The additional four thousand acres the Air Force sought to secure in 1993, it should be noted, was on and around Whiteside Mountain, and is in addition to the Groom Mountain takeover cited earlier. Several groups have protested the government's action, principally because Whiteside has become a favorite, if somewhat inaccessible, vantage point from which UFO buffs can watch activities at the installation about twelve miles away. It's also a favorite spot to look for UFOs in the clear skies of the desert night.

[9] Glenn Campbell, *An Area 51 Viewers' Guide*, 1.2 ed. (May 20, 1993).

Setting aside the Lazar story for the moment, what could be going on at this installation that merits such exhaustive efforts?

George Knapp is the Las Vegas television reporter who brought Bob Lazar (alias "Dennis") to public attention. He is bright, intense, and every inch the professional TV journalist. In an extensive interview Knapp told us that, ". . . for forty years it [Area 51] has been the location of choice for . . . the most secret projects of the world that our military is looking into."

The implication here is that not only are we testing our own designs, but also weapons or weapons systems captured or otherwise acquired from other nations. Whatever they are, they are being tested and scrutinized by the engineers and strategists that work at the installation.

"It's perfect for that," says Knapp. "It's ringed by mountains; it's in the middle of nowhere; it's adjacent to the nuclear test site; and it's exactly what you would look for if you were going to test things like the Stealth bomber, the U–2 [and] the SR–71. And because of that, because of the nature of the programs that are there, it has extremely severe security measures."

If Knapp is right about the kinds of activity that go on there, it would seem that "severe security measures" are justified. But the use of deadly force? Could you get shot just for watching a strange-looking airplane take off or land? So far as we know, no one has yet been met with deadly force although the security measures in place would make such an eventuality a very real possibility.

With a reporter's practiced insight, Knapp described the system for us. "It has three different security forces that patrol the area," he said. "It has surface-to-air missiles in case planes fly over that aren't welcome there. It has motion detectors in the ground. It has ammonia detectors that can sense the smell of ammonia in human skin. It has surveillance cameras to see who's looking down on the base. It is a very secure location."

It is the very fact that this level of security exists in the middle of the Nevada desert that piques the interest of many investigators. It's understandable for a prudent government to seek to protect military secrets. But the security measures at Area 51, many believe, go far beyond such prudence, extending even to endangering private citizens on public land as far away as ten miles from the perimeter of the installation.

Norio Hayakawa, former regional director of the Civilian Intelligence Network, a California-based group, has organized many trips to the remote desert area surrounding Groom Lake. On one occasion he says he was, ". . . pursued dangerously by this helicopter. They are prepared," Hayakawa told us, "to use whatever force is necessary to keep the people as far away as possible from this area."

His firsthand experience with the security surrounding Area 51 has convinced Hayakawa that there is, literally, more going on there than meets the eye. "In 1991," he recounts, "I led an investigative group from Southern California, including some journalists, to this area. After we witnessed what I believe was some type of test flight or possibly maneuvering of these objects, I was leading a caravan of seven cars on this dirt road. Suddenly a black, military helicopter with no insignia came over and approached our cars. [They] came in front of our cars . . . about ten to fifteen feet above [us]. At no time," Hayakawa continues, "were we trespassing the military area. We were well away from the military zone, and we were on public land. We had every right to be [there] . . . yet we were harassed by this military helicopter."

The degree of security at the area has convinced Hayakawa that the government is test-flying several state-of-the-art aircraft that "almost resemble flying saucers," some of which could even be the rumored Aurora spy plane allegedly built by Lockheed. Other craft Hayakawa believes are being tested in the area include the TR–3A, commonly known as the "Black Mania," and several diamond-shaped aircraft called "pumpkin seeds" by insiders. This latter craft, according to Hayakawa, uses some sort of pulse detonation propulsion system.

"There is no doubt in my mind," says Hayakawa, "that this Nevada facility is where the leading-edge technology is located . . . the leading edge in propulsion systems, in computer applications, and even . . . in medical technology."[10]

Could that leading-edge technology include some sort of flying disk? Some investigators are convinced that whatever else might be going on there, "saucer"-type aircraft are definitely part of the equation.

Gary Schultz, director of the Southern California-based Secret Saucer Base Expeditions, claims that on February 28, 1990, he watched in awe as what seemed to be a metallic disk-shaped object suddenly appeared over the Jumbled Hills (another identifying landmark) south of Area 51 and flew toward Groom Lake. "There is no doubt about it," Schultz says, ". . . some select U.S. pilots are regularly being given instruction in maneuvering several disk-shaped craft at Papoose Lake."[11]

It should be pointed out that it isn't just UFO groups that have made these observations. In April 1992 the mainstream press got into the act and in a significant way. According to Norio Hayakawa, an NBC news crew was sent to the area to report on the landing at Groom Lake of the super spy plane, Aurora. While waiting for that event they accidentally succeeded in videotaping the first flight of what Area 51 observers call "Old Faithful," a mysterious object seen virtually every day precisely at 4:45 A.M. The crew was standing at the black mailbox, looking south toward the Jumbled Hills. The footage was taken with a night-scope camera and was broadcast on the NBC Nightly News with Tom Brokaw on April 20, 1992. NBC News reported that

---

[10] A shocking update: The truth about Area 51, UFO *Encounters*, 1992, p. 58
[11] Ibid.

they had videotaped a test flight of a new U.S. aerial craft that had definitely defied the laws of physics.[12]

John Lear, son of the designer of the famous Lear Jet, and an accomplished test pilot in his own right with many years of government service, conducted a session at a UFO conference in Los Angeles in 1993. In that session he described things he had personally seen near Papoose Lake while in the company of Bob Lazar. He declined to be interviewed for this book, citing the fact that his public pronouncements had already cost him dearly in terms of contracts with the Department of Defense. But he did say that whether anyone believed his story was irrelevant. He had seen what he had seen. If people wanted to ignore it, that was their problem. Then he interjected something new into the controversy. "I have come to believe," he said, "that there are some things the people do *not* have a right to know."

Normally we wouldn't even mention someone who didn't want to be interviewed, but as it turns out, John Lear may have been the man who opened up this whole can of worms. According to George Knapp:

> I first got involved in doing this UFO stuff when a guy named John Lear came into the station . . . trying to tell my managing editor about UFOs, possibly alien technology, being out in the desert at Area 51. The managing editor was having no part of it. I was eavesdropping, as always, and I said, 'Let me take a look at this stuff.' And I put John on this little public affairs program that I was producing at the time, and the response from the audience was incredible. [I] put him on again. The response was even bigger. He started telling stories about alien technology at Area 51 [and] I didn't believe it, but I decided to

---

[12] Norio Hayakawa, UFOs: The Grand Deception and the Coming of the New World Order (Gardena, CA: Civilian Intelligence Network), January 1993.

take a look at it. The more I delved into it, the more people I came across who said they had seen this alien technology. People who had walked into hangars and saw discs [sic] sitting under tarps. [Then] Bob Lazar came along, and that's when I knew I had a story, because instead of just saying, 'I've seen flying saucers,' he told me what they were and where they had come from.

So, having taken the guided tour of the Area 51 complex, we wind up right back where we started, with Bob Lazar. Can he be believed?

It depends on who you talk to. Glenn Campbell, for example, says:

"There are a lot of problems with the Bob Lazar story. The most notable is that his educational credentials don't check out. He claims to have gone to MIT and Caltech and that plainly isn't true. You can remove a student's records, say from the registrar's office, but can you kill off every professor he once took classes with or kill off every student?"

Campbell does concede, however, that ". . . the area does seem to be highly secret, and workers at Groom Lake have told me that, yes, when they were there, this area, S–4, was a highly secret area. Something big was going on there, but the workers I talked to don't know what."

George Knapp acknowledges that, "trying to verify his [Lazar's] records has been almost impossible. I've been stonewalled," he says, "basically every step of the way. He claims he worked at Los Alamos National Lab. It took me two years before Los Alamos would acknowledge that he actually was there, and even after that they claim that he was not an employee of the lab but a subcontractor."

According to Knapp, sticking with this story has not been easy. ". . . [Bob is] a very uncooperative guy, even with me, and I've known him for a long time. He doesn't give a hoot whether the UFO community believes him or not. In fact he can't stand most UFO . . . researchers." But having said that, Knapp seems to find more to accept than reject in Lazar's story. "I've known the guy for years. He hasn't disappeared, the story that he's told has stayed the same all the way through. It's the same story he told the court, by the way, when he got into legal problems. If he were a con man, that would have been the time to come clean, because if they had caught him lying about his background, he could [have gone] to jail. He didn't. He stuck to the story that he had worked at Los Alamos Lab, that he had worked for the U.S. Navy up at Area 51, and that he had worked on flying saucers . . . the judge commented that he found it believable."

Frank Joseph, in an article entitled "UFOs: The Best Evidence," describes Lazar as a "soft-spoken professional who very reluctantly consented to appear . . . [on KLAS-TV]."[13] He also reminds us that, "Lazar voluntarily submitted to hypnosis and polygraph tests to determine his credibility. The extensive examinations conducted by clinical experts repeated[ly] demonstrated that he was telling the truth."

With regard to the absence of any scholastic or work records, Joseph said: "After Lazar disclosed the secret of Groom Lake . . . both he and his wife's lives were threatened and his educational and employment records began to disappear. 'They're trying to make me an un-person,' Lazar said. Even while he was employed by the federal government, Lazar was subjected to psychological and physical terrorism. Military police would suddenly jam the barrel of an M–16 rifle into his stomach, warning him never to divulge what he saw in Area 51."

After the programs were aired on KLAS-TV, the real "Dennis," who Lazar later said was his supervisor at S–4, called with a single, sinister question: "Do you have any idea," he asked, "what is going to happen to you now?"

[13] Frank Joseph, UFOs: The Best Evidence, *Unicus*, 2(3), p. 13.

Except for the series with George Knapp and his own video, Lazar has been very reluctant to grant interviews. One notable exception was a UFO conference actually held in Rachel, Nevada, at the Little A'le'inn, on May 1, 1993. In a casual give-and-take with the interviewer, Lazar gives some insight into his feelings about everything that's happened since his first public revelation of the story. The interview was published in the MUFON UFO *Journal*, October 1993. Some of the questions and answers are quite revealing.

Q: What was the ratio of security people to scientists out there?

BL: (Laughing) A million to one.

Q: Why?

BL: I have no idea. . . . you're secure in a test site already, and it's not like there's going to be an invasion team coming over the hill. I have no idea what the level of security was for.

Q: Your coworkers at S–4, did you detect an arrogance or ego on their part?

BL: No. Not at all. They really feel privileged, as I did when I was there, to be involved with it. And we kind of pushed off everyone else. The feeling was something like, "you're right, this *should* be a secret. To hell with everyone else. (Laughs) . . . believe me, when you're involved with it, you feel like, "hey, we're *it*!" That's really the attitude I had when I was there.[14]

All other arguments aside, those responses appear to convey a certain genuineness. Bob Lazar may, indeed, be a con man, but if he is, he is at least entertaining. It is also

[14] John Kirby, An interview with Robert Lazar, MUFON UFO *Journal*, No. 306 (October 1993), p. 10.

interesting to note that Lazar arrived at the conference in a car with Nevada license plates that read, "MJ–12." Apparently Mr. Lazar has not lost his sense of humor through all his trials and tribulations.

And what of Area 51 today? Thousands of UFO enthusiasts make the trek to the black mailbox every year. Many of them claim to have seen flying saucers or UFOs of various types. Hundreds of photographs and miles of videotape of these peculiar sightings exist. But are they seeing an alien technology? Is there anything that can be learned from these difficult, often cold and miserable trips into the desert?

Except for some members of Congress who might want to know where all the money is going, George Knapp doesn't think so. "If they ever had it," he says, "any kind of alien technology [that] was out there, I'm fairly certain . . . [it's] not there anymore. It makes no sense for them to have it there . . . because so many people are going out there to look for it. So if there was alien technology there, it's gone."

According to Knapp some "congressional personnel" did visit Groom Lake on the premise of checking on rumors about the spy plane Aurora. Two of them wanted to see Papoose Lake. "One wasn't allowed to go," he said, "because of a freakish, blinding snowstorm. The other was told there was nothing at S–4 except a lot of radioactivity from past programs. Curiosity about whether there are hangars built into the mountain may never be satisfied."[15]

The base, however, is real. We know this if for no other reason than the Russians have taken satellite photos of it. One of those photographs appeared on the cover of the March 1994 issue of *Popular Science* magazine. "The Russians," Knapp says, "have been taking pictures of Area 51 for many years. In fact, we've signed an Open Skies treaty that

---

[15] *MUFON Symposium Proceedings* (Seguin, TX: Mutual UFO Network, 1993), p. 238.

allows dozens of other nations to fly over and take all the pictures they want, but we, the people who foot the bill . . . aren't supposed to know about it."

Glenn Campbell suggests the whole controversy could be done away with in a single afternoon. "Why can't the military march a few journalists through there?" he asks. "Show them the lake bed, show them that there's nothing there?" But he answers his own question. "The fact is, the area does seem to be highly secret."

Norio Hayakawa thinks he knows why. "I have come to the conclusion," he says in a published article, "that our government, especially under the auspices of such top-secret agencies as the U.S. Naval Research Laboratory and DARPA (the Defense Advanced Research Projects Agency), now has the capacity to simulate and even 'stage' fake extraterrestrial landings by building believable disk-like craft and [to] create an alien threat if they really want to . . . for some reason or another."[16]

The idea of some kind of grand conspiracy doesn't carry much weight with George Knapp. In fact he attributes much of the confusion about what's going on at Area 51 to what he calls "blatant profiteers, religious zealots, or hopelessly gullible saucer nuts." He does, however, have a kind of "conspiracy" concept of his own; one that explains why Bob Lazar was hired in the first place and why he has been allowed to continue to tell his tale of super saucers and other worldly propulsion systems.

"If you take Lazar out of the Area 51 story," he told a MUFON symposium group, "it is still a story. There are too many other witnesses who claim knowledge of the program. But, if you keep him in the story, and if you can discredit him, you cut a wide swath across all UFOlogy. [You] cast doubt on the crashed saucer theory [and] forever wipe out the silly rumor about UFOs in the Nevada desert. [You also]

[16] A shocking update: The truth about Area 51, UFO Encounters, 1992, p. 58.

get in a few shots at MJ–12 while you're at it and scare the dickens out of anyone else who might someday want to talk about secret programs they've worked on.

"By picking someone like Bob for their program, by letting him see certain documents even before his clearance had been upgraded, by messing with his mind, they had a perfect, built-in safety valve. By discrediting him you give UFO luminaries an excuse to attack [and] you give the lunatic fringe something to embrace and embellish. You almost guarantee that no official in his right mind [will] get near this mess to find out what really might be going on."[17]

What really might be going on seems to be the question of the year. And there is yet another theory, proposed by Bob Lazar himself in his videotape. But in order to get the full impact of this idea, we have to go back about thirty years.

You'll remember we asked you to keep in mind, the star map drawn by Betty Hill after her abduction experience. Under hypnosis Betty was able to describe her abductors in considerable detail. She also said she saw a strange diagram on one of the walls of the ship she was in. Her captors told her it was the star system from which they came. Betty was able to reproduce the diagram with what she felt was considerable accuracy. At the time it was regarded as an odd curiosity at best, and, at worst, a fanciful contrivance.

In 1966, however, Marjorie Fish, an Ohio schoolteacher and amateur astronomer, became aware of Betty Hill's map. She concluded that it could be verified and began searching for a similar set of stars in then-current astronomical publications. According to two German MUFON researchers, Fish had completed a three-dimensional model of the nearer surroundings of our sun by 1968. It included stars up to 10 parsec distance (1 parsec = 3.262 light years). In 1969 an

---

[17] MUFON *Symposium Proceedings* (Seguin, TX: Mutual UFO Network, 1993), p. 237.

updated edition of the *Catalogue of Nearby Stars,* by W. Gliese, was printed. With this new data some of the star positions could be corrected, and Marjorie Fish found a pattern of stars similar to that in Betty Hill's map. It was now very logical.[18] Betty Hill, who couldn't read a star chart if her life depended on it, had somehow created an almost perfect rendering of a star system, thirty-five light years away and still undiscovered at the time she drew it.

A couple of decades later Bob Lazar would tell the world that while working at S–4 he was shown official briefing documents stating that the beings who gave us the secrets of the flying saucer came from the Zeta Reticuli system. He went on to describe these beings in much the same way as had Betty and Barney Hill: They were three to four feet tall, with grayish skin, large heads and almond-shaped, wraparound eyes. According to Lazar:

"These beings said that they had been visiting Earth for a long time and presented photographic evidence, which they contended was over 10,000 years old. There was an exchange of hardware and information in central Nevada until 1979, at which time there was a conflict that brought the program to an abrupt halt."

Lazar seems to be suggesting that someone from "out there" has a plan to try and help us along. Somehow it all sounds vaguely familiar. The SHAPE "Assessment" report, according to Robert Dean, concludes some sort of plan is being implemented by extraterrestrial visitors. According to Zechariah Sitchin's reading of the Sumerian texts, visitors from another world have been giving earthlings a technological, perhaps even a biological boost for hundreds of thousands of years. Is Bob Lazar just the latest to chronicle these activities?

---

[18] Joachim Koch and Hans-Jurgen Kyborg, *New Discoveries in Betty Hill's Star Map* (Berlin: Author, 1993), p. 2.

But Lazar had said something truly startling—that there had been an "*exchange*" of information. If the documents that Lazar insists he read are accurate, we are not only being visited, someone—some military leader or government official—has met with our "guests" and found a way to communicate with them. Could this be the secret the military is so eager to protect at Area 51?

Remember Bob Lazar's description of the underground facility at S–4? It is inside a mountain with nine giant hangar doors colored and textured to blend with the natural surroundings. We don't want to get too far ahead of ourselves here, but, incredibly, this description matches the one given by some people who claim to have been kidnapped by the occupants of UFOs and taken to a mysterious underground facility.

Robert Dean adds another note of intrigue that is also consistent with Lazar's account of the classified documents he was permitted to read. "Abductees," Dean told us, "have been taken to places that they have assumed were underground facilities. Abductees have also reported that they have seen what appeared to be *U.S. military people* [emphasis mine] involved in this abduction." Could all of this be going on under the smothering cloak of secrecy at Area 51?

If only a fraction of what we have presented in this chapter is true, the government has plenty of reasons to maintain the virtually impenetrable security at the Groom Lake operating location. But whether it is true, the fact remains that public demand for an explanation of what's going on at Area 51 is growing every day. Just about everything we know about the place is hearsay, but the questions keep coming. Is there an alien spacecraft locked beneath the desert floor? Is it possible that behind the tightest ring of security in our history there actually exists proof of life on other worlds?

Questions like these are not easily dismissed from the public mind.

There is another question that continues to insinuate itself into the controversy despite nearly fifty years of investigation and denials: If there are alien spacecraft at Area 51, how did we get possession of them? Is it possible they were retrieved from the crash site at Roswell, New Mexico?

If such an event is conceivable, we will find out about it in the next chapter.

CHAPTER 5

ROSWELL REVISITED

> >> The intelligence office of the 509th Bom-
> bardment group at Roswell Army Air Field
> announced at noon today, that the field
> has come into possession of a flying
> saucer.
>
> Roswell Daily Record, Roswell, New Mexico, July 8, 1947

On the evening of July 2, 1947, near Roswell, New Mexico, Mac Brazel, the foreman on the Foster ranch, was making his way through a blinding rainstorm to the range shack where he could bed down for the night. The desert storm had rolled in about sundown, and the rain was coming down in sheets.

A nighttime thunderstorm in the desert can be one of the most beautiful and frightening events you can experience. Usually brief, such storms are spectacular. Brilliant bolts of lightening snap out of the sky and illuminate the landscape for an instant, while great peals of thunder roll across the land in total darkness. Occasionally, a thunderbolt will crash to earth and an instant later, while light still floods the sky, a crack of thunder will follow. When that happens, you know the lightening has struck close by, sometimes close enough to make the hair on your arms fairly tingle.

This was not the first thunderstorm Mac Brazel had ever been in, and he was pretty sure it wouldn't be the last.

Suddenly there was a loud, explosive sound cut through the storm. Brazel jerked back on the reins and spun around in his saddle.

Nothing! He stared into the gathering darkness in all directions, but saw only the slashing rain. Couldn't have been thunder, he thought, or I'd have a lightning bolt in my lap. He pulled his hat down a little tighter, gave his horse the spurs, and continued on toward the shack.

The next morning Brazel was up at first light. The storm was completely gone, leaving behind the fresh, clean smell of the desert and the promise of a cooler day. He was grateful for that. July on the high desert of New Mexico can be blistering hot, and even a small flock of sheep can raise a choking dust cloud. Mac had sheep all over the range, and the storm would have likely scattered them from hell to breakfast. Then there were the windmills and fence lines that would have to be checked. He'd probably be all day getting the ranch back together again. He tightened the cinch on the saddle, dropped the stirrup into place, and lifted himself up on the horse's back.

He might have wondered how long he'd be in the saddle that day. He might even have been concerned about accounting for all the sheep so he could take off the Fourth of July holiday. He certainly didn't know he was about to ride out into the desert and change the way people think about the world.

Thanks largely to the tireless efforts of Dr. Stanton T. Friedman, a nuclear physicist whose chance encounter with a TV journalist in 1978 set him on a journey of discovery, the story of the UFO crash near Roswell, New Mexico, is well documented. Dr. Friedman and Don Berliner, an aviation/ science writer, published their findings in 1992 in a book titled *Crash at Corona*. Then, in 1994, Kevin D. Randle, a captain in the Air Force Reserve, along with Donald R. Schmitt, director of special investigations for the Center for UFO Studies,[1] published the results of nearly ten years of investigation in their book, *The Truth About the UFO Crash at Roswell*. Although the two studies do not agree in all particulars, they both support the main contentions that form the basis for what is now widely viewed as one of the U.S. government's most blatant, and very nearly successful, cover-ups. In addition, at least two full-length feature films have been made on the subject and been widely distributed.

It is not our intention here to revisit all the details of the Roswell incident. Rather we intend to add new information relating to the crash and its aftermath that is not likely to be found in anything published or produced before mid-1995. For the reader who may not be familiar with the story, however, the following is a summary of the events researchers now believe took place.

Mac Brazel rode out onto the range and discovered a field littered with some kind of metallic-looking debris, unlike anything he had ever seen. Later that day he picked up some of the metallic pieces and drove over to his neighbors, Floyd and Loretta Proctor, who had a ranch some twenty miles away. They took a long look at the chunks of "metal" Brazel had with him and shook their heads. They'd never seen anything like it, either. The Proctors suggested he take the material into town and tell the sheriff about it.

Mac Brazel still had work to do, so he spent the next couple of days making sure everything was taken care of at the ranch before driving the nearly seventy-five miles south to Roswell. When he pulled his truck up in front of the sheriff's office, it was the afternoon of July 6. It had been

---

[1] The Center for UFO Studies was created by renowned astronomer J. Allen Hynek, whose first association with UFOs was to debunk them. His work led him to a different conclusion and to the establishment of the J. Allen Hynek Center for UFO Studies (CUFOS) in Chicago.

nearly three days since Brazel had heard an "explosion" above the crashing thunderstorm.

George Wilcox, who was the sheriff of Roswell at the time, examined the strange material Brazel had brought, then he decided somebody better have a look at the crash site. He dispatched two deputies to go to the scene and, probably thinking it was some sort of military device that had come down in the storm, notified the headquarters of the 509th Bomb Group at Roswell Army Air Field. That phone call set in motion a series of events that would alter the character of this small New Mexico town and many of its residents forever.

It is important to note here that the people of Roswell, New Mexico, were very familiar with the workings of the military. At that time, the 509th Bomb Group was the world's only nuclear strike force. It also may be safely assumed that the residents were familiar with the need for military secrecy. After all, the *Enola Gay*, the B–29 that had dropped the atomic bomb on Hiroshima, had been hangered there. In fact, the powdered gypsum dunes of White Sands, New Mexico, had been the first spot on Earth to feel the searing heat of an atomic blast. The citizens, in all likelihood, would not think twice about turning anything out of the ordinary over to the military. It's also likely that had the military handled the whole affair differently, none of the witnesses would have questioned the need for secrecy. Still imbued with the patriotic zeal of World War II and living in a world suddenly very jittery over its newly acquired means of self-destruction, the good people of Roswell could have been counted on to go along with whatever the government or military officials asked them to do.

Within minutes of the sheriff's phone call, the base intelligence officer, Major Jesse Marcel, arrived at the sheriff's office. With him was a counterintelligence officer, Captain Sheridan Cavitt. The major talked to the sheriff and Brazel, looked over the unusual debris Mac had brought with him, and immediately called his commanding officer, Colonel William Blanchard. The commander wasted no time in ordering both Marcel and Cavitt to take Brazel back to the site and conduct a thorough investigation.

Major Marcel and Mac Brazel climbed into the major's Buick staff car, with Cavitt following in an army truck. By the time they completed the dusty trip back to the ranch (much of the drive was over dirt road), it was after dark. The three men spent the night in sleeping bags at the range shack, looking forward to an early start the following morning. In the meantime the sheriff's two deputies had returned to Roswell. They didn't find the debris field, but they had stumbled onto a large, circular burn area in a pasture. It caught their attention because of its unnatural, dark-brown color. When they walked over to the spot, they could see that this particular patch of ground had been subject to such an intense heat that the sand had been fused into glass. They ruled out a lightning strike because of the size and nearly round shape of the burn. Phylis McGuire, Sheriff Wilcox's daughter, remembered her father telling her the melted area was about the size of a football field.[2]

The three men in the range shack were unaware of the deputies' discovery. They spent the next day gathering as much of the scattered metallic bits and pieces as they could. Brazel estimated that the debris-covered area was about three quarters of a mile long and 250 yards wide.

It was late when the men got back to Roswell. Flushed with excitement, Major Jesse Marcel hurried into the kitchen of the small home he shared with his wife and son, Jesse Marcel, Jr. Even though it was nearly 2 A.M., he awakened them both. According to Jesse Marcel, Jr., now a doctor living in Montana, it was an exciting evening.

In several interviews since the death of this father, the

---

[2] *UFO Secret, The Roswell Crash.* New Century Productions, Anthony R. Iascone, executive producer, 1993.

younger Marcel has reiterated the same sequence of events. His father, Major Marcel, he said, was on his way to deliver the debris to the air base but stopped off to show him and his mother what they had found. The 1942 Buick staff car, according to Jesse, Jr., was "loaded with the stuff," and his father brought in a box containing several pieces of the debris. He spread it on the floor like a jigsaw puzzle, trying to give it some definition or shape but that didn't work. There was no clue what object the material may have come from. The Marcels had to be satisfied with handling this strange metallic debris. Of particular interest to young Jesse was a small rectangular piece, approximately a foot long and a half-inch wide. It was in the shape of an I-beam. What caught the boy's eye was a row of characters of some sort that appeared to run the full length of the beam. They were not characters he could read, but were more like the Egyptian hieroglyphics he had seen in school. Years later, Jesse, Jr., under hypnosis, would describe the characters. His memory of what they looked like can be seen, if you're ever in Roswell, on plastic souvenir replicas of the I-beam Jesse, Jr., said he handled.

Marcel isn't the only living witness who handled pieces of the debris. Frankie Rowe, whose father was a volunteer fireman, was at the Roswell firehouse. A state trooper who had helped in the clean-up brought in a piece to show some of his friends.

In a recent television interview, Frankie Rowe said the trooper had "a piece of the material wadded up in his hand. It was just a tiny ball, and when he dropped it on the table, it spread out like it was liquid or quicksilver. And there was not one wrinkle in that. And I do remember that we all got to touch it . . . we all got to pick it up. You could bend it; it made no crinkle, no noise. It was very thin. Very shiny . . . very silvery color. It was about . . . maybe a foot square. And I have no idea what happened to it."[3]

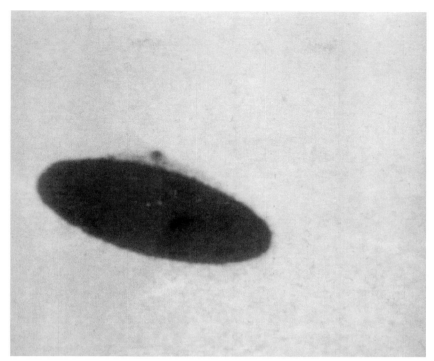

These famous photographs were taken over a farm in McMinnville, Oregon, in May 1950. Project Blue Book was unable to discount them as hoaxes. (Courtesy of J. Allen Hynek Center for UFO Studies)

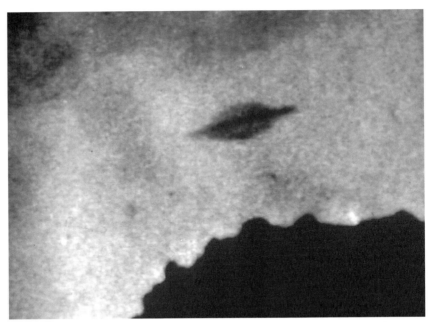

A "daylight disk" photographed in Trindade, Brazil. (Courtesy of J. Allen Hynek Center for UFO Studies)

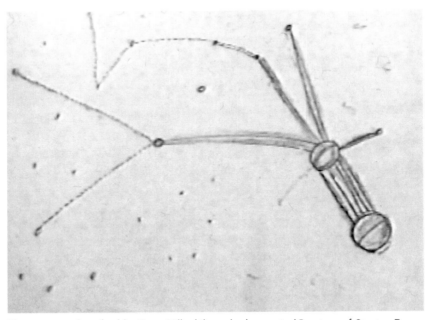

The star map described by Betty Hill while under hypnosis. (Courtesy of Stanton T. Friedman)

Mac Brazel, the Foster ranch foreman who discovered metallic debris and called authorities. (Courtesy of New Century Productions, Inc.)

Stone relief discovered in 1935 in Palenque, Mexico. It seems, stunningly, to depict an astronaut at the controls of a rocket. (Courtesy of Sun International Pictures, Inc.)

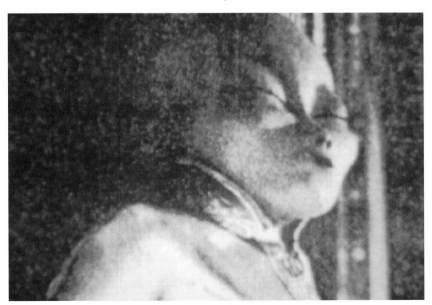

This mysterious photo has been suggested to be an alien body recovered from a 1947 flying disk crash at either Roswell or San Augustine Flats, New Mexico. (Courtesy of Ralph E. Heick)

Brigadier General Roger Ramey and Colonel Thomas J. DuBose identify metallic fragments found near Roswell. (Courtesy of the Bettmann Archive)

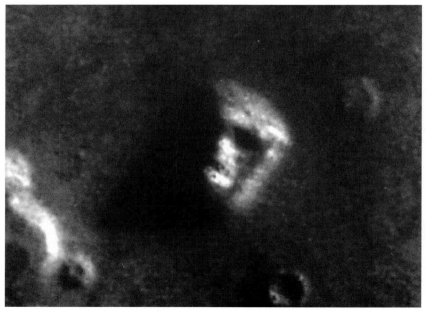

NASA photograph taken by the *Viking* probe and digitally enhanced by Dr. Mark J. Carlotto to show structures on Mars in the shape of a face. (Courtesy of Mark Carlotto)

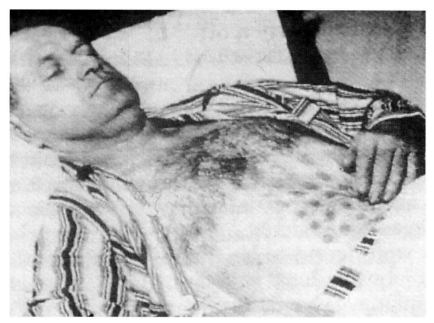

Stephen Michalak, who said he was burned by a blast of hot air from the grille-covered opening on a UFO in 1967. (Courtesy of Chris Rutkowski)

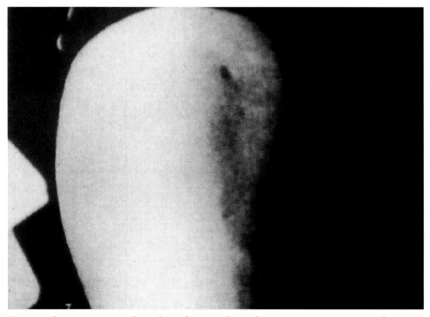

Scars and puncture wounds such as the one shown here are common among those claiming to have been abducted by UFOs. (Courtesy of Budd Hopkins)

The original Project Blue Book staff. Major Hector Quintanilla, Jr. (seated), First
Lieutenant William Morley, Sergeant Harold T. Jones, typist Hilma Lewis, and secretary
Marilyn Stancombe (standing, left to right). (Courtesy of J. Allen Hynek Center for UFO
Studies)

Respected astronomer J. Allen Hynek, who began his investigation of Project Blue
Book as a skeptic and became a believer. He is considered the father of the modern
UFO movement. (Courtesy of J. Allen Hynek Center for UFO Studies)

UFO Sightings by Engineers

to the detailed report by the crew of General Mills balloon technicians headed by aerologist ion I), dozens of professional engineers and technicians have reported UFOs. As indicated clude a cross-section of technological fields. Many are uniquely qualified to evaluate the a omeha in comparison to known devices or atmospheric effects.

(All rep

Witnesses	Field	Description
David A. Kenney, two others	Instruments Engineer, Aviation Co.	Oval UFO in steady flight at high altitude.
Several	Aircraft technicians	Oval object, apparently rotating [Section
Victor G. Didelot	Aircraft Instrumentation	Elliptical or oval UFO, sudden vertical as
Charles B. Moore, Jr., Others	Aerology, balloon technicians	Elliptical UFO tracked with theodolite [S
Guided missile unit	Missile tracking	Two white round UFOs paced missile [Se
Six	Balloon technicians	Two discs, approached rapidly, circled ba
Alford Roos	Mining engineer	Two discs descended, hovered, shot away.
J. J. Kaliszewski, others	Aeronautical research	Maneuvering UFOs observed during ballo

A large spectrum of society has witnessed UFOs, as detailed in these excerpts from reports in Project Blue Book. (Courtesy of J. Allen Hynek Center for UFO Studies)

UFO Sightings by Scientists

(All Reports on File at NICAP)

Name	Field	Description
"top astronomer"	Astronomy	Elliptical object which hovered, wobbled, asce [Section II.]
Carl A. Mitchell	Physics	Three luminescent greenish discs one second across sky from N to S and over horizon.
Clyde W. Tombaugh	Astronomy	Circular pattern of rectangular lights, keeping
Seymour L. Hess	Meteorology Astronomy	Disc or sphere in apparent "powered" flight.
John Zimmerman	Geology	Silvery discs looping around aircraft, disrupt
J. D. Laudermilk	Geochemistry	Disc moving with wobbling motion passed behi minimum speed computed to be 720 mph.
Walter N. Webb	Astronomy	Bright glowing light moving in undulating path
W. Gordon Graham	Astronomy	UFO "like a smoke ring, elliptical in shape, a pinpoints of light along its main axis;" sailed to E. [5.]
Dr. Charles H. Otis	Biology	Formation of rocket-like objects leaving cons

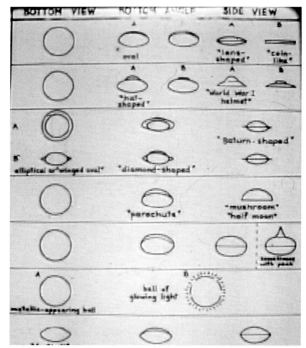

UFO shapes were categorized in Project Blue Book, as shown here. (Courtesy of J. Allen Hynek Center for UFO Studies)

Betty and Barney Hill hold an article entitled "The Interrupted Journey," their account of a 1961 abduction by aliens. (Courtesy of Stanton T. Friedman)

There was something else strange about the material the intelligence officer found. In an interview made in 1979, shortly before he died, Jesse Marcel, Sr., told the interviewer:

> It was something I had never seen before. . . . But something that is more astounding is that the piece of metal that we brought back was so thin, just like the tinfoil in a pack of cigarette paper. I didn't pay too much attention to that at first, until one of the GIs came to me and said "You know the metal that was in there? I tried to bend that stuff and it won't bend. I even tried it with a sledge-hammer. You can't make a dent on it." He said, "It's definite that it cannot be bent and it's so light that it doesn't weigh anything." And that was true of all the material that was brought up. It was so light that it weighed practically nothing.[4]

Appropriately perhaps, it was Jesse Marcel, Sr., who, after thirty years of silence, was the unwitting catalyst who reopened the investigation that has since focused worldwide attention on Roswell, New Mexico. In 1978 in a casual conversation between Dr. Stanton Friedman and a TV station director in Baton Rouge, Louisiana, Marcel's name was mentioned as a man who had ". . . handled pieces of those things." Dr. Friedman, who had been lecturing at Louisiana State University on the subject "Flying Saucers Are Real," didn't quite know what to make of the statement. But when the station director told him that he and Marcel were old ham radio buddies and that Marcel was a "very reliable" person, Friedman decided it was worth following up. At the time Marcel was living in Houma, Louisiana.

---

[3] Ibid.
[4] Stanton T. Friedman and Don Berliner, *Crash at Corona* (New York: Marlowe & Company, 1992), p. 100.

The very next day Friedman gave him a call, and the long search for the truth about what happened at Roswell began.[5] Marcel and the counterintelligence corps officer, Cavitt, had indeed been the first military men on the scene, of that there is no doubt. The only question that needed to be answered, and still needs to be answered, is on the scene of what?

Colonel Blanchard, quite probably due to the reports of Major Marcel and Captain Cavitt, was convinced there was more to the incident than just scattered junk. The bits and pieces had to have come from something, and judging by the amount of material scattered about, that "something" was probably still out there. The colonel ordered Major Marcel to do an air search and to take Mac Brazel with him.

On the morning of July 8, nearly a full week after Mac Brazel had heard an explosion in the rainswept darkness of a desert downpour, the last piece of the puzzle was about to fall into place. A group of archaeologists, seeking clues to ancient Indian tribes and hoping to find a few artifacts, wandered into the New Mexico desert and into UFO history. Dropping down into a protected arroyo, they came upon a singularly horrifying sight. A circular craft unlike anything any of them had ever seen before was partially imbedded in the wall of the ravine. Scattered about were four bodies. They were small, not more than four feet tall and very slender. Their heads, by human standards, were much too large for the frail-looking bodies. Standing amidst the wreckage, almost close enough to touch the bodies, was a lone man.

By this time the airplane carrying Mac Brazel and Major Marcel had apparently spotted the wreckage also. Brazel helped the major direct ground troops to the area.

The man already at the site when the group of archaeologists stumbled on the scene was a civil engineer, Grady

---

[5] Ibid., p. 8. (The reader should not be confused by the difference in names. "Roswell" was where the official investigation and subsequent press releases were handled. "Corona" is the area in New Mexico closest to the actual crash site.)

Barnett, who was doing survey work for an irrigation project. A former military officer in the 313th Engineers and by
all accounts an honest and straightforward man, Barnett was
stunned by what he had found. Years later the former second
lieutenant would take a close friend named Vern Malthais
into his confidence. In an on-camera interview in 1993,
Malthais recounted that conversation.

> He said I'm going to tell you something that I'm not sup-
> posed to divulge . . . he come across this object on the
> ground which was the shape of a flying saucer, and it had
> split open. So he jumped out of his pickup and went down
> there. And there was [sic] four beings laying on the
> ground, and they were in a sort of a silver-colored suit,
> and they were about three to four feet high, and the suits
> were rather tight fitting . . . and the shape of the heads of
> the beings on the ground were hairless with a sort of a
> pear-shaped head and the hands were exposed.
>
> He had just barely arrived and there was an archaeol-
> ogy team that had come up there . . . just a little bit after
> Barney, and then the military come [sic] in and sur-
> rounded the area and they called all those people that
> were there, the archaeology team and Mr. Barnett and
> they briefed them . . . that this was not to be divulged to
> anybody, that they were not to say one word about it . . .
> and forget that they had ever seen anything.[6]

Meanwhile, back in Roswell, things were beginning to
heat up. When Colonel Blanchard received a report that an
actual craft had been found, he sealed off all three sites. All
roads leading into the ranch where the debris field and the
circular burn area had been discovered were put under military guard. He placed the crash site itself completely under
control of the army. No civilian nor any civilian vehicles
were permitted anywhere near the spot.

[6] UFO Secret, *The Roswell Crash*. New Century Productions, Anthony R. Iascone,
executive producer, 1993.

But in a classic military "snafu," the army lost Mac Brazel. In all the excitement and hubbub, the man who had started the whole thing dropped out of sight.

About this same time, to everyone's surprise, Colonel Blanchard called his public information officer, First Lieutenant Walter Haut, and instructed him to issue a press release, spelling out what had taken place. Lt. Haut prepared the statement[7] as ordered and delivered copies to both Roswell newspapers and the town's two radio stations. By 4:00 P.M., the afternoon of July 8, the *Roswell Daily Record* published the story, based on Lt. Haut's press release, with a banner headline.

RAAF CAPTURES FLYING SAUCER
ON RANCH IN ROSWELL REGION!
No Details of Flying Disk Are Revealed

The intelligence office of the 509th Bombardment group at Roswell Army Air Field announced at noon today, that the field has come into possession of a flying saucer.

According to information released by the department, over authority of Maj. J.A. Marcel, intelligence officer, the disk was recovered on a ranch in the Roswell vicinity after an unidentified rancher had notified Sheriff Geo. Wilcox here, that he had found the instrument on his premises.

Major Marcel and a detail from his department went to the ranch and recovered the disk, it was stated.

After the intelligence officer here had inspected the instrument, it was flown to "higher headquarters."

The intelligence officer stated that no details of the saucer's construction or its appearance had been revealed.

---

[7] Here Friedman and Randle part company. Friedman is convinced Barnett found a "second" crashed saucer and actually appeared just ahead of the military at a spot 150 miles west called the Plains of San Augustin. While accepting the Barnett story as genuine, Randle concludes nothing happened on the plains. In a later interview Walter Haut, long since retired, told reporters he was "given the press release and told to deliver it to the local media."

Here was a clear, unambiguous report that appeared to describe with a fair amount of detail what had taken place in the desert.

Hours before the newspaper hit the streets, however, the two local radio stations had already put the story on the air. Frank Joyce, an announcer for KGFL, picked up the release from the news desk and read it. Incredulous, he called Haut's office at the base, suggesting it probably wasn't a good idea to release that kind of a story. Lt. Haut replied: "No, it's OK, I have the OK from the CO [Colonel Blanchard]."[8]

Joyce aired the story and put it on the Western Union line to United Press (UP). The UP issued the story as a bulletin, and within minutes the phone lines were jammed. Joyce also claims he received a call from someone at the Pentagon who " . . . was really pretty nasty" and who suggested that a number of very unpleasant things would happen to him if he continued to air that story. When Joyce told him it was an "official" Army Air Force press release, the line went dead.

KSWS, the other Roswell radio station, also was dealing with a thorny problem. The station was a Mutual/ABC affiliate, and as a matter of course, shared important stories with the network. Lydia Sleppy, a teletype operator at the station, was typing in the story as it was being dictated by a reporter named John McBoyle. Suddenly she was interrupted by the warning bell and a line of type began to appear on her machine. It read: "This is the FBI. You will cease transmitting."[9] She did, but she continued to take McBoyle's report in shorthand.

Among other things the story said:

> . . . the many rumors regarding the flying disk became a
> reality yesterday when the intelligence office of the 509th

---

[8] Stanton T. Friedman and Don Berliner, *Crash at Corona* (New York: Marlowe & Company, 1992), p. 76.

[9] Ibid.

Bomb Group of the 8th Air Force, Roswell Army Air Field, was fortunate enough to gain possession of a disk through the cooperation of one of the local ranchers.[10]

Out at Roswell Army Air Force Base a number of other events were happening in rapid succession. Major Marcel was ordered to report immediately to "higher headquarters" in Fort Worth and to bring some of the debris with him. Never one to question orders, Jesse Marcel filled a box with some of the material he had found and headed for the flight line. Planes were also coming into Roswell from Washington, D.C., and Fort Worth, where headquarters for the Eighth Air Force was located. The excitement in the area was palpable. Almost everyone was touched in some way by what was going on.

Another story about flying saucers was also on the front page of that special edition of the *Roswell Daily Record*, but it was largely overlooked in all the excitement. In retrospect this story, though on the surface having nothing to do with Roswell, may have been the more important of the two.

Dateline Portland, Ore., July 8, UP—The [*Portland*] *Oregonian* said today that Maj. Gen. Nathan F. Twining, chief of the AAP material command, told it flatly that the "flying saucers" are not the result of experiments by the armed services.

Neither the AAF nor any other component of the armed forces had any plane, guided missile or other aerial device under development which could possibly be mistaken for a saucer or formation of flying disks.

Interestingly, General Twining issued his statement from Kirtland Army Airbase in Albuquerque, New Mexico. Speculation was rife among members of the press corps that what were really being seen were secret military machines. If any-

---

[10] Ibid.

one in Roswell or anywhere else, thought what they now had in their possession was U.S. military ordinance, General Twining's remarks should have put the notion to rest. In point of fact the general was referring to a spate of flying saucer reports that had been coming in all spring and summer. The general was stating unequivocally that there was no U.S. military craft of any kind that could meet the specifications of the aircraft being sighted. Whether General Twining was in New Mexico because of the excitement at Roswell is unknown.

On the evening of July 8, Major Jesse Marcel, Sr., was ushered into the office of Brigadier General Roger M. Ramey, commander of the Eighth Air Force. Major Marcel placed his box of debris on the general's desk and was invited to join the general in an anteroom to "look at a map." When Major Marcel and General Ramey came back into the office, the box Marcel had brought with him had been replaced by another box containing material the major quickly recognized as the remnants of a weather balloon.[11]

It is not known what conversation passed between the two officers, but the general had already called reporters. Photographs of Major Marcel with the scraps of weather balloon were taken and widely circulated. The Army's official line? The major and his commanding officer, Colonel Blanchard, had simply goofed.

On July 9, 1947, the *Roswell Daily Record* published the following headline:

GEN. RAMEY EMPTIES ROSWELL SAUCER

The first four paragraphs of the story that accompanied the headline are reproduced verbatim.

Fort Worth, Texas, July 9 (AP)—An examination by the army revealed last night that a mysterious object found on

[11] Ibid.

a lonely New Mexico ranch was a harmless high-altitude weather balloon—not a grounded flying disk.

Excitement was high until Brig. Gen. Roger M. Ramey, commander of the Eighth Air Force with headquarters here, cleared up the mystery.

The bundle of tinfoil, broken wood beams, and rubber remnants of a balloon were sent here yesterday by army air transport in the wake of reports that it was a flying disk.

But the general said the objects were the crushed remains of a ray wind target used to determine the direction and velocity of winds at high altitudes.

Back in Roswell, First Lieutenant Walter Haut, the public information officer who had written and/or delivered the original press release, was stunned. There is some indication that the 509th Bomb Group commanding officer, Colonel Blanchard, was also taken by surprise. Nevertheless, the army being what it is, they all went along with the general's story.

Lieutenant Haut later resigned his commission and settled in Roswell. In 1993 he was asked if he knew why General Ramey had suddenly decided to change the story. Haut replied: "I think that not only was I set up, I think Colonel Blanchard was also. About the only reason that I can think of is they wanted to cover up the story and keep all of this information confidential."

If, after Jesse Marcel, Sr., and Walter Haut told their stories, there was anyone left who still believed the "weather balloon" explanation, they were in for yet another surprise in the person of Thomas J. DuBose, who was serving as chief of staff to General Ramey at the time of the Roswell incident. He had retired from the U.S. Air Force in 1959 with a rank of brigadier general. General DuBose, long after his retirement, told investigators that he had been ordered by General Clements McMullen, deputy commander,

Strategic Air Command, to have the debris flown from Roswell to Fort Worth, then on to the Pentagon. McMullen said he would send the material by personal courier to Benjamin Chidlaw, commanding general of the Air Materiel Command at Wright Field, later Wright-Patterson Air Force Base and home of the famous "Hanger 18," the storage hanger where UFO debris from Roswell was supposedly housed.

Some reports have suggested that General McMullen also ordered Colonel DuBose to "come up with something" that would satisfy the press and that the weather balloon story was the colonel's invention. DuBose, however, denies that. Before he died he told investigators:

" . . . we knew that it [the weather balloon] was a cover story and it . . . whose idea it was I haven't the vaguest. But we used that in order to assuage the curiosity of the press."[12]

Who came up with the weather balloon story is almost irrelevant. What is of far more importance is that General DuBose, if he was telling the truth, confirms conclusively that army brass, clear up to the Pentagon, were directly involved with the events transpiring in Roswell.

Meanwhile, back in Roswell, the army was frantically searching for the missing Mac Brazel. He was the wild card in the cover-up story that was being dealt to the public. They would probably have been even more nervous had they known that Walt Whitmore, co-owner and manager of radio station KGFL, had offered him a place to stay for the night.

Judd Roberts, Whitmore's partner in the radio station, recalled what happened.

"He [Walt] found him and suggested they go out to [Walt's] house, which was on the extreme side of Roswell at that time. And we felt it would give us an opportunity to get some information, which we would have liked to have had."[13]

[12] Ibid.
[13] Ibid.

Ultimately the military found Brazel, and to everyone's surprise, put him under "house arrest." He was subjected to an intense debriefing that lasted for hours and, for some reason, included a complete physical examination.

Walt Whitmore had, in fact, recorded an extensive interview with Mac Brazel while he was staying in his home, but, unfortunately, no one ever got to hear it. On the morning of July 9 station KGFL received a telephone call from Washington, D.C. Judd Roberts recalled the conversation:

"The suggestion was made to us that if we wanted to keep our license we would not use the interview on the air, because that would give us about twenty-four hours to find something else to do besides the radio business."[14]

Roberts wasn't sure, but he believed the call came from someone either in the office of Clinton Anderson, then U.S. Secretary of Agriculture and a former congressman from New Mexico, or from the office of New Mexico Senator, Dennis Chavez. In any case the phone call had the desired effect. The recorded interview with Brazel was "lost." Whitmore may have erased it to make certain it never got on the air, no one knows. Unfortunately no one is around today who can tell us what the ranch foreman might have said. Frank Joyce, the KGFL newsman who had spoken to Brazel on the phone the day before, did say that Mac Brazel had changed his tune after his debriefing.

On the evening of July 8, Joyce said, Mac Brazel, in the company of military officers, showed up at the KGFL studios with a completely different story about the crash. Essentially Brazel now agreed that what he had found could have been a weather balloon after all. Joyce, who was at the control board while Brazel made his statement, was incensed. He told Brazel he didn't believe this new story, but Mac stuck to

---

[14] *UFO Secret, The Roswell Crash*. New Century Productions, Anothony R. Iascone, executive producer, 1993.

his guns. Joyce pointed out several inconsistencies between what he was now saying and what he had said earlier. Finally Mac replied, "It'll go hard on me."

Brazel walked out of the station and climbed back into the car with the officers. For some reason he was housed at Roswell Army Air Force Base for several days before being allowed to go home.

Some have speculated that Brazel's change of heart was the result of serious threats to himself and his family, which would not be unthinkable given the testimony of other witnesses. But there may have been another reason. Loretta Proctor told investigators that Mac Brazel left the Foster ranch shortly after this whole affair. He was reported to have purchased a cold-storage locker plant in another community, and some neighbors reported seeing him driving a new pickup truck. Others insist Mac Brazel was not the kind of man to accept a bribe, and he certainly never broke the security oath the military insisted he take.[15]

Brazel's sudden turnaround was only the beginning of a host of curious events and contradictions. For example, why would the military expend all the power at their command to seal off and keep hidden a weather balloon? Even more curious; a crashed weather balloon could probably be gathered up and put in the trunk of a car. Why, then, did it take nine airplanes and numerous crates and packages to transport what was left of it when General Ramey already had most of the debris in his office?

According to the flight records in and out of the Roswell base during this period, the following flights took place:

JULY 6:   From Roswell to Fort Worth
            From Roswell to Washington, D.C.

---

[15] Stanton T. Friedman and Don Berliner, *Crash at Corona* (New York: Marlowe & Company, 1992).

JULY 8:   From Roswell to Wright Field in Dayton, Ohio

From Washington, D.C., to Roswell (a sealed box was picked up)

From Roswell to Fort Worth

JULY 9:   From Roswell to Los Alamos (three flights)

From Roswell to Fort Worth

JULY 10:   From Wright Field to an unknown destination

It is this last flight that has given rise to speculation that something from the Roswell crash might have been taken to Area 51.

But there was something else, something the weather balloon story didn't cover at all. Weather balloons don't carry personnel, even small ones. What happened to the bodies that several witnesses claim to have found at the scene?

Civil engineer Grady Barnett, you'll remember, said all of the beings he saw at the crash site were dead. But Sheriff Wilcox told a slightly different story. Barbara Dugger, granddaughter of George and Inez Wilcox, vividly remembers the stories her grandmother passed on to her before she died. According to Mrs. Dugger, her grandfather had also seen the bodies of small beings, unlike anything he had ever come across before.

"Grandaddy," she told us, "said their heads were large and the little suit they had on . . . was like . . . . silk or something." But the real shocker came when she asked her grandmother if they were alive or dead: " . . . and she said, I think one of them was alive."

This means that of all the witnesses, only Grady Barnett, the members of the archaeological group, and Sheriff George Wilcox claimed to have seen bodies. But apparently there were others who did see something other than mechanical bits and pieces. This part of the Roswell story has reverberated through nearly five decades, and in just the past few months has begun to reenergize the controversy as never before.

Let's go back to that fateful week in July 1947 one more time.

Glen Dennis was a mortician who worked for the Ballard Funeral Home in Roswell. Like most of the citizens of the community he had a comfortable and pleasant working relationship with the military. The funeral home had a contract to provide mortuary services to the base, and Dennis was often called to help out in difficult situations.

Sometime around noon on July 8, Dennis received the first of a series of calls from someone at the base. Over the next few hours he was asked a number of puzzling questions. What was the availability of small caskets, the size you might use for a child? How quickly could they be delivered? But even more disconcerting were the questions about methods of preserving bodies. How long before a body would begin to decompose? What could be used to slow the process? Dennis told the caller he had used dry ice successfully on several occasions, which seemed to satisfy the person's curiosity. But if there had been a major accident resulting in deaths, Dennis wondered why he hadn't been notified. After all, those services were part of the funeral home's contract.

A few hours later, as a result of a minor mishap involving an airman, Glen Dennis drove over to the base to take the young man in for treatment. Upon arriving at the infirmary he was surprised to see ambulances there. Usually, in the case of a serious accident, he would have been one of the first people called in to assist, particularly if they were dealing with bodies. As he walked by the ambulance he glanced in the back, fully expecting to see a stretcher with a body on it. Instead he saw objects that looked like "half canoes," with unusual writing on them.

He went inside with his charge and no one paid much attention to him, probably because he was a familiar figure in and around the hospital. But as he walked down a corridor a door opened, and a young nurse whom Dennis had been seeing with some frequency came out. According to Dennis, she appeared to be terrified, and the stench that wafted through the open door was gut wrenching.

"You've got to get out of here, now," she told him, "or you'll be in big trouble."

"Why?" he wanted to know. "What's happened?"

"Just leave, quickly. You shouldn't be here."

She turned and went back into the room. Dennis didn't know what was going on, but he decided to take her advice. He was a few seconds too late.

"What the hell is he doing here?"

Dennis turned to see a burly red-headed officer with eyes like tracers.

"Get him out of here. Now!"

This time he almost made it to the doors when he heard the officer scream again.

"Bring that sonofabitch back here. I'm not through with him yet."

Two soldiers grabbed Dennis by the shoulders and shoved him into a small room. The red-haired officer was close behind. What followed was a steady stream of threats and verbal abuse aimed at the bewildered mortician. The officer told him if he ever told anyone about anything he had seen there at the base hospital his life wouldn't be worth living. Dennis, not particularly happy with the officer's expletives, told him he was a civilian and there wasn't a damn thing the army could do to him. At which point a sergeant in the room reminded him that it was a big desert, and it would take a long time for anybody to find his bones.

Dennis left the hospital, shaken and angry. A few hours later the military called and told him, "You open your mouth [about this] and you'll be so far back in the jug they'll have to shoot pinto beans [into you] with a bean shooter." Dennis said he just laughed and told them to "go to hell."[16]

The next day Dennis heard from the nurse again. The two of them had more than just a casual relationship; they had been seeing each other regularly and had even talked about marriage. According to Dennis she called and asked him to meet her at the officer's club for lunch. By the time he arrived he thought she was "about to go into shock." She was extremely distraught and worried about him having been there.

"It's amazing what's going on," she told him, "you wouldn't believe it."

The nurse then began to describe three small bodies that had been brought in to the base hospital. Two of them were badly mangled (they had been out on the high desert for almost a week, remember), but one of them, she told him, was "really in pretty good condition."

Dennis listened in quiet amazement. The bodies had been found in the strange, canoe-shaped objects he had seen in the rear of the ambulances, some one or two miles from the crash site.[17] It was assumed the containers were escape pods of some sort.

The nurse then drew some sketches of one of the "alien's" hands. It had four fingers, and on the tips of the fingers were tiny suction cups. She gave the sketches to Dennis with a warning never to let anyone see them. The only reason she had been there, she told him, was because the two doctors examining the bodies had commandeered her. They needed the help of a nurse.

Dennis drove her back to the barracks. It would prove to be the last time he would ever see her. When he tried to contact her later, he was told she had been transferred to England. He wrote to her at the appropriate APO number and received only a brief note in reply, saying she would

[16] Ibid.

[17] This would tend to support Friedman's contention that there were two crash sites instead of one, as Grady Barnett explicitly described finding bodies scattered near the crash.

explain everything later. His next letter was returned unopened. The outside of the envelope was stamped *Deceased.*

Dennis placed the sketches she had given him in the Roswell Air Force Base files at the mortuary. When he left some years later, he neglected to take them with him. The funeral home eventually went out of business, and the original sketches were lost. Everything associated with the nurse, except for Glen Dennis, seems to have vanished completely.

The release of the weather balloon story seemed to satisfy the mainstream press, and although a number of UFO enthusiasts kept hammering away at the official government line, the matter was largely forgotten until Friedman's chance encounter with Jesse Marcel, Sr. The ensuing research and investigations resulting in statements (in some cases, deathbed confessions) of eyewitnesses who had kept silent because of threats to themselves and their families, or in some cases, bribes, reawakened an interest in what had really happened in Roswell, New Mexico, in July 1947. Today there are few who still believe the Air Force story about a weather balloon. In 1993 the government tried to shore up the sinking balloon by issuing an updated version. It was not an ordinary balloon that crashed in Roswell, they said, but another type of balloon designed specifically to detect high-altitude radiation. They were concerned about the Soviets exploding A bombs in the atmosphere. That version didn't get much attention, either.

Recently Congressman Steven Schiff of the first congressional district in New Mexico sent a request to the Secretary of Defense, asking for all pertinent information about the incident at Roswell. He was concerned with the growing accusations of what was essentially a government cover-up.

"The response I got," he said in a filmed interview, "was a very terse letter that said, 'We have referred your letter to the National Archives.' The National Archives then said, 'We don't have any information about the Roswell incident,' which I was convinced the Defense Department had to know before sending me there. So in other words I thought I was getting the runaround."

But Congressman Schiff didn't let it go at that. He called the General Accounting Office (GAO), the official investigating arm of Congress. In July 1995 the GAO issued its report. They had, they said, examined classified and unclassified documents from the FBI, the CIA, the Department of Energy, and the White House Office of Science and Technology. There was no information on Roswell. Even the outgoing messages from Blanchard, Marcel, Cavitt, et al., to their superiors, had been destroyed.

Dr. Friedman didn't believe that was a sufficient answer. "We're only talking about outgoing messages," he said. "What about analysis of materials? How about autopsy reports? How about eyewitness testimony? There ought to be a ton of other paper."[18]

Kevin Randle was also unimpressed with the GAO findings. "There is no question," he says, "that film exists . . . when you have an event like this, you're going to film every aspect of it. We've been told by people who participated in the cleanup of both the debris field and the impact site that photographs were taken, film was taken. All of this exists somewhere.[19]

A number of witnesses are also reluctant to accept the notion that everything relating to the incident has simply disappeared and that no one in authority knows anything about the events in which they were so intimately involved.

Jesse Marcel, Jr., who is himself a respected physician and Air Force reserve pilot, says, "I'm positive there is infor-

---

[18] *Alien Autopsy: Fact or Fiction?* Vidmark Entertainment, Robert Kiviat, executive producer, 1995.
[19] Ibid.

mation being withheld from the American public concerning the Roswell incident."

Frankie Rowe, daughter of a Roswell fireman, also saw and handled pieces of the debris. In an emotional interview, she tells of being visited by members of the military who threatened her life if she ever spoke of it. Finally, working through forty years of anger and fear, she says, "I'm hoping they will someday release the information."

Walter Haut puts it more succinctly: "Tell us what actually happened."[20]

But the government so far has shown no willingness to do so. Even the GAO is stymied. According to their report to Congressman Schiff, they have no way to continue the investigation.

It might have ended there, but in the summer of 1995, something happened that would challenge the official silence. A producer of documentary films in London, England, was canvassing all the living military photographers he could find who had been in the service in the '50s. He was looking for Elvis Presley film for a documentary on the rock and roll king's years in the military. What he found was far more electrifying than rock and roll.

[20] Ibid.

CHAPTER 6

ALIEN AUTOPSY

> >> What I have seen here does not appear
> to be a human being.
>
> Dr. Cyril Wecht, Chairman,
> Department of Pathology, St. Francis Central Hospital

R ay Santilli is an English producer of film documentaries and an expert on the rock and roll music of the
fifties and sixties. On one of his forays to the United
States he and a partner, Gary Shoefield, were seeking collectors of Elvis Presley memorabilia, including old
film taken during the years Elvis was in the service. They
had managed to put together some sixteen or seventeen separate film clips from five different sources before Santilli
made his most stunning call.

He had been given the name of an ex–U.S. Army cameraman, now in his eighties, who was said to have filmed a
number of military shows as well as far more important
events. It was believed this particular cameraman had car-

ried a top-secret clearance. The clearance was not likely to have anything to do with Elvis Presley, but it did speak well for the cameraman. Someone who was called on for top-secret jobs was likely to have been pretty good at his craft. The better the film, the better his documentary.

Based on recent interviews with Santilli and some of his comments gleaned from various Internet forums and discussions, we have pieced together a likely scenario for his amazing discovery.

Santilli probably called the cameraman (whom he calls Jack Barnet, a pseudonym invented to protect the man's real identity), introduced himself and his project, and asked if he had any film he could buy or at least purchase the rights to. As it turned out he did have, and yes, he would be willing to sell it. The cameraman presumably suggested that he had other film Santilli might be interested in and offered to let him look at it.

Santilli was delighted. He offered to drive over to "Barnet's" home and pick it up. When he arrived, the old man ushered him into a room that contained his personal archive—a cardboard box filled with assorted cans of film. He produced the Elvis footage, and they struck a bargain.

Had Santilli merely written a check, turned around, and left, the world of UFO investigations would be much quieter today. But there was the other film the old man seemed anxious to have Santilli look at. There is no record of this meeting and Santilli has been very protective of the cameraman but, based on what he has said about that first meeting, we imagine the conversation went something like this.

"What is it you say you do?" Barnet asked.

"I make documentary films," Santilli replied in a clipped British accent, "dealing with music mostly."

"Uh-huh!"

"Why do you ask?"

"Well," the old man seemed hesitant, "I do have the

other film I mentioned on the phone, but it's probably not in your field of interest."

"Well, one never knows. Just what does the film cover, anyway?"

"It's an assignment I had a long time ago, back in the late forties, actually." Barnet shifted uncomfortably, and Santilli had the distinct feeling the man regretted having mentioned the other film. Suddenly Santilli's curiosity was aroused.

"The late forties, you say? Were you back in the states or overseas?"

"Uh, no . . . I was here. I mean I, uh, it was in Fort Worth, Texas, and a place near Roswell, New Mexico."

Ray Santilli was not a big UFO fan, but the mention of Roswell got his attention. Someone had just published a book on it, or maybe it was a movie. Anyway, he recognized the name and associated it with some kind of controversy. For a producer of documentaries, controversy is like manna from heaven.

"I might be interested," he said, trying to mask his growing excitement, "is there something here I could look at?"

"Oh yes," Barnet replied, "right here."

He reached into the cardboard box, moved a few canisters out of the way, and produced what appeared to be a very old roll of 16mm film. It looked like standard army issue. Carefully he removed the film from the canister and handed it to Santilli, who held it up to the light and slowly unrolled it, a few frames at a time. He blinked, adjusted his glasses, and looked again. Without being aware of it, he had stopped breathing and the back of his throat went dry.

"Is this real?" he whispered.

"Oh, yes," Barnet replied, "very real. I took every bit of it and a whole lot more that went to Washington."

Santilli's hands were shaking as he rewound the film and tenderly placed it back in the canister. "Is this the only one?"

"No, I have six . . ." he looked over his shoulder at the

box, "no, seven more rolls. They were taken in different places. That one was shot at the Fort Worth Army Hospital just after the Fourth of July in 1947. And there's some other footage on there that I took near Roswell."

"How can you remember so precisely?"

"You think you'll remember today?" Barnet asked, a trace of a smile on his lips."

"Yes, yes, I see what you mean."

According to the cameraman, this was actual footage which he personally took at the autopsy of an *alien being* recovered from the crash of a UFO near Roswell, New Mexico, in July 1947.

As Santilli tells it, the cameraman was ordered to fly to Roswell on an urgent mission. At Roswell he was required to film the recovery of several "beings," some of whom were alive. He was also ordered to film the autopsy of one of them, which is believed to have taken place in Fort Worth only because the base hospital at Roswell Army Air Field lacked the facilities for such specialized work.

Most of the film went straight to Washington, D.C., but some of the rolls he felt needed special processing. In those days it was not uncommon for the cameraman to do much of his own film processing.[1] Barnet told Santilli that sometime later, when the film was fully processed, he tried hard to get Washington interested in these additional rolls. Whoever it was he contacted apparently had no interest in either the incident or the film. His requests to have them picked up went unanswered. The canisters remained in the cardboard box, eventually to be forgotten or, at the very least, relegated to some obscure corner of his mind. Perhaps rummaging around in the cardboard box looking for the Elvis film reminded him of what was there, or maybe, because of his

---

[1] *Alien Autopsy: Fact or Fiction?* Vidmark Entertainment, Robert Kiviat, executive producer, 1995. (Some critics of the story insist that Kodak did all the film processing for the government. Santilli disputes that notion, particularly where "national security" film was being handled.)

age, he decided this might be the last chance to make the film public. Santilli just happened to be in the right place at the right time.

The above scenario, of course, presumes that the cameraman is real and that the film Santilli saw that fateful day is genuine. There are those who believe something else quite different took place before Ray Santilli announced to the world that he had found actual film footage of U.S. doctors or pathologists, performing an autopsy on an alien being.

According to the alternate scenarios, Santilli's company produced the film, doctored it up to look fifty years old, and put it in circulation to take advantage of the sudden upsurge in interest in the whole business of UFOs, particularly the Roswell incident. Or, someone else produced the film and cut a deal with Santilli to release it for a piece of the action. In either case the presumption is the film is a hoax and couldn't possibly be authentic. Regardless of which scenario is chosen, Santilli would have to be a crook or a dupe or both.

Whether the question is resolved in the pages of this chapter is largely up to you. We will give you a summary of both positions that is as current as last night's cruise of the Internet, where the "Autopsy Film" or "SUE" (Santilli's *u*nidentified *e*ntity) is the subject of nightly discussion. Santilli himself participates in some of the exchanges.

The first general exposure of Santilli's film came in a one-hour video presentation entitled, *Alien Autopsy: Fact or Fiction?*, produced by Vidmark Entertainment, and aired in the United States in 1995 as part of the television series, *Sightings*. The video features Jonathan Frakes (Commander Riker of *Star Trek: The Next Generation*) as the host. In addition to the material aired on *Sightings*, the video version carries the full autopsy film, purportedly unedited and uninterrupted, at the end of the presentation. As of this writing the video can be rented at most video/rental outlets across the country.

It is difficult, perhaps impossible, to convey the disturbing sense of trepidation that comes with first viewing the video. The grainy, black-and-white quality of the film and the cold, stark setting does little to alleviate those feelings.

Three men, dressed in white radiation protective suits, including gloves and a head covering with a rectangular glass viewing plate, move efficiently around a naked body that gives the appearance of at least being humanoid. One of the men is believed to be the cameraman, who was required to wear the same protective gear as the surgeons. Occasionally a fourth man is glimpsed through a glass window in one wall. He also appears to be dressed in surgical gear, but his face is covered only by a standard surgical mask.

The body is approximately four feet tall and fairly stout. The abdomen area is somewhat distended and the legs and thighs appear to be quite muscular. There is no hair on the body whatsoever. The head is larger than one might expect, with large, dark eyes that look slightly oriental. The nose is small, as are the ears, which are much lower down toward the jaw line than you would expect to see on a human being.

There is no navel that can be discerned nor is there any male genitalia or secondary female organs. Therefore, the sex of the being cannot be determined solely on outward appearances.

The being has six toes on each foot and six somewhat elongated fingers, including an opposable thumb on each hand. The forearm appears to be longer than the upper portion of the arm, which, along with the extra length of the fingers, seems to distort what we would describe as a "normal" symmetry.

The large eyes are open. Indeed, it is not clear that the eyes are capable of closing. The small mouth also gapes open in death.

The most immediately discernible wound is a huge, jagged hole in the upper right thigh area. Some have suggested the wound is the result of scavengers or wild animals that got to the body while it lay exposed in the desert near Corona, or perhaps Soccoro, New Mexico. As the cameraman moves around the body, we see that the right hand is almost completely severed at the wrist, and there appears to be a wound beneath the right armpit.

The room itself is devoid of any decoration, as might be expected. On one wall is a 1940 style, G.E. electric clock. On another wall, to the left of the glass window, is a black lucite telephone with a rotary dial.

The body is lying on what appears to be a stainless steel table. Drainholes are clearly visible. A utility table stands at right angles near the head of the table upon which the body is lying. The utility table holds a tray of surgical instruments, neatly laid out and within easy reach of the surgeons. Included in the tray is an old style hand saw used for removing the cranial cap. The only other furniture in the room is a smaller table, covered with a white cloth, which holds a bunsen burner next to a flask of some sort, two metal bowls, a test tube stand containing five test tubes, and a large beaker partially filled with a dark, ominous-looking fluid. Everything appears to be exactly as it should be for a 1947 operating room.

In eerie silence the men in white suits move about the corpse. From time to time we see only the back of one of them, indicating he has moved in front of the cameraman. Indeed neither of the surgeons appears to give the least notice to whomever is shooting the film. The single exception comes at one point in the procedure when one of the surgeons appears to be gesturing angrily at the cameraman.

The area near the leg wound is carefully inspected and the knee joint is manually manipulated with great care. Eventually one of the men takes a scalpel and makes a long, straight incision from the sternum to the pelvis. We also see an incision from the lower part of the ear down the neck to the collar bone. A layer of something is removed from the eyes. Ultimately the skin on the skull is peeled back and the cranium is opened. The chest and stomach are also opened revealing . . . what?

To those not used to such things, which we assume is most of us, it is a grisly sight. And in a world where global communication is instantaneous, it took only a matter of hours before those who believed the film to be authentic and those who were convinced it was fake began to line up and start firing at one another.

It should be noted that the producers of the commercial release went to great lengths to present a balanced view of the film's authenticity, or lack thereof. Santilli himself takes a very benign view: "All we're doing," he said, "is placing [the film] in the public domain and saying, here it is. Please investigate."[2]

He needn't have extended the invitation. A thorough investigation was bound to follow the release of the film, whether welcomed or not.

There is, in fact, more on the film than just the autopsy. This footage is also generating its own controversy. Like all good military cameramen, Barnet used up the entire roll before removing the film from the camera and inserting new film. A portion of the autopsy film contains footage of some of the recovered wreckage as well. Was this portion shot at Roswell? At Fort Worth Army Air Field? Perhaps it was taken at the infamous Hangar 18? Only the cameraman knows for sure, and so far he isn't talking to anyone but Santilli. In some ways this part of the film is even more fascinating than the medical examination of the body.

Given what we know of the government's response to the incident at Roswell and the "vacuum cleaner" tactics employed in rounding up even the tiniest scrap of material recovered from the crash site, the cameraman's story takes on an air of plausibility. Only through some accidental or fortuitous oversight could this particular cameraman (or anyone

---

[2] Ibid.

else for that matter) have gotten away with not one, but several canisters of the most sensitive footage imaginable.

But what do the experts think of the film? Phillip Mantle, Director of Investigations for the British UFO Association, (BUFOA), said: "If he is telling the truth, and I have no reason to doubt that [he is], it is the most momentous event in human history and he [the cameraman] owes it to mankind to tell his story."[3]

Although Santilli has stated publicly that he doesn't trust the credibility of U.S. companies with large defense contracts, apparently someone involved with the production of the *Sightings* presentation did contact the Kodak film company. Laurence Cate, identified on the film as an "Eastman Kodak sales representative," confirmed that the film stock "could be" from 1947. The code mark imbedded in the film identifies it as being either 1927, 1947, or 1967 stock. Later independent analysis narrowed it down to 1947. The 1927 stock would have produced a much grainier product, the 1967 stock not grainy enough.

So the raw film at least appears to be of the right kind and the right period. But what about the subject matter? Allen Daviau, a well-known Hollywood director of photography, doesn't think the content is genuine.

"I have to say that what we're seeing here is a hoax. What we're seeing here is somebody photographing this, intentionally letting the image go out of focus. It just doesn't make sense that he would go in and make no adjustment on the focus."[4]

But Dr. Roderick Ryan, a former navy combat cameraman, believes that this flaw is one of the film's surest signs of authenticity.

"The fact that it lost focus," he says, "is consistent with the type of equipment they had to be using. The cameras in

[3] Ibid.
[4] Ibid.

general use at that time by the military were 'Filmo' cameras made by Bell & Howell. The camera did not have through-the-lens focusing. So if it had maintained focus, there could be the possibility it could have been done with modern-day equipment."[5]

Paolo Chrechi Usai, the Eastman House senior curator, seems to think that the trouble and expense involved in faking this film would simply be more than the effort was worth. "You cannot fake a motion picture that easily," he says. "It would take an amount of technical know-how, of sophistication that would make the operation not worthwhile."

The program producers also spoke with Stan Winston, Academy Award–winning creator of the creatures in *Jurassic Park* and *Alien*, two films that feature highly sophisticated techniques for creating various entities. At first Winston thought he was looking at a body that had been created as a "prop." After examining the image closely, he conceded that if the body wasn't real, he would be "real proud of creating an image like that." Members of his creative team were even more effusive in their praise, pointing out that such things as the uniformity in wetness and the drippage were effects they were never able to do. The unevenness of the skull suggested it was not created on a mold, yet the skin texture appears to be very even, as you would expect with a real cadaver.

"My hats off," Winston said, "to the people who created it . . . or the poor alien who's dead on the table." Winston went on to say, "Nothing about this [film] feels phony. If you came to me and said that you created this illusion, you'd be working here, [he snaps his fingers] like that."[6]

Having spent most of my adult life in the motion picture business, I have to say that that offer may be the carrot that brings this particular rabbit out of the hat. It's hard for me

[5] Ibid.
[6] Ibid.

to imagine anyone in the industry receiving that kind of praise and not wanting to step up and take credit for his or her work. Then, of course, there's the money. Creatures created by Stan Winston and his group command enormous sums. After all, they are the real stars of the pictures for which they are created.

Assuming for the moment that the body seen in the film is not artificial, could it be simply a deformed human? It has been suggested that a certain chromosomal disorder, for example, can result in six fingers and toes.

Dr. Cyril Wecht, chairman of the Department of Pathology at St. Francis Central Hospital, examined the film and came away perplexed. Although admitting that the two pathologists or surgeons in the film appeared to know what they were doing and had probably performed many autopsies, Dr. Wecht was still puzzled by what he saw of the being itself.

"I have never performed an autopsy on anybody that even closely resembles the being that we see on the film," he said. "I cannot relate these structures to abdominal content . . . I have great difficulty correlating this with any human body that I have seen. The brain is not a human brain."

Obviously baffled, Dr. Wecht was nevertheless unwilling to put his full stamp of authenticity on what the film purports to be. "I am . . . extremely reluctant to say it, but what I have seen here does not appear to be a human being. I would prefer to say it is 'humanoid.' I won't say it's from another planet."[7]

Dr. Chris Melroy, senior lecturer in forensic pathology at the University of Sheffield in England, while admitting that ". . . the basic procedures being carried out [on the film] are those that one would do in an autopsy," questioned why, if this was really an alien being, only two hours were spent on the autopsy?[8] The reference is to the apparent elapsed

[7] Ibid.
[8] Ibid.

time on the wall clock in the operating room. One astute observer in a discussion on the Internet pointed out that according to the clock, the autopsy could have taken four- teen hours or even twenty-six hours. This observation would seem to be consistent with the film itself. From time to time the roll of film ends in a "whiteout," again, charac- teristic of the B & H Filmo 70, which often came to a stop with the shutter open. According to the cameraman, he might have taken as many as thirty rolls of film.

As we mentioned earlier, some of that film was used to capture images of the wreckage, which is assumed to have come from the crash sites near Roswell. If so, it provides a much more intricate view of the craft that carried the aliens than anything previously seen or described by witnesses to the Roswell incident.

The film shows several tables of wreckage, all neatly laid out and tagged. Included are a number of I-beam segments, much larger than those seen by Jesse Marcel, Jr., which also contain neat rows of indecipherable characters. The charac- ters on these I-beam fragments also appear to be raised or embossed onto the "metal."

But of perhaps even greater interest are three, relatively large panels with handprints embedded in the material. Each panel has a left and right handprint with an arc above each one. The handprints correspond to the six-fingered hands of the "alien." In the arc above each handprint and at strategic locations in the handprint itself are what appear to be holes or buttons of some kind. This feature of the panels has given rise to speculation that these were control panels for the craft. Each panel appears to be approximately two feet long, ten to twelve inches from top to bottom, and three to four inches thick. A person in the film picks up each one of them to give the cameraman a better and more precise view. And in fact the viewer is treated to several clear close-ups of both the panels and the I-beams. In some the numbering system on the tags is clearly visible, though obviously not understandable.

In a lengthy discussion of this debris published on the Internet, March 1, 1996, by a man named Dennis Murphy, a number of enticing possibilities are raised. For example at the root of the I-beam, that is, where the web and the flanges meet, there doesn't appear to be a radius. That means the web and flanges meet at right angles, something that would almost certainly create cracking with our current technology. Mr. Murphy says he knows of no manufacturing process that could produce this structure. Another tricky problem is created by the raised lettering on the web of the I-beam. Murphy rules out extrusion or milling because of the acute right angles. Some of the I-beams in the film have more than two right-angled roots, making raised lettering impossible to produce. Yet the lettering is obviously raised. Rolling, molding, and casting all fail as possible manufacturing methods for the same reason. The standout question keeps coming up: If the film is faked, how did the fakers do it?

Furthermore, the mysterious panels do not appear to be identical. The left- and right-hand indentations are not the same size. On one panel the left hand appears to have a longer palm indentation than does the right. Also the curved indentation above the left hand in at least two of the panels appears to be closer to the finger indentations than does the one on the right. One explanation, according to Murphy, is that each panel is custom made for the hands that will use it. There also appear to be different numbers of buttons associated with different panels, which suggests each panel controlled a different set of functions.

All of this is pure speculation, of course. There is no way to say conclusively that the panels are control devices. Nor is there a pattern in the lettering on the I-beams that is subject to interpretation. But the letters are definitely there in the photographs and they are definitely raised. The inescapable reality is, hoax or not, something or somebody went to a great deal of time and expense to create what is on this truly remarkable piece of film.

On March 24, 1996, Ray Santilli participated in a world-wide Internet conference on the Autopsy Film, conducted by the Encounters Forum. Among other things Santilli confirmed that the cameraman has provided additional details that are subject to verification, but the information is being withheld until Santilli and his group can check it out. He also indicated that the cameraman claims to have filmed *three* autopsies. But for those who have heard rumors that President Harry Truman appears somewhere in one of them, those expectations were dashed. Santilli says flatly that he has no film of Truman.

He did, however, raise the possibility of a new television special being prepared by a "major broadcaster." If this is accomplished, it may include a firsthand presentation of the cameraman's whole story, including a map the cameraman has marked that should clear up the exact location of the crash site once and for all.

Santilli says he has been contacted by certain agencies in the U.S. government but he won't say which ones, and he characterizes Eastman Kodak as being generally uncooperative. He also betrays a certain level of frustration with people who seem to reject the film out of hand.

"I have no desire to continue a fight," he said, "when I am not able to fight back or use ammunition [I have]. In addition, I don't really care. As you all know this is not my subject. The sad thing is that the film holds the real answer to what happened in 1947. But what will the leading UFO investigators have to investigate when the answer has been provided?"

Santilli's frustration is undoubtedly justified. Many investigators, particularly in the UFO community, seem to have written off the film. Their fear is that if it is a fake, aligning their organization or efforts too closely with it will result in even further ridicule of what they consider to be very important research.

Kent Jeffrey, coordinator of the International Roswell Initiative, is typical of that view. "My guess is that this was done by somebody strictly for money. I think eventually it will be shown to be a hoax. By that time Santilli will have collected his royalties from TV companies throughout the world, and he will have made the majority of his sales of videos."[9]

Paolo Cherchi, who thought the cost of faking such a piece of film would probably be more than it was worth, takes a more open view. "If it is a true document," he says, "it is a document of exceptional importance. If it's a fake it should be hailed as one of the most extraordinary fakes ever put together by a filmmaker."[10]

My own experience as a filmmaker tends to support this view. If the film is not authentic, it could not have been produced by the people we see moving about on the film. As has been pointed out, some very highly skilled technicians would have to be involved in fabricating the creature. It could not be a one-person job. Then there is the matter of research. Every prop, if indeed they are props, appears to be perfect for the time the film was said to have been shot. I can assure you that creating something that will stand up to the kind of intense scrutiny being afforded this film is not a matter of happenstance or good luck. Someone would have to do extensive research not only on autopsies, but military autopsies of the period. Normally this means contacting a lot of people and asking very specific questions. Given the notoriety this footage has received, it seems reasonable to expect that someone, somewhere would stand up and say, "Wait a minute. I gave so and so a lot of information about the operating rooms at Fort Worth air base."

[9] Ibid.
[10] Ibid.

We have already alluded to the matter of "professional pride" and the huge rewards that could be reaped by creators of the "alien," if, in fact, it was created. It is fair to note the same would be true for the producer, director, and crew of the film. Praise from the industry's most prominent creator of strange creatures is hard to come by and could quite literally be the key to the career vault. If this is a hoax, my guess is someone before long is going to stand up and loudly claim credit for putting it together.

On the other hand, if the film is genuine, the implications for our society and the world in general are overwhelming. Governments worldwide will be forced to confess that they have been lying for years or confess that they are monumentally inept and incapable of dealing with reality in any meaningful way. Either way the very fabric of society would undoubtedly change forever. Whether that change would be for the better is perhaps the most significant question of all.

Like everyone else, we will have to wait for the final verdict that a host of investigators are still seeking avidly. In the meantime it is possible that the film has already provided more answers than anyone expected.

The doctors doing the autopsy have reportedly been identified as Dr. Detlev Bronk and Dr. Lloyd Berkner. An enlargement of a notebook in the film supposedly shows the name "Dr. Bronk" written on it. The mysterious cameraman is also reported to have named Detlev Bronk as one of the people who gave him orders. All of that would be only a curiosity except for one important fact. In 1987 the names of twelve men alleged to be part of a secret organization established by President Truman following the Roswell incident were released to the public. These men, it was claimed, were the political and scientific keepers of *all* government-held information regarding UFOs. Under the code name MJ–12, or "Majestic 12," they secretly conducted far-reaching investigations into all aspects of extraterrestrial events in the

United States. Prominent on that list of the first appointees to this super-secret, super-elite group are Dr. Lloyd Berkner and Dr. Detlev Bronk. (Both are long since deceased.)

Was or *is* "Majestic 12" an actual organization with unlimited funds and great political clout? We'll attempt to answer that question in the next chapter.

CHAPTER 7

MAJESTIC 12

>> **A Top Secret Research and Development/ Intelligence operation responsible directly and only to the President of the United States.**

Uice Admiral Roscoe H. Hillenkoetter, U.S. Navy

J aime Shandera was a member of a research team look- ing into the reality of so-called flying saucers. Shan- dera was working closely with a man by the name of William L. Moore who claimed to have many con- tacts with "insiders," presumably in Washington, D.C. A number of them had given Moore the impression they would be willing to help him make sure certain facts about UFOs were made available and released to the public. The efforts of Shandera and Moore were well known to that portion of the community euphemistically referred to as UFOlogists. Beyond that association, however, neither Moore nor Shan- dera could be classified remotely as "household names."

One December day in 1984, all of that changed. Shandera and Moore became the focus of a controversy that is still going on.

Like most great controversies this one began in a very mundane fashion. The postman delivered a small package to Shandera's home in Burbank, California. The package was double wrapped in plain brown paper and bore no return address, but the postmark indicated it had been mailed in Albuquerque, New Mexico. Inside the brown wrapper there was a smaller package, and inside that, in a sealed wrapper, was a roll of exposed but undeveloped 35mm film. Upon developing the film Shandera discovered two sets of eight negatives each. The sets were separated by several blanks. The second set was an exact duplicate of the first. When he looked at the finished prints Shandera was shocked to see eight pages of official looking documents purporting to be "briefing" papers for President-Elect Dwight D. Eisenhower. The date on the briefing memo was November 18, 1952. Even more surprising was the fact that the pages described, in an almost matter-of-fact way, the crash and recovery of not one but two flying saucers near Roswell, New Mexico, in July 1947. Included were references to alien bodies and even live alien beings. The documents also included a brief memorandum from then President Harry S. Truman to his Secretary of Defense, James V. Forrestal, dated September 24, 1947, instructing him to set up a super-secret project that would go by the code name "Operation Majestic Twelve."

With the exception of the Truman/Forrestal memo, which bore "Top Secret, Eyes Only" stamps, all of the other documents were labeled, "Top Secret/*Majic*—Eyes Only."

Shandera, a movie producer, must have blinked in disbelief. Here, after years of study, research, in-depth investigation, and swirling controversy, was *proof* that at least two flying saucers had crashed and been recovered by the government along with their occupants. According to the document the government had not only known about it but had gone to great lengths to cover it up.

Or was it proof?

The manner in which the documents were revealed was almost guaranteed to feed the fires of doubt, not extinguish them. Shandera also knew that Moore was considered by many at the time to be the premier Roswell investigator. His own association with Moore, while extending back over a decade, was more obscure. Why send the film to him? Why not send it directly to Moore?

Shandera contacted Moore immediately and sent him prints taken from the negatives. If these documents were authentic they put an end to the mystery of Roswell and opened up the government to unprecedented charges of cover-up and outright lies.

But what if they were phony?

The list of names of the men that comprised the "Majestic 12" included some of the nation's most prominent scientific and political figures, and at least one surprise of monumental proportions. Moore decided to keep the information under wraps for awhile, at least until they could find out more about it. The last thing the Roswell investigation needed at that point was another "startling discovery" that turned out to be a hoax.

In point of fact there had been rumors about a top-secret government organization called "MJ–12" floating around for years. Some UFO researchers called them "The Maji" or "The Majestic Twelve." But until now there was nothing to support the claims. Rumor had long held that the group was set up by President Truman following the rash of UFO or flying saucer reports that flooded the nation in 1947, culminating, in the public mind at least, with the crash and recovery of "something" in Roswell, New Mexico. These twelve men, it was alleged, had the final say on anything having to do with extraterrestrial investigations. They held a high military rank by protocol and could come and go as they pleased on any military base in the world. They were experts in the fields of astrophysics, astronomy, mathematics, medicine, linguistics, military strategy, engineering, diplomacy, and international protocol. They were, if one listened to the rumors, a group of twelve men who could be considered the best of the best in their field.

But until Jaime Shandera opened that package in December 1984, there was nothing tangible to suggest the rumors were anything more than just rumors. A sort of American "James Bond" tale times twelve. But if this organization did exist its members *knew*, beyond any shadow of a doubt, that UFOs were real, that they were of extraterrestrial origin, and that they were piloted by humanoid beings. It was even possible a method of communicating with them had been found.

What Shandera saw when he looked at the prints taken from that anonymous roll of film are reproduced in their entirety in the photo section of this book exactly as they were received by him. Also included is a reproduction of a document discovered in the National Archives in 1985 by Shandera and Moore. This document is known as the Cutler/Twining memo and will figure significantly in the investigation.

It should be pointed out that even after almost ten years of exhaustive study, no one is yet prepared to state flatly that these are photographs of *genuine* government documents. Several detractors, however, are not so cautious. They have stated flatly that these are nothing more than elaborate frauds. We encourage you to look them over carefully before going on.

You will notice that everything about the documents seems genuine at first glance. The names, the signatures, the dates all correspond with what is known to be fact or believed to be fact based on current research. The reference to the crash of a second object on December 6, 1950, near El Indio Guerrero on the Texas–Mexico border was something of a surprise. Roswell investigators, however, particularly Stanton Friedman, had long championed the idea of a second crash although much closer to the site and time of the Roswell crash.

Still it was not the idea that a super-secret group of scientists were involved with examining more than one downed craft that made Moore and Shandera cautious about releasing the documents. It was one of the names that appeared on the list of MJ–12 members. This particular name also figured prominently in the text of one of the documents, and based on everything they thought they knew, it simply should not have been there.

Moore had been sharing information about the Roswell crash with Stanton Friedman for some time and knew of the thoroughness of his work. He was also familiar with Friedman's reputation for no-nonsense fact finding.

Friedman, whom I met personally, along with his arch rival, Philip Klass, at a MUFON symposium near Austin, Texas, in 1994, is a formidable champion for the ideas and discoveries he believes stand up to intense scrutiny. However, he has demonstrated a willingness, even an eagerness to quickly discard anything that fails this test. Friedman was precisely the kind of man Moore needed to examine the authenticity of the Majestic 12 documents.

Dr. Friedman was contacted, shown the documents, and asked if he would be willing to try and authenticate them. He quickly agreed. Moore and Friedman then went to the extraordinary measure of requesting a grant of $16,000 from the Fund for UFO Research, an independent group that provides funding for selected UFO research. The money would be used by Friedman in the authenticating process. This meant the Fund board would have to review the documents, which also meant the cat, so to speak, was out of the bag. It was now 1987. Up to that time, the photographs had remained in the private and secret possession of Shandera, Moore, and Friedman for nearly three years.

Almost as soon as the documents were made public, there were critics who denounced them as a fraud. Philip

Klass became the chief spokesman for those anxious to declare the documents a hoax though he was by no means the only skeptic. He was, however, the most vocal. That in itself was not too surprising. Klass and a Harvard professor named Donald Menzel were considered two of the most formidable debunkers of anything even remotely related to UFOs.

Those of you who read the briefing documents carefully will recognize Donald Menzel as the third name from the bottom on the list of original members of Operation Majestic Twelve. This was the name that had everyone shaking their heads in disbelief. Dr. Donald Menzel was also the man referenced on page four of the documents in the discussion on the origin of the spacecraft. Not only was the appearance of his name an anomaly in that context, but the arguments the document suggested he put forth were completely out of character with his very public pronouncements.

Until Friedman began his research on Majestic 12 in 1987, Donald Menzel, the eminent Harvard professor, was believed to be the premier UFO skeptic. He wrote books on the subject and argued strongly against the whole idea of extraterrestrials. Robert Hall, a member of the board of the Fund for UFO Research and one who voted to approve the Friedman grant, had known Menzel for some time. Hall was initially skeptical of the whole package primarily because Menzel's name was included. In an article published in 1991, defending the issuance of the grant, Hall said:

"I had watched Menzel in action as an ardent debunker and had tended to attribute his unscientific rantings to a passionate zeal to put down irrationalism and defend science. But this interpretation never quite made complete sense. His anti-UFO arguments often were so bizarre that I could not understand how a scientist could make them or how his scientific colleagues could 'buy' them."

Friedman was likewise stunned to see Menzel's name included on a team of scientists who ostensibly *knew* that

UFOs were real and of extraterrestrial origin. Not only was his name included in this elite group, he was apparently a leading *exponent* of the notion.

According to the documents, many of the MJ–12 scientists were convinced that the flying saucers came from another planet, perhaps Mars, but some, " . . . *most notably Dr. Menzel* [emphasis mine] consider it more likely that we are dealing with beings from another solar system entirely." It was a contradiction of monumental proportions, but the documents were what they were. And if they were authentic there would have to be some kind of an explanation.

In fact Dr. Friedman's research uncovered a completely different man than the one who had consistently and stridently set himself against all aspects of UFO thought or investigation. According to Friedman's report, issued in 1990, Dr. Menzel was a Harvard professor of astrophysics, a well-known astronomer and an expert on solar eclipses. His first negative book on UFOs was published in 1953 (significantly, perhaps, in light of subsequent findings), and he published two more books after that, loudly proclaiming he could explain every sighting.

But after considerable digging, Friedman discovered that there was another side to Dr. Menzel. He found that he had, " . . . a longer, continuous association with the National Security Agency and its predecessor Navy group than anybody else, that he had a "Top Secret, Ultra" security clearance, that he had done work for the CIA, that Menzel had even written several letters to Senator John Kennedy, at least one of which dealt with what was happening in the NSA [National Security Agency], during the Eisenhower Administration, and that he was a world-class expert on cryptanalysis."[1]

Friedman also learned, from a former graduate student of Menzel's, that the professor not only lived a double life, he

---

[1] Stanton T. Friedman, *Final Report on Operation Majestic 12*, Fredericton, New Brunswick, Canada (April 1990).

relished it. Well into the presidency of John F. Kennedy he continued to advise the White House on matters of national security and NASA.

As it turned out the arguments over the authenticity of the documents did not turn on Menzel's involvement after all. Critics instead turned up a page-by-page laundry list of what they referred to as "anomalies." Leading the list of debunkers was and is a group that calls themselves the Committee for the Scientific Investigation of Claims of the Paranormal (CSICOP). Through press releases, a series of "white papers," and articles in a publication called *The Skeptical Inquirer* (*SI*) virtually every aspect of the MJ–12 briefing documents have been attacked.

Also under attack is another document discovered in 1985 in the National Archives by Moore and Shandera. This Top Secret memorandum, dated July 14, 1954, was from Robert Cutler, special assistant to the president, and addressed to General Nathan Twining, informing him of a change in date of an MJ–12 briefing. If authentic the Cutler/Twining memo could go a long way toward validating the earlier documents. The Cutler/Twining document did something else. If authentic it proved conclusively that President Eisenhower had kept Operation Majestic Twelve intact and functioning. From the standpoint of the critics, this memo must also be shown to be a hoax if, in fact, the briefing documents are a hoax.

Once again, the circumstances under which the document was discovered brought its authenticity into question. Shandera and Moore were searching through more than a hundred boxes of recently declassified documents in Records Group 341 at the National Archives in Washington, D.C. The onion-skin copy was found *between* two folders, and as a White House document it was completely unrelated to RG341. To further add to the controversy, it was found in box number 189. At first that fact carried no significance but Moore remembered a puzzling postcard he had received from New Zealand with a return address of Box 189, Addis

Ababa, Ethiopia. Friedman concluded the document was planted by someone who intended it to be found by Moore. But by whom? Could it have been the same person who sent Shandera the film? Remember, at this time Moore had not released the "briefing" documents to the public. Who knew he had them? These matters remain unresolved.

Under the best of circumstances it is not an easy task to prove the authenticity of any document. The problem is compounded when all you have is a photograph of those documents. This means, of course, that the actual ink and paper cannot be verified. Other methods must be used to test for authenticity. In the case of the MJ–12 briefing documents the critics placed them, as it were, under a microscope. This is as it should be. Friedman, who prior to publishing his findings could also be counted a skeptic, likewise examined even the most minute detail of each photograph.

Philip Klass was and remains the principle antagonist (though by no means the only one) of the papers' authenticity, writing primarily in the publications cited previously. Klass is a professional writer and is frequently published in the highly respected Washington magazine, *Aviation Week & Space Technology*. Because of his professional credentials, Klass tends to receive a high level of acceptance from the news media.

In one of his *SI* articles Klass raises the question of why the film was sent to Shandera in the first place, " . . . who has never published any papers on UFOs and does not even consider himself a UFOlogist? How could the sender of the film even know that Shandera and Moore were friends and that the contents would find their way to Moore?"

Friedman points out that Shandera had joined Moore and himself in studies on UFOs as early as 1980. Moore and Shandera, he said, "shared information" for at least four years, a fact that was widely known in the UFO community and should have been known to Klass.

But perhaps the most telling complaints about the documents, according to Klass and other critics, are those pertaining to the various "date formats" that are used in the several documents. To be specific, there are three different date formats that appear. The first and most prevalent is the day followed by the month, a comma, and then the year, e.g., 24 September, 1947. When this format is used, a "0" precedes any single digit date, e.g., 07 July, 1947. In at least two cases the month is typed in capital letters. A second date format uses the day, followed by an abbreviation of the month (in capitals), all followed by an abbreviated form of the year and a period, e.g., 30 NOV. '47. In one instance (our example) a period follows the month. The third date format appears only once, on the Truman/Forrestal memo. In this instance the month is spelled out, followed by the day, a comma, and the year followed by a period, e.g., September 24, 1947.

We spell out these dates in such detail only because the critics claim that these differences would never be tolerated if the memos were genuine. The anomalies also seem to be the principal barriers to the authenticity of the documents. Other objections have so far failed to hold up to the kind of scrutiny to which the documents themselves have been subjected. For example, all of the "players" appear to have been available on the dates and times specified. One would expect, in the case of a forgery, that at least one or two of the people involved could be shown to have been somewhere else at critical times. Nothing like that has developed.

Beyond just the date format, Klass attacks the Truman/Forrestal memo by suggesting it was atypical of what Truman "would have" said. According to Klass, "it *would have* read more like the following:

> Let's find out where in the hell these craft are coming from, whether they pose a military threat, and what in the hell we can do to defend the country against them should they attack . . . .[2]

[2] MUFON *Symposium Proceedings* (Seguin, TX: Mutual UFO Network, 1988), p. 214.

Quite apart from what Klass thinks Truman might have said, it should be pointed out that Friedman was unable to locate a single, official Truman memorandum that is worded in such a fashion. Klass did concede that the Truman signature appeared to be authentic but suggested that with modern copying technology, it would have been a simple matter to substitute the phony text over a genuine signature and make a clean copy.

A similar charge was leveled against the Hillenkoetter memo by prominent Roswell researchers, Kevin Randle and Donald Schmitt. They suggested, among other things, that the admiral would never have permitted his name, Roscoe, to be used (he supposedly hated his name); that the memo did not bear his actual rank, vice admiral; and that the tone of the memo was atypical of Hillenkoetter. Therefore, he didn't write the memo.

The researchers took every criticism seriously. They began an extensive search into other Hillenkoetter documents that were known to be authentic. They discovered that the admiral frequently used his first name and that the use of "admiral" in lieu of "vice admiral" was no more unusual than using the term "general" in lieu of "major general" or "brigadier general." In fact the practice was and is quite common in any but the most formal transmissions.

The matter of the tone of the memo was more problematic. Because, unlike the Truman/Forrestal memo, it was comparatively lengthy, the researchers turned to an expert, Roger W. Wescott, professor of linguistics at Drew University in New Jersey, to analyze the Hillenkoetter memo. Wescott's examination involved a comparison of the memo's language and writing style with twenty-seven verified authentic examples of Hillenkoetter's writings obtained from the Truman Library. According to Professor Wescott, "There is no compelling reason to regard any of these communications as fraudulent or to believe that any of them [was] written by anyone other than Hillenkoetter himself."[3]

Apart from a great many suggestions by Klass and others that they somehow know what the various individuals named would have done, or should have done, or logically would do, the hard scientific arguments seem to fall back on the date format anomalies. Even this objection does not stand up to serious scrutiny. Friedman, after examining hundreds of documents in the various libraries and collections noted above, points out that as far as date formats are concerned:

"Formats and styles vary all over the place for the same office. One folder of letters and memos of the Office of the Secretary of Defense had seven different date formats. I have seen single pages with three different date formats."[4]

So much for the date anomalies.

As Friedman himself has pointed out, however, proving that the skeptics are wrong doesn't necessarily prove that the documents are genuine. While that is true, it would be hard to imagine nine pieces of paper that have been pored over with more intensity than these documents. One exchange of letters between Friedman and Klass illustrates how intense the scrutiny has been.

On January 16, 1989, Philip Klass wrote to Dr. Friedman about the Cutler/Twining memo. Remember, this document was discovered independently of the briefing papers. Klass' contention was that the typeface used in the memo (pica) was inconsistent with the elite typeface used in all executive memos; therefore the Cutler/Twining memo could not be authentic. Among other things he said:

> I challenge you to produce known-to-be-authentic White House/business letters/memoranda written by Cutler or Lay during the 1953–55 time period which use a typeface identical in size and style to that used in the alleged Cutler/Twining memo of July 14, 1954.

[3] Ibid., p. 227.
[4] MUFON *Symposium Proceedings* (Seguin, TX: Mutual UFO Network, 1993), p. 81.

To provide motivation for your prompt response for an article I plan to write, I herewith offer to pay you $100.00 for each such letter you can provide in the next 60 days, with an upper limit of $1,000.00 if you supply 10 different letters that meet the above conditions.

On January 20, 1989, just four days later, Friedman responded:

Subject: MJ–12/White House Typewriters
Reference: Your completely inane comments of
             January 16, 1989
The postman must have known how pleased I would be to get yet another example of your ineptness as an MJ–12 document researcher since it only took 4 days to get your silly material here.

I am enclosing copies straight from my files of various Lay and Cutler material . . . first ones at hand, but just the tip of the iceberg. You will note that Pica is quite common, that on June 19, 1951, Lay signed both PICA and ELITE memos, that on Feb. 19, the date was ELITE and the memo and sign off PICA.

I look forward to your check and will not charge you for copying the various memos. . . .

Apparently the government offices in question had plenty of typewriters capable of both pica and elite type. Typeface, it would seem, cannot be used either to prove or disprove the authenticity of the documents. Klass would have to come up with some other reason why the Cutler/ Twining memo was a forgery. As a matter of fact, he did. The memo was not signed.

Further investigation revealed that Cutler was out of the country when the memo was written. That being the case an aide must have prepared it, but who? In one of his many forays into documents at the Eisenhower Library, Friedman discovered a memo dated July 3, 1954, in which Cutler instructed James Lay, Executive Secretary of the National Security Council, to "Keep things moving out of my basket." On July 16, 1954, another memo from Lay to Cutler strongly suggests Lay is doing just that. "Will try to have everything tidy and not too much pressure on you when you arrive," he writes. The lack of a signature or even the /s/ indicating an original had been signed, far from being an indication of a forgery, instead supports the document's authenticity. A signature found on a memo prepared while Cutler was out of the country would have been a signal that something was amiss.[5]

Virtually every aspect of the MJ–12 documents has undergone and, in some cases, is still undergoing the same intense scrutiny. To the best of our knowledge the conclusions presented to the Fund for UFO Research are as valid today as they were when they were submitted in 1990. In his final report Friedman wrote:

> With regard to questioned documents the burden of proof is on those who claim that the documents are forgeries as opposed to those who say the documents may be genuine. After several years of sometimes very intense research with regard to the Operation Majestic 12 documents, I have still been unable to find any argument of the dozens put forth that demonstrates that any of the three primary documents are fraudulent. I have been able to demonstrate that there is a very great deal of information in them not known to anybody not on the inside at the time the documents were received. Therefore I am forced to conclude that the documents are genuine.[6]

[5] Stanton T. Friedman and Don Berliner, *Crash at Corona* (New York: Marlowe & Company, 1992).

[6] Stanton T. Friedman, *Final Report on Operation Majestic 12*, Fredericton, New Brunswick, Canada (April 1990).

Friedman's conclusion notwithstanding, critics remain unconvinced. Unlike the Roswell incident, where a number of living witnesses have come forth and admitted their involvement in the cover-up, no government official, scientist, or past or present member of MJ–12 has stepped forward and said, "I was there. I am/was one of them." Some Canadian researchers, however, have uncovered a conversation that comes very close to such an admission.

Grant Cameron and Scott Crain teamed up in 1987 as a result of the announcement of the briefing documents. Cameron had spent ten years investigating the flying saucer research of Canadian scientist, Wilbert B. Smith. He felt that his efforts might finally be paying off. According to Cameron and Crain's study and report[7] they located an informant (unnamed) who acknowledged the existence of MJ–12 and who admitted to having attended secret meetings at Wright-Patterson Air Force Base concerning UFO phenomena.

Among a great many other items, their continuing investigation also uncovered a transcript of a discussion between Dr. Robert I. Sarbacher and Wilbert B. Smith that occurred during a meeting held in Dr. Sarbacher's office in Washington, D.C. The meeting was to discuss matters of national security with members of the Canadian Embassy staff. At the time Dr. Sarbacher was a science consultant on the U.S. Department of Defense's Joint Research and Development Board. The date was September 15, 1950.

The transcript, it should be noted, was discovered by Arthur Bray, author of the book, *The UFO Connection*, among Smith's personal papers after the Canadian government downgraded his work on geomagnetics from "Top Secret" to "Confidential."

---

[7] Grant Cameron and T. Scott Crain, Jr., *UFOs, MJ-12 and the Government* (Seguin, TX: Mutual UFO Network, 1991).

SMITH: I am doing some work on the collapse of the earth's magnetic field as a source of energy, and I think our work may have a bearing on the flying saucers.

SARBACHER: What do you want to know?

SMITH: I have read Scully's book[8] on the saucers and I would like to know how much of it is true.

SARBACHER: The facts reported in the book are substantially correct.

SMITH: Then the saucers exist?

SARBACHER: Yes, they exist.

SMITH: Do they operate as Scully suggests, on magnetic principles?

SARBACHER: We have not been able to duplicate their performance.

SMITH: So they come from some other planet?

SARBACHER: All we know is, we didn't make them, and it's pretty certain they didn't originate on the earth.

SMITH: I understand the whole subject of saucers is classified.

SARBACHER: Yes, it is classified two points higher than the H-bomb. In fact, it is the most highly classified subject in the U.S. Government at the present time.[9]

Here, then, may be independent corroboration for at least part of what the MJ–12 briefing documents suggest. A highly-placed government official confirmed to a Canadian scientist, highly regarded for his work in geomagnetics that

[8] Frank Scully, *Behind the Flying Saucers* (New York: Henry Holt, 1950).

[9] Grant Cameron and T. Scott Crain, Jr., *UFOs, MJ-12 and the Government* (Seguin, TX: Mutual UFO Network, 1991).

the flying saucers did exist, were most likely from another world, and that the topic was the most highly classified project in the U.S. government.

Smith apparently had no better luck in following up on this information than had some of his U.S. counterparts. Sometime later he said:

> They [the military] collected much data, classified it, and buried it so effectively that no one else could get at it, and those that might have been able to sort the matter out found themselves deprived of the basic data and had to content themselves with the bit that escaped the clutches of the military.[10]

It is not known whether he meant the U.S. or Canadian military.

After all the controversy, the man who began the project may yet have the last word. President Harry S. Truman, in a press conference shortly before he left office, was asked a question pertaining to United States involvement with the flying saucer phenomenon.

"I can assure you," the president said, "that flying saucers, given that they exist, are not constructed by any power on Earth."

The arguments and the investigation have apparently been ongoing, at least since 1947. And it seems clear from the investigation outlined in this chapter that many of our brightest scientists were convinced these strange craft were coming from another planet. Early on, you'll remember, several members of this elite group thought Mars might be the most likely source for alien forays to earth.

Assuming for the moment that MJ–12 does or did exist, wouldn't it also be logical to assume that the scientists involved would make some effort to find out if our nearest

[10] Ibid.

planetary neighbor was the source of such a vexing problem? The question then becomes, has the United States or the former Soviet Union, which we now know had a keen interest in UFOs, made any serious attempts to discover what, if anything, is to be found on Mars?

The answer may surprise you as we continue our investigation in the next chapter.

CHAPTER 8

THE MARS CONNECTION

>> There before me in black and white was the . . . serene image of a human-like face against the background of the Martian land surface.

Uincent DiPietro, electrical engineer

The one technological certainty in our discussion of UFOs is that today human beings of the planet Earth are a space-traveling species. Whatever doubt there may have been about that was erased in July 1969 when the *Eagle* moon lander touched down on the lunar surface. If the moon had been populated, someone would have surely reported seeing a UFO. But we should also remember the comment broadcast worldwide as Commander Neil Armstrong stepped off the ladder of the *Eagle* spacecraft and stood in the ancient dust of the moon's surface: "That is one small step for man, one giant leap for mankind." Even though we have become a space-traveling species, we have taken only the tiniest of baby steps.

To put this in perspective, go to a park or some other large open space and put an orange down in the center of it. The orange represents the sun. Now measure twenty-five feet out and put a pin in the ground. The head of the pin represents the Earth. To travel that distance in terms of real space, at a speed of 36,000 miles per hour, would take 107 days. To reach Pluto, another, even smaller pinhead 1,200 feet from the orange, would take fifteen years. If we wanted to continue our journey and travel to the nearest star, the trip would take us 80,000 years just to get there and another 80,000 years for the return trip. The miniature step to the moon, a microscopic speck just a fraction of an inch from the tiny pinhead that represents Earth, barely meets even the definition of a "baby step."

Still, metaphorically speaking, we have come light years from the technology available to the best minds in the world in 1947. By the end of World War II humanity had advanced to the point where progress could be measured in decades. Today we measure progress in years, sometimes even months. This evolution is nowhere more evident than in the field of technology. A serious article on computer science written just two decades ago predicted that within fifteen years computers would weigh *"no more than 1.5 tons"* (emphasis mine). Today a computer that weighs five pounds, and has more computing capacity than the behemoths of ten or fifteen years ago, is considered "heavy."

For the scientists who comprised MJ–12 to suggest in 1947 that they were dealing with a phenomenon that might be originating on Mars took extraordinary courage and foresight. If Dr. Donald Menzel, professor of astrophysics at Harvard University, did indeed seriously suggest they might be dealing with something originating in another solar system, he was eons ahead of his time.

The question, then, is not so much what would the MJ–12 scientists have done to test their theories, but what *could* they have done? The answer is, not much. The ability of scientists to study Mars had not progressed a great deal beyond Boston astronomer Percival Lowell's photographs and sketches made in the early 1900s. In 1947, what was generally thought to be a system of canals and oases was still the subject of controversy, and the technology to prove or disprove various theories of martian terrain was still two decades away. In 1939, just prior to World War II, a hint of an immense green area was supposedly discovered. It wasn't until 1954 when Earth and Mars were at their closest opposition, that scientists would have a chance to really study the red planet. An international "Mars Patrol" was organized, cosponsored by the National Geographic Society and the Lowell Observatory, in an attempt to get a better view of what was calculated to be 200,000 square miles of green anomaly on the planet's surface. In early 1954, seventeen nations trained their telescopes on the red planet, fully expecting great things from their observations. Many Mars experts were hoping for photos to confirm that the long, straight lines were actually canals, as many believed. Some theorists even suggested that because many of these straight lines ran for hundreds of thousands of miles, it meant there was or had been intelligent life on Mars. They reasoned that two points connected by a straight line on the surface of a sphere simply does not occur in nature.

Dr. Earl Slipher of the Lowell Observatory directed the international committee that observed Mars from 1954 to 1956, the two years it was closest to Earth. In 1956 public announcements relating to the canals and the green anomaly and anything else the study might have produced were eagerly awaited. Unfortunately, no announcements from the committee were ever made. The matter was quietly dropped without any explanation.

Given this level of scientific knowledge even as late as 1956, it is not too surprising that the MJ–12 group in 1947 seriously speculated that flying saucers might be coming from Mars. What is surprising is the fact that there are some serious investigators today who think they may have been right.

By the time the Eisenhower briefing document was written, technology was rapidly changing. A scant four years following the close of Slipher's Mars Patrol, the Soviet Union was preparing to send an unmanned spacecraft to Mars. Their efforts began a long string of dismal failures, broken by a few successes, that continues to this very day.

In October 1960 the Soviets launched two spacecraft, neither of which reached Earth orbit. Those failures can easily be attributed to the infancy of rocket and space technology. Then in October 1962 they tried again. This time the craft reached orbit but died there. They tried again in November of that year and actually got a craft on its way. They called it *Mars 1* and proudly announced it would fly by Mars in June 1963. If, in fact, this probe did fly by the red planet as it was designed to do, no one will ever know. Just ten weeks before it was scheduled to arrive at its destination, the Soviets lost all contact with *Mars 1*.

Meanwhile, the United States was planning its own attempts to reach Mars. NASA's *Mariner 3* was launched in November of 1964. But the craft's protective shroud wouldn't open, and the craft was trapped inside and rendered useless. The Soviets, seemingly unwilling to give up, tried once more. They launched a probe called *Zond 2*, also in November 1964. Its purpose was to fly by Mars, but again, in April 1965, they lost contact with it. American space scientists began to joke, although somewhat nervously, about the "Great Galactic Ghoul" lying in wait to gobble up anything on its way to Mars. After five years and six tries, Earth scientists were still no closer to Mars than Dr. Slipher and his committee had been in 1956.

But November 1964 marked a turning point. *Mariner 4* was launched and completed the first successful flyby of Mars in July 1965. *Mariner 4* returned twenty-two images of the red planet and was the beginning of a series of highly successful missions. In 1969 *Mariners 6* and 7 completed flybys, returning over 200 photographs that began to detail the planet's surface. Alas, Lowell and Slipher had been wrong. There were no canals on Mars nor anything that appeared even remotely green.

In 1971 NASA successfully placed *Mariner 9* in orbit around Mars. The Great Galactic Ghoul, it seems, had been defeated. Or had it?

The Soviets, still trying to regain leadership in the space race following the United States' spectacular triumph in putting a man on the moon in 1969, announced they were going to *land* on Mars. Accordingly Soviet scientists launched *Mars 2* and *3* in 1971. Each of these craft carried "rovers," small, remotely operated vehicles that could be sent across the planet's surface after touchdown. The two Soviet spacecraft arrived at Mars roughly two weeks after *Mariner 9* had dropped into orbit. Their landing sequence, automatically preprogrammed, could not be changed. *Mars 2* flew into the teeth of one of the great Mars dust storms and crashed. *Mars 3* landed safely, however, and deployed its rover. The Soviets can forever claim to be the first to send pictures back to Earth from the martian surface. It was to be a short-lived triumph, however. Within two minutes of being deployed, the rover's transmitter went dead. The Galactic Ghoul was back in business. It would make itself felt again with a vengeance in just a little over a decade.

In 1975, NASA successfully launched the *Viking 1* and *2* probes. Taking volumes of photographs from Mars orbit, the two *Viking* craft sent back the most striking images ever seen of the surface of Mars. Huge volcanoes were identified as well as a canyon that would dwarf our own Grand Canyon on Earth. After studying the images, several scientists would announce that in all likelihood the surface of Mars was once covered with water. Harold Masursky of the U.S. Geological Survey has concluded that running water must have existed on the surface of Mars in "relatively recent times, geologically speaking," leading some scientists to suggest Mars may have been habitable as little as 10,000 years ago. Keep that number in mind; it will take on disturbing significance.

But of the thousands of photographs sent back by the *Viking* probes, only two have captured the world's imagination. They have also ignited a controversy that is still unresolved today. Identified as *Viking* frame 35A72 and *Viking* frame 70A13, taken as the probe soared over a plain on the surface of Mars known as Cydonia, these two photographs clearly show what has been termed "the face" on Mars. According to many observers, these two images are "most likely" the result of intelligent creation.

NASA quickly discounted the photographs as nothing more than tricks of light and shadow, suggesting at first that the face only appeared on frame 35A72 and that other pictures taken of the same area with a different lighting angle show no indication of a face. The heretofore highly successful method of ridicule was employed. NASA pointed to other representations of features on Mars they called "Kermit the Frog" and the "Happy Face," which they said proved the face was only an illusion. They summarily announced that the matter wasn't worth any further investigation.

But Vincent DiPietro, an electrical engineer with twenty years of experience in digital electronics and image processing, didn't see it that way. In his own words:

> I was thumbing through the archives of the National Space Science Data Center. There before me in black and white was the . . . serene image of a human-like face against the background of the Martian land surface. The title was certainly not misleading; It simply said 'HEAD.'[1]

DiPietro was looking at *Viking* photo 76H593/71834. He presumed that since it was so easily available in the NASA archives, the agency scientists would have verified it. He

---

[1] DiPietro, Molenaar, and Brandenburg, *Unusual Mars Surface Features*, 4th ed. (Glendale, MD: Mars Research, 1988), p. 13.

quickly discovered that NASA had *not* verified the photo, and, furthermore, wanted nothing at all to do with it.

Greg Molenaar, a Lockheed computer scientist and acquaintance of DiPietro, also found the photograph intriguing. Molenaar suggested a method of improving the image quality, and a partnership was born. If NASA was not going to do anything to verify the image, they concluded, it was up to them.

"We decided to blend our computer hardware and programming skills," DiPietro said, "toward the study of this single image."

They had the photo number (76H593) and the "picnell" number (35A72) (orbit 35, camera A, 72nd frame), which was enough information to let them request the original digital tapes from the Jet Propulsion Laboratory (JPL) in California. In January 1980 Molenaar and DiPietro began processing the tapes on their own photo-recording equipment.[2]

The completed computer enhancement came to the attention of Richard Hoagland, a former NASA consultant. He believed the mile-wide feature might be artificial, that is, formed by other than natural means. The more he investigated the face the more convinced he became that it could be an artifact from an ancient civilization. But how to prove it?

The work being done by DiPietro and Molenaar was truly groundbreaking. They developed an entirely new process they called "Starburst Pixel Interleaving Technique" (SPIT for "spitting image"), which resulted in much higher resolution of the frame. What they really needed, however, was another picture or, better yet, several more pictures taken from different angles.

NASA was still maintaining that the two men were literally grasping at shadows. Dr. Gerald Soffen, the *Viking* image team chief, was quoted in David Chandler's book, *Life on Mars*, as saying there was a second image made a few

---

[2] Ibid.

hours later that portrayed only an ordinary mesa. That sent DiPietro and Molenaar back to the *Viking* library. They couldn't find any photos that had been taken a few *hours* later, but their search did yield another image taken thirty-five *days* later over the same area, identified by NASA as the Cydonia plain. This frame, 70A13, (orbit 70, camera A, frame 13), was taken by the same satellite, and the face appeared again. Not only did this image confirm 35A72, but additional features began to emerge. According to Molenaar: " . . . there was [the] face with a higher sun angle, showing more detail than before . . . And images of the eyes showed pupils and [the] mouth area showed teeth. We were very impressed."

Slightly embarrassed by the find, NASA nevertheless remained immovable in their rejection of the photographs as anything more than a naturally formed feature of the martian landscape.

The discovery of the second frame had a different effect on Hoagland. He began to investigate the phenomenon in earnest. Hoagland enlisted the aid of Erol Torun of the Defense Mapping Agency and Dr. Mark Carlotto of Analytical Sciences Corporation and formed the Mars Mission. In the early 1970s, NASA was preparing the *Mars Observer*, a new probe that was intended to take a closer look at Mars than any craft previously launched. A new camera, the Mars Observer Camera (MOC), designed specifically for this satellite would have the capability of imaging objects as small as a coffee table from orbit with at least fifty times the resolution of the *Viking* probes.

Hoagland's Mars Mission was primarily an effort to make certain the MOC would reimage the plains of Cydonia, the geographic area where the face was located. They were interested not in just the face but in the entire region. Frame 70A13 had given them a look at something that was perhaps even more exciting than the enigmatic humanoid image even NASA was now referring to as the face.

"About ten miles away from the face," Molenaar told us in an interview, "[are] a couple of pyramids, and the strange thing about those pyramids is their very regular triangular shape. At the corner of each corner there appears to be a buttress and on close examination the buttress itself is pyramid shaped. This would be really, really remarkable for this to be a natural formation." The largest of these pyramids, a five-sided structure that clearly stands out from the others, was dubbed the D & M pyramid after its discoverers, DiPietro and Molenaar.

Richard Hoagland, a science writer by profession, began a tireless effort to discover the whole truth about the mysterious Cydonia region of Mars. So far, his effort has produced two, full-length videos, *Hoagland's Mars—The NASA–Cydonia Briefings* and *Hoagland's Mars, The Terrestrial Connection*. His book, *The Monuments of Mars*, was published in 1987 and reissued in 1992 in anticipation that the *Mars Observer*, scheduled for launch in 1992, would settle the issue once and for all. In spite of continued stonewalling by NASA officials, Hoagland, with the help of New Jersey Congressman, Robert Roe, had finally gotten the agency to commit to reimaging Cydonia.

Unfortunately it wasn't going to be that easy.

A member of Hoagland's Mars Mission team, Dr. Mark Carlotto, was adding his own imaging expertise to the work of DiPietro and Molenaar. According to Hoagland, " . . . he decided to use a state-of-the-art 3-D computer modeling technique which now strongly indicates that the face could, in fact, be a real three-dimensional, human-looking sculpture. A sculpture fifteen hundred feet high and over a mile long."

But it was more than just the face now; it was the amazing symmetry of the D & M pyramid and several other geometric-looking structures in the immediate vicinity that Hoagland dubbed "the city."

Pyramids on Mars, as it turns out, were nothing new. *Mariner 9* had sent back some startling photographs of an area astronomers called Elysium, which clearly showed pyramid-like formations. Carl Sagan made much of this in his famous PBS series, *Cosmos*, in which he called for further unmanned exploration of Mars and, "the pyramids of Elysium."

Cydonia, however, with its face and now its "city," was on the other side of the planet. DiPietro and Molenaar began a search for photographs of the area surrounding Cydonia. They wanted to find out if there were other, similar planetary features totally unrelated to either the face or the city. Their search uncovered ten photographs representing some 400,000 square miles of the surface of Mars around Cydonia. All ten of them had been taken during the same two orbits that produced the images of the face. After carefully examining these photographs, literally millimeter by millimeter, the researchers could find nothing even remotely similar to the planetary features in the immediate vicinity of the face. However, some of the researchers did discover similarities. To everyone's amazement, they found those similarities on *Earth*.

Hoagland had begun to develop a complex geometry based on the location of the face, the pyramid, and several other "structures" that all seemed to be related to the position of the face. It was, he said, "the discovery of . . . a highly specific and redundant mathematical and geometric *proof* that Cydonia is 'real,' and the apparently successful 'decoding' of the *meaning* of this Cydonia mathematical proof neatly resolves into the geometric properties of a *circumscribed 'tetrahedron'*—the simplest of the five classical 'Platonic solids.'"[3]

Hoagland developed a complicated geometric theory grounded in the tetrahedron, a four-sided pyramidal struc-

[3] Richard Hoagland, *The Monuments of Mars* (Berkeley, CA: North Atlantic Books, 1992), p. xvii.

ture, with each side forming an equilateral triangle circumscribed within a sphere. He believes the points at which the
baseline of the tetrahedron touch the sphere, whether the
apex is pointing up or down, pinpoint certain anomalies
throughout the solar system. For example, the giant storm
on Jupiter falls at a latitude predicted by this theory, as does
the Hawaiian archipelago with its constant volcanic activity
on Earth. Hoagland also gives great weight to the angles,
tangents, and cosines that are replicated in specific latitudes
on Mars and Earth.

In the process of analyzing this geometry, Hoagland and
his colleagues made an amazing discovery. In the southwest
of England, the ancient, man-made structure known as Silbury Hill has loomed over the horizon since time
immemorial. Nearby is Avebury, believed to be a centuries-
old fortress with tall earthen walls protecting an inner
mound. This area contains a remarkable connection to the
structures at Cydonia that according to Hoagland, is
founded in the solid facts of geometry.

"The angles and positions of the ancient features,"
Hoagland points out, "including where the cliff would be
and where the tetrahedral pyramid would be, and angles to
other key things in this vicinity all seem to match, including
the very size of Silbury Hill, in terms of its exterior moat."

The question for Hoagland was, were all of these structures built by the same race of beings, human or otherwise?
And if so, does this constitute new evidence that intelligent
life could have once thrived on the planet Mars?

Meanwhile other researchers on Hoagland's team were
coming up with some interesting findings of their own. First
they copied the left half of the Cydonia face, made a mirror
image of it and pasted it on the other side. The results were
interesting but inconclusive. Then they did the same thing
with the right half. The result was a clear image of a lion's
head. When placed side by side with a photograph of the
Sphinx at Giza, the resemblance was unmistakable. Hoagland
wondered if this was a mere coincidence or if the image

was trying to tell them something, perhaps even something profound.

Hoagland's team had already noted a number of similarities between the location of the D & M pyramid on Mars and the whole Cydonia complex, with features in and around the pyramid complex at Giza here on Earth. He decided to take a closer look at the pyramids of Giza and specifically at the Sphinx.

He soon discovered that certain scientists were questioning the long-accepted notions as to the age of this ancient artifact. According to J. David Davis, an author and ancient historian, " . . . recent archaeological and geological findings show that the Sphinx is at least 10,000 years old and maybe [even older]."[4] There's that number again.

"The Sphinx," Hoagland says, "appears to be much much more heavily weathered than we have any right to expect from only '5,000 years' of desert weathering. The kind of weathering we see on the Sphinx is best explained by the action of running water. You need rain to get that degree of erosion. Twelve feet of it in some places, and that amount of [rain] has not fallen in Egypt for ten, maybe fifteen or twenty thousand years.

"Now that raises a wonderful problem. It means that we're now looking at a monumental work of art created at a time when nobody else on the planet Earth is supposedly able to do anything of that magnitude or scale. There's no other contemporary civilization to pin it on. So, who did it?"

Hoagland was raising some very perplexing questions. Could both of these artifacts—one on Earth and one on Mars—have been made by the same race of beings? If so, who or what are these faces on the Sphinx and on Mars intended to represent? Is the key to understanding the face on Mars the fact that the Sphinx of Egypt is a combination

---

[4] Charles E. Sellier, *Mysteries of the Ancient World* (New York: Dell Publishing, 1995).

of hominid and feline . . . half man, half lion? Or is it all merely coincidence and strange optical illusions?

All of this was too much for Dr. Michael Malin, the University of Arizona contract scientist responsible for the imaging process on the *Mars Observer*. The attention that was being focused on Cydonia was detracting from what he considered the genuinely scientific aspects of the mission. He went on record with his opinion that there were no artificial structures on Mars; furthermore, it was not the mission's objective to look for life there.

About this time another professor from Arizona weighed in with his observations. Stanley McDaniel, professor emeritus from Sonoma State University, had begun his investigation with " . . . considerable skepticism." But professor McDaniel was a man who was as objective as he was thorough. He personally contacted the independent researchers, DiPietro, Molenaar, and Hoagland and members of Hoagland's team. He also reviewed NASA documents and responses to questions posed by the independent investigators. His conclusions were published in *"The McDaniel Report"* subtitled, *On the Failure of Executive, Congressional, and Scientific Responsibility in Investigating Possible Evidence of Artificial Structures on the Surface of Mars and in Setting Mission Priorities for NASA's Mars Exploration Program.*

In the preface to his 196-page report (including Appendix) professor McDaniel states:

> I became aware not only of the relatively high quality of the independent research, but also of glaring mistakes in the arguments used by NASA to reject this research. With each new NASA document I encountered, I became more and more appalled by the impossibly bad quality of the reasoning used. It grew more and more difficult to believe that educated scientists could engage in such faulty reasoning unless they were following some sort of hidden agenda aimed at suppressing the true nature of the data.

The rhetoric was definitely beginning to heat up.

In the meantime in an unprecedented display of international unity, the United States, the Soviet Union, and thirteen European nations participated in yet another attempt to learn more about Mars. In October 1988, *Phobos 1* and *Phobos 2* (named after one of the martian moons) were launched from Baikonur in the USSR. Even though the probes were launched from the Soviet Union, British and American scientists were on hand in the mission control center in Kaliningrad, the first and perhaps the last time any such show of cooperation has been attempted.

Phobos 1, like so many previous attempts, met with some form of disaster and was lost. (One report suggested a Russian technician accidentally turned it off.) But *Phobos 2* made it to Mars and seemed to be operating perfectly. A number of images were sent back to Earth from the probe, now circling Mars in the same orbit as the project's namesake, the moonlet Phobos. On March 1, 1989, photographs were received at mission control that showed a strange grid work of some sort on the surface of Mars. When the infrared images were overlaid on the optical photos and enlarged, the result was something that looked very geometric and very *un*natural. For some reason never explained, Russian mission control did not release any other images for the next twenty-four days.

Then on March 26 *Phobos 2* sent back images taken just south of the martian equator. They showed a long, elliptical "shadow" aligned with a long linear strip on the surface. It was defined as a shadow because scientists could see other surface characteristics through it. But perhaps even more significantly, it was *moving*. It was a shadow, but of what? The next day, March 27, something caused *Phobos 2* to shut down. An "accident" was reported by Soviet authorities; the probe was no longer sending images back to Earth. The last images received, so far as the international team knew, had been of the strange, elliptical shadow.

Three weeks later in a news conference, A. S. Selivanov, department head of the Soviet Space Agency, made the following rather curious and unsolicited comment:

"It does take a minimum of precision criteria to obtain on the image these spots, which some would like to call *flying saucers* [emphasis mine] that appear within individual fields of the infrared range. Actually, at first we were saying that there was no flying saucer, that truly, all that we saw could be explained in natural, understandable and physical terms."

Five months later in September of 1989, British television did a special on the *Phobos* mission. In the words of the reporter:

"Scientists are also puzzled by this shadow, pictured on the surface of Mars by both optical and heat-seeking cameras. They're convinced it's a shadow because they can see objects on the surface beneath, but a shadow of what? Finally there's the mystery of the vanishing spacecraft. The Russians are yet to release the last pictures transmitted by *Phobos* before it lost contact with ground control. But the Russians have said that it shows an object coming toward the spacecraft. An object which, in their words, *should not have been there* [emphasis mine]."

Is it possible that *Phobos 2* actually caught a glimpse of the Galactic Ghoul before it was rendered useless? Could it be that there is something on the planet Mars, intelligently controlled and capable of shutting down our probes and satellites? So far, and in spite of the international makeup of the enterprise, the Russians have refused to release those final photos sent back to Earth by *Phobos 2*.

Perhaps the scientists of MJ–12 were right after all, and Mars is, at the very least, a way station of some sort for interplanetary vehicles. Zechariah Sitchin thinks that was definitely the case in the past and very likely could be the case today.

According to Sitchin, "The Sumerian tablets refer to the 'station planet Mars' as 'the travelers ship.' I have taken it to mean that it was at Mars that the Annunaki from Nibiru[5] transferred to smaller spacecraft to reach Earth orbiting stations, not once every 3,600 years, but on a more frequent schedule. The actual landing and take-off from Earth were performed by smaller shuttle craft."

Sitchin reminds us that if there was a prehistoric, extraterrestrial culture that used Mars as a stopping off point to keep in touch with Earth, the only evidence of any such beings is found in the writings of the people of Sumer and their tales of the Annunaki. Sumer, it should be noted, was located where the present-day nation of Iraq now exists, at roughly the same latitude on Earth as Cydonia is on Mars.

Which brings us back to the controversy generated by the "face" photographed by NASA and investigated exclusively (so far as we know) by independent researchers and experts.

Following the strange loss of *Phobos 1* and *2* in 1989, more attention than ever was focused on the upcoming *Mars Observer* mission. As the countdown to the launch date continued, Hoagland and his group continued to press for a firm commitment to reimage the entire Cydonia plain and to look closer at the pyramids of Elysium as well. NASA continued to waffle, but they did make one significant change in their policy. After nearly four decades of permitting the public and commercial television networks to carry the images of NASA-funded projects live as they are broadcast back to Earth, they announced that due to an agreement with the MOC (Mars Observer Camera) inventor, there would be a six-week delay in the public release of any photographs from the *Mars Observer*.

The independent investigators were incensed. NASA was, after all, a publicly funded agency, and these were publicly

---

[5] According to Sitchin's theories, Nibiru is the planet in a huge elliptical orbit that comes into our solar system every 3,600 years. When it nears Mars its inhabitants, the "Annunaki," come to Earth to check on our progress and, from time to time, impart new knowledge.

funded projects. Entirely apart from the obvious opportunity this gave officials to hide, delete, or doctor any photographs coming out of the mission, NASA, it was argued, had no right to make a deal of any kind that would accrue to the private benefit of any individual to the exclusion of all others.

As it turned out, the argument was not with NASA after all, but with the now, not so funny, Galactic Ghoul, or whatever it is that doesn't want us to get any closer to Mars than we already are.

"The *Mars Observer* mission," according to Greg Molenaar, "may have been doomed before it even left the ground."

Molenaar was referring to Hurricane Andrew that hit the coast of Florida just about the time the *Mars Observer* was being prepared for launch. The spacecraft was prepared for such an onslaught, but something that still hasn't been explained took place.

After the storm, according to Molenaar, " . . . technicians checked the probe to make sure it had not been damaged by the storm. The nitrogen system was equipped with special filters to prevent dust and debris from being taken into the system, and the cameras were in a separate compartment. In spite of this bits of paper and dust and debris [were] found in both compartments. It looked," Molenaar continued, "like someone had swept the floor, taken a dustpan and dumped it into those compartments. It's unlikely that Hurricane Andrew would have been responsible for all of that damage."

But if not the hurricane, then who? There are many experts who now believe that the forces protecting the secrets of Mars may be right here on the planet Earth. Why else would NASA change the policy of releasing live data that has stood for almost forty years? Does it *know* something it doesn't want the independent investigators to find out? If not, this reversal of policy is an absolutely sure way to make everyone think it does.

Vicki Cooper-Ecker, editor of UFO *Magazine*, suggests that the reversal in policy might be due to NASA's long and close relationship with the Department of Defense. According to Cooper-Ecker, "They have been, I believe, under a lot of national security restrictions. And there is very much evidence, I believe, [of] backtracking [and] coyness on behalf of NASA and their involvement with UFOs."

In any event, on September 25, 1992, one of the most sophisticated space probes of its kind was launched into outer space. The *Mars Observer* was designed and programmed to approach, photograph, and carefully study the red planet in far greater detail than ever before. On August 21, 1993, at precisely 6:00 P.M. Pacific Standard Time, the radio signals from the *Mars Observer* stopped. The *Mars Observer* probe, over seventeen years in the making at a project cost of nearly one billion dollars, went silent—suddenly, completely, and as of the date of this writing, irrevocably.

The *Mars Observer* might have given us definitive answers to the question of intelligent life on Mars. As of now the billion-dollar satellite appears to be lost somewhere in the vast reaches of space.

Professor Stanley McDaniel, author of *The McDaniel Report*, believes there is a very practical justification for NASA's attitude. According to McDaniel, "Some people have speculated that NASA is afraid that it will lose funding if it even so much as hints that it might imagine that there are artifacts on Mars or elsewhere in the solar system. I think they believe Congress would think this was so far-fetched they would withdraw funds."

Professor McDaniel, when preparing his lengthy report, may have stumbled upon another reason for the government wanting to cover up any real proof of extraterrestrial life that is or has been in contact with Earth. Included in his report are excerpts from a Brookings Institute Report prepared for Congress in 1961. On page 215 of the Brookings Report it states: "While face to face meetings with [extra-

terrestrial life] will not occur within the next 20 years, artifacts left at some point in time by these life forms might
possibly be discovered through our space activities on the
Moon, Mars or Venus."

The Brookings Report goes on to point out that,
"Anthropological files contain many examples of societies
sure of their place in the universe which have *disintegrated*
[emphasis mine] when they had to associate with previously
unfamiliar societies espousing different ideas and different
life ways . . ."[6] On the next page the preparers of the report
speculate on ways such information might either be dissem-
inated or *withheld* from the public.

Professor McDaniel, it should be pointed out, is not
making excuses for NASA's performance. To the contrary.
The opening statement in his report, issued following the
untimely demise of the *Mars Observer*, reads as follows:

> The apparent failure of the *Mars Observer* mission is all
> the greater loss to science because of its inability to return
> data on the Martian land forms whose natural origin has
> been called into question. If NASA's current failure to
> assign appropriate priority to these land forms remains in
> effect for future missions to Mars, science stands at risk of
> being denied what might be the greatest scientific discov-
> ery of all time; and NASA itself is at risk of committing the
> most egregious act of scientific irresponsibility of all time.
> Indeed, NASA has already, by its ridicule of the indepen-
> dent investigation and its failures in the area of proper
> research on the land forms, effectively compromised the
> scientific process.[7]

To be sure, not everyone believes the *Mars Observer*
really died. Richard Hoagland stated publicly that he thinks

[6] Stanley McDaniel, "The McDaniel Report," 1961, p. 215.
[7] Ibid.

a miraculous "save" will occur. At the very least, it's fair to say he *hopes* it will. Hoagland, far from seeing the discovery of alien artifacts as damaging to society, views it as a rare, perhaps even a *planned* event of transcendent importance. According to Hoagland:

> Cydonia was probably constructed to communicate some very fundamental information. We believe now that we are looking at the outlines of a whole new physics, how the universe functions. A kind of grand unified theory as it were, given to us, communicated even on the photographs taken by *Viking*, by the geometric layout of the structures.[8]

If that is true, science would do well to try to decipher the message with all possible speed. It appears, however, that NASA will maintain a lofty disdain for anything that smacks of "unearthly" civilization. Their scientists insist that, in spite of Hoagland's rather elegant mathematics, their only interest is in discovering more precise data on the "scientific" characteristics of the planet. Do not expect them to rephotograph or reexamine the Cydonia plain anytime soon.

It might be possible however, to make the same kind of discovery on our own planet. Some scientists have speculated that Mars was habitable as few as 10,000 years ago. The Sphinx is now believed to be at least 10,000 years old. Sitchin is confident from his translation of the Sumerian texts, which refer to events taking place at least 10,000 years ago, that Mars was a transfer point for extraterrestrials coming to Earth. Is it all just a fantastic coincidence? Could it be that the similarities between the pyramids on Mars and the pyramids at Giza will yield some as yet undiscovered key to our past . . . and to our future? That is the challenge of our next chapter.

---

[8] *Hoagland's Mars, Vol. II*, B. C. Video, Inc., New York, 1992.

CHAPTER 9

PYRAMIDS— THE ALIEN CONNECTION

Certainly Richard Hoagland and the members of the Mars Mission team had been looking at the same stark features on the surface of Mars that everyone else was seeing. But their thinking, along with those of men like DiPietro and Molenaar, was far different from that of the NASA officials, or for that matter, many so-called mainstream scientists who simply dismissed the whole idea as "nonsense."

What the Mars Mission group seemed to want was recognition of the *possibilities* presented by the sudden, almost serendipitous appearance of the face. By the time the *Mars Observer* literally disappeared from the scene and dashed the hopes of everyone interested in settling the issue of whether the face was of "natural" origins, the argument had been going on for seventeen years. What's more, neither side showed any signs of softening.

Then suddenly the focus of the discussion began to shift away from the basic configuration of the face to the even more radical idea of a possible direct connection to the Earth.

"The key to our apparently successful solution to the riddle of Cydonia," said Hoagland in Volume II of his *Mars Mission* video, "turned out not to be the face at all, but a two-mile long, half-mile high, five-sided pyramid located a few miles away."

Could this mean, he wondered, that there was a message of some sort tucked away in the angles and structures of what seemed to be another intelligent construction on the planet's surface? Many scientists are convinced that the language of mathematics will likely prove to be the only truly universal language. The question is, can we decipher it? Can we learn to speak it?

In February 1971 the United States launched *Pioneer 10*, an unmanned space probe designed to reach farther and last longer than any other probe launched to date. One of the unique things about *Pioneer 10* was our attempt to include a message to whomever or whatever might find the probe should it be drawn into another solar system and discovered by inhabitants of some other planet. The message was a combination of pictographs, geometric designs, and mathematical symbols (the rectangle, circle, arc, etc.) that would tell these beings we were male and female, we lived on a relatively small planet that was the third planet from our sun, and we were peaceful. Not a word was used on the message. When you stop and think about it, using words would have made no sense at all.

Hoagland's team was already convinced that the structures at Cydonia were, " . . . intimately connected to each other by an identical geometry." And geometry, according to Hoagland, " . . . is the key, the one true signature of intelligent life that planetary scientists now look for on all planets. In simple terms: intelligent life creates things, things like buildings, cities, pyramids . . . that are inescapably composed of repeating *geometric* structure.

"The Face on Mars, its nearby pyramids, the entire Cydonia complex," Hoagland claims, "is simply brimming with this elegant, repeating geometric structure."[1]

The team had already noted the similarity between the Cydonia complex and the Silbury Hill complex near Avebury in England. The similarity between certain configurations of the face and the Sphinx near the Great Pyramid of Giza had likewise pointed them in the direction of the Giza Plateau. Perhaps it was time to take a closer look at the controversy that had begun to well up over the dating of the Sphinx. The question was, is there any reputable scientific proof for the earlier dating?

John Anthony West, a writer and Egyptologist, had been studying the Sphinx for nearly fifteen years when he began to be more and more concerned with an anomaly in the weathering of the Sphinx that the current scholarly suppositions could not explain. Specifically, there was a great deal more weathering than might be expected over 4,000 to 5,000 years. More importantly, much of it seemed to have been caused by the action of running water. West eventually succeeded in getting a geologist of international repute to examine the Sphinx firsthand. Dr. Robert W. Schock, tenured professor of geology at Boston University, took a team of scientists to Egypt and conducted extensive tests. He reported on his findings to the Geological Society of America (GSA) conference in 1991:

> Based on this chain of reasoning . . . we can estimate that the initial carving of the Great Sphinx, (i.e., the carving

[1] Richard Hoagland, *The Monuments of Mars* (Berkeley, CA: North Atlantic Books, 1992).

of the main portion of the body and the front) may have
been carried out [sometime between] 7,000 to 5,000 B.C.
This tentative estimate is probably a minimum date, given
that weathering rates may proceed non-linearly . . . the
possibility remains open that the initial carving of the
Great Sphinx may be even older than 9,000 years . . .[2]

This report called into question not only the traditional
dating of the Sphinx, but the dating of the pyramids as well.
The community of Egyptology was in for yet another shock.

Dr. Herbert Haas, director of the Radiocarbon Laboratory at Southern Methodist University, has devoted a great
deal of effort to establish accurate dates for the construction
of the pyramids as well as other ancient constructions. He
announced that, according to established carbon-dating
methods, the Great Pyramid is at least 400 years *older* than
Zoser's "bent" pyramid. The significance of this discovery
cannot be overstated. If the carbon-dating results were accurate, they turn the traditional theory of pyramid construction on its head. For thousands of years it was supposed
that the Great Pyramid was the crowning achievement of
several generations of trial and error on the part of the pyramid builders. The step pyramids, Zoser's bent pyramid
(so-called because of it's irregular shape) and dozens of
smaller pyramids were all supposed to have been the early
attempts to solve the problems of pyramid construction,
ending in the monumental triumph of the Great Pyramid of
Khufu.

On the other hand, for many years a small band of theorists had proposed an alternative explanation. The Great
Pyramid, they suggested, already existed when the Egyptians appeared on the scene. All other pyramids (some 80 of
them), scattered along the west bank of the Nile, were simply failed attempts to copy the original. Zoser's bent

[2] *Hoagland's Mars, Vol. II*, B. C. Video, Inc., New York, 1992.

pyramid was the most classic example of the inability of Egyptians of the old kingdom to duplicate the feat. It now appeared that these theorists were right.

Perhaps we should take a moment here to define just exactly what it is that makes the Great Pyramid and its companions on the Giza Plateau so special. To begin with, the Great Pyramid is the largest human construction on the planet. It covers nearly fourteen acres at its base and rises to a height of nearly 500 feet. It is composed of some 2,300,000 limestone blocks, each weighing from two and a half to ten tons, rising upward at a precise angle of 51° 52'. The exterior casing stones, now almost all removed, were at one time highly polished and covered the entire structure with a smooth, gleaming surface. The stones were shaped to such fine tolerances that a knife blade could not be inserted between them. Imagine a work of optical precision on a scale of acres.

To be sure, the pyramid complex at Giza did not require the discovery of a giant feline-hominid face on Mars or a series of pyramidal structures at Cydonia to generate controversy. Since the first historical record of these amazing structures was made by the famous Greek historian Herodotus sometime around 425 B.C., they have been the subject of debates regarding their purpose and origin. According to Herodotus, the Great Pyramid of Khufu (also called Cheops or simply, the "Great Pyramid") was built in just twenty years by teams of 100,000 men working in three-month shifts. These were either loyal subjects of the pharaoh or slaves, or a combination of both.

This account supposes that the huge stones were quarried from a gigantic limestone formation nearby. Modern Egyptologists also hold that the quarried blocks were dragged or rolled over the sand on logs to the Giza Plateau. The writings of Herodotus also suggest that some kind of huge leverage device was used to raise the stones to each succeeding level. Here Egyptology parts company with the

Greek historian. Many modern theorists believe the structure was raised by virtue of an earthen ramp that was constructed as the pyramid rose and was then dismantled from the top down, allowing workers to put the casing stones in place as the ramp receded.

But why are we left to theorize? The Egyptians were prolific record keepers, and their form of writing is found everywhere. Curiously, in spite of their great penchant for carving everything they did in stone, the Egyptians did not leave us any hieroglyphs about the construction of the pyramids. Not a word about who or when or why they did it. The pyramids are left to speak for themselves, which they do, according to some experts, in the elegant language of mathematics. Strangely enough, it was not a scientist but a conqueror who first saw the need for trying to decode the language of the pyramids.

Roughly two thousand years after Herodotus made his journey to the Nile delta, Napoleon Bonaparte, with a small army of scholars, scientists, artists, and mathematicians, stood before the awesome structures and asked the same questions. How were they built and why? How long did it take? It was Napoleon's army of savants that began what has since become a science itself. Napoleon's scholars set about measuring, calculating, and theorizing about the pyramids. By the time Napoleon's army arrived on the scene, much of the facing—the beautiful polished white limestone that covered the exterior of the pyramids—had been removed to help build the city of Cairo. That defacing made it possible for the French scientists to measure and calculate the weight of individual stones used in the construction. The results stunned Napoleon. He is supposed to have mused that there were enough stones in the Great Pyramid to build a wall around all of France seven times.

Today scientists of several different disciplines put computers and calculators to work and still can't solve the puzzle to everyone's satisfaction (or perhaps to *anyone's*). But as we suggested in the previous chapter, a whole new breed of scientist, as well as various groups of self-styled investigators, are now poring over the thousands of pieces of information that have been gathered over the centuries. They are attempting to see if somewhere in all this data there is not an *alien* connection.

It might be helpful here to highlight some of the more obvious bones of contention between the traditional view of the modern Egyptologist and the views resulting from some of the more recent investigations pertaining to the Great Pyramid of Giza.

For one thing, no one in any scientific discipline has been able to explain the huge, seventy-five-ton granite "spirit" stones in the heart of the pyramid. Why are they there? What was their purpose? More importantly, perhaps, how did they get there?

Furthermore, there is the whole question of how the huge stone blocks used to build the pyramid, weighing from two and a half to ten tons, were quarried, transported over the sand, and raised to a height of nearly fifty stories. There are two distinct schools of thought here, and over hundreds of years neither of them has achieved anything like a consensus. In fact some modern researchers say they are both impossible theories.

Then, of course, there are the dozens of finer points having to do with mathematics, geology, geography, and astronomy that seem to fly in the face of the conclusions of traditional Egyptologists. This is where our principal interest lies, but keep in mind that dozens of volumes have been written exploring every aspect of what has come to be called "the language of the pyramids." Our main concern is, is it the same language as that being deciphered from the pyramids of Cydonia?

The Egyptologists, of course, prefer to ridicule any suggestions that the pyramids are anything other than giant tombs for ancient Egyptian kings. Those who think they may have served some more ancient and practical purpose are referred to as "pyramidiots."

Zechariah Sitchin, on the other hand, who " . . . has a profound knowledge of modern and ancient Hebrew . . . the Old Testament . . . history and archaeology of the Near East . . . [and] attended the London School of Economics,"[3] states flatly that, "It appears that the Giza Pyramids were built as beacons by extraterrestrials as part of the landing corridor ending at the space port in the Sinai desert."[4]

There is an enormous gap between those views—almost as wide as the distance between Earth and Mars. It may be that the only way to bridge that gap is by deciphering the mathematical codes discovered in the Cydonia complex and the pyramid complex at Giza.

The one undeniable aspect of the whole debate is the fact that the pyramids are there. Even so there are a number of experts who insist the ancient Egyptians not only did not but *could not* have built these marvelous structures. In fact many scientists agree that physically, mathematically, and scientifically, the Great Pyramid could not have been built by human labor at all. Some argue that if the pyramid weren't already there we wouldn't have the scientific know-how and capability to build it today, at least not to the exacting and precise standards to which it was constructed. Yet it exists, as undeniable as the sunrise.

Setting the theories aside for the moment, let's try to put this controversy in perspective in terms of those facts that are scientifically beyond question. It helps to realize, for instance, that the Great Pyramid contains enough stone to build thirty-five Empire State buildings, with several tons left over. In spite of the pyramid's great size and bulk, its alignment to true north is virtually perfect, being off absolute true north by just three minutes of arc. Further-

---

[3] *MUFON Symposium Proceedings* (Seguin, TX: Mutual UFO Network, 1991).
[4] *UFO Diaries*. Sun International Pictures, Salt Lake City, 1995.

more, to this day the precision of that alignment has never been duplicated. The closest that modern science and construction method have come is in the Paris Observatory, which is off true north by six minutes of arc.

"The Great Pyramid," according to Joseph B. Gill, author of *The Great Pyramid Speaks to You*, "is more truly oriented to the cardinal directions, as we know them, than any other pyramid. This is a difficult feat, even today, when we realize true and magnetic north do not coincide and the latter also wanders." He adds, "Let there be no mistake these points were designed. They are not coincidental nor accidental construction quirks. Neither were they required nor necessary for the established tomb purposes."[5]

As noted above, the base of the pyramid covers more than thirteen acres, each side measuring 756 feet. The sides soar upward some 452 feet (probably closer to 480 feet before the casing stones were looted) at a precise angle of 51° 52'. Amazingly, the sciences of geology, mathematics, and astronomy seem to reach their zenith with the construction of the Great Pyramid. Weighing some fourteen *billion* pounds, it sits on a plot of desert that just happens to have a solid base of limestone underneath the sand. In 5,000 years, the Great Pyramid, weighing 700,000 tons, has settled less than one-half inch. It is also situated on the prime meridian of Earth, its east-west, north-south axes intersecting the only lines of longitude and latitude in the world that equally divide the Earth's land masses and oceans. Could this have all been just a monumental (no pun intended) series of coincidences?

Knowing where to put the pyramid and how to align it was only the beginning of the problem. After all, that could have been done before a single stone was put in place. Keeping the four sides in alignment as the structure rose is an

---

[5] Joseph B. Gill, *The Great Pyramid Speaks to You* (New York: Philosophical Library, 1964).

even greater achievement. The side of the Great Pyramid deviated from straight alignment by only about one quarter of an inch, a feat impossible to duplicate even today! Nor is that the end of the wonders to be noted in this marvelous masterpiece of construction. Europeans argued for centuries over whether the Earth was flat. Yet in the design and construction of the Great Pyramid we are faced with indisputable proof that the ancient Egyptians, or whoever built this monument, could calculate the longitude and latitude of the Earth as a sphere.

These facts deal with only the external dimensions of the Great Pyramid. Several indisputable facts must be pointed out that relate to its interior construction. For example, a narrow passageway slopes downward at precisely twenty degrees for several hundred feet only to arrive at a dead end in an obviously unfinished chamber. The ascending passageway slopes upward at precisely the same angle. Midway up this ascending passage is another passageway that levels off and ends in what is called the Queen's Chamber. This room, like all of the others in the Great Pyramid, is empty and devoid of any decoration, except for a sixteen-foot-high niche carved enigmatically in the east wall.

From this level passageway upward is an area in the pyramid called the Grand Gallery, an architectural marvel that has puzzled and astonished architects and builders for centuries. This passageway opens up to a breathtaking 157 feet in length and 26 feet in height. Blocks of limestone, some weighing twenty to thirty tons, are cut, polished, and positioned to a tolerance of 0.01 inch. What's more the walls are built to a precise slope. Sixty-two inches wide at the floor, it narrows to forty-two inches at the top.[6] British astronomer Richard Anthony Proctor, points out that "Had an ancient astronomer wished for a large observation slot precisely bisected by a meridian through the north pole, so

[6] Barbara Mitchell, *Pyramids* (St. Paul, MN: Greenhaven Press, 1988).

as to observe the transit of the heavenly bodies, [he would have requested of an architect] a very high slit with vertical walls, preferably narrower at the top; a gallery whose aperture, thanks to the reflected light of the polar star, could be designed so as to be exactly bisected by a true meridian."

The Grand Gallery meets those specifications precisely and in so doing takes us directly to the King's Chamber. Again, like the Queen's Chamber, this room lacks any decoration, but its dimensions are amazing in their mathematical precision.

The walls are of pink Aswan granite. Nine slabs of granite make up the ceiling with a total weight of probably 400 tons. Above that ceiling are four more flat ceilings, each one constructed of several granite slabs, approximately seventy-five tons each. Above those ceilings is the granite A-shaped ceiling, probably designed to keep the great weight of the pyramid from crashing down on the chamber.

The only artifact ever discovered in this room (we are dealing here only with what we know, remember) is a coffer, some refer to it as a sarcophagus, cut from a single block of rose granite and hollowed out to exact dimensions. This brings us to one of the most recent scientific undertakings with regard to the Great Pyramid.

Robert Bauval, a construction engineer, and writer Graham Hancock, have begun to focus on some of the features of the Pyramid of Khufu that have so far been largely overlooked, like the so-called sarcophagus in the King's Chamber. To begin with it is a solid block of rose granite that has been cut, hollowed out, if you will. In and of itself, that fact is only a curiosity. What captured their imagination was a simple, straightforward question. What tools or method *could* the ancient Egyptians have possibly used to accomplish this remarkable task?

Chris Dunn, a drilling expert, points out that in primitive societies the granite would have been hollowed out with a bow drill, using sand or diamond abrasive to advance the drill into the rock. This, method, Dunn says, would have taken too many years. He believes the builders must have used some kind of power tool.

Power tool? In 2500 B.C.?

Dunn points out that to accomplish this feat today drillers would advance the drill into the granite at a rate of $^2/_{10,000}$ of an inch per revolution of the drill. He believes that whoever cut this granite box, with its squared corners, smooth sides, and flat bottom, must have been advancing the drill at an even faster rate. What tool could the ancient Egyptians have had that would let them do such remarkable work? The answer is nowhere to be found. Moreover, the Egyptians, if indeed it was Egyptians who did it, were able to cut and polish not only granite, but diorite, the hardest stone in nature. In some cases these mysterious builders drilled out the inside of diorite vases to a depth that modern-day tools couldn't even reach.[7]

Bauval and Hancock made another interesting discovery, an observation that would have been impossible without the aid of computers. With all the precision evident in the pyramids of the Giza Plateau, the smaller of the three structures is curiously out of alignment with the other two. Noting the position of the three stars in Orion's belt, in the constellation of Orion, Bauval wondered if perhaps the layout of the pyramids wasn't in fact a "star map" of this constellation. Orion does figure prominently in ancient Egyptian religious writings. When he checked it out, it was close, but not quite there, at least not as the stars would have appeared in 2500 B.C. Taking into account the changes that appear to take place in the heavens, caused by the wobbling of the Earth on its axis, a phenomenon known to astronomers as "precession," Bauval discovered that the position of the three pyramids precisely duplicates the position of the stars in

[7] *Ancient Mysteries of the Pyramid and the Sphinx*, A & E, (*Ancient Journeys*, May 1996).

Orion's belt as they appeared in 10,500 B.C. Amazingly, when viewed as a star map, the position of the Nile relative to the pyramids also precisely matched the Milky Way relative to the stars in Orion's belt during that same epoch. But there was more.

John Anthony West, whom you'll remember was praised by Richard Hoagland for his pioneering and unflinching work in dating the Sphinx, joined Bauval and Hancock in their quest for the truth about the age and meaning of the Giza monuments. Among other things, they confirmed the action of water erosion on the base of the Sphinx. West also points out that the head of the Sphinx is in much better condition than the body; furthermore, when the huge statue is taken as a whole, the head appears to be much too small for the proportions of the monument. Could it be that the head was originally that of a lion, and at some point was recarved by an Egyptian king to represent himself?

But why a lion? Going back to the computer the investigators discovered that the astronomical epoch marked to be the ascension of the constellation of Leo occurred around 10,000 B.C. Furthermore, the constellation, as it appeared on the Egyptian horizon during this epoch matches, with astonishing similarity, the dimensions of the Sphinx, if, in fact, it was carved as a lion between 11,000 and 10,000 B.C. These findings, strangely enough, match the geological weathering of the Sphinx to a degree that would seem to eliminate coincidence.[8] Does this mean the Egyptologists are totally mistaken?

The indisputable fact is that no mummy of any kind—no king, queen, or commoner—has ever been found in any pyramid. In the case of the Great Pyramid there is no indication that anything even remotely like the funerary embellishments of the great pharaohs was ever there. But certain mathematical constants are there. The Great Pyra-

[8] Ibid.

mid is of a height that suggests dynamic geometry and a shape that directly implies static geometry. The King's chamber is a perfect "golden rectangle," which provides the necessary information to construct the Fibonacci series and the logarithmic spiral (discovered by Descartes) which is a function of *pi*, long thought to have been the discovery of the Greeks.[9] Could the Egyptians of the old kingdom have invented these complex mathematical theorems?

But perhaps too much has been made of all of this.

According to Kurt Mendelssohn, in his book, *The Riddle of the Pyramids*, the Egyptian architects, " . . . never did anything more sophisticated than to build pyramids according to the simple gradients of 4:1 and 3:1. This [4:1] is the mysterious ratio used in pyramid construction and which, at the same time, leads inevitably to an angle of elevation of 51° 52'. In other words," says Mendelssohn, "the pyramid builders discovered the transcendental number, *pi* (3.141) without trying and without knowing." Because this culture was not capable of geometry, the fact that they built with *pi* is only a coincidence.

That settles the matter for Mendelssohn. "Having disposed of the idea," he continues, "that the Egyptians of more than 4,000 years ago revealed in building pyramids an enigmatic command of advanced mathematics, we can return to the generally accepted interpretation that the pyramids were pharaonic tombs."

Well, perhaps not quite yet.

---

[9] The golden rectangle, in its simplest terms, is a rectangle where the center point of either of the longer sides is precisely equidistant from each of the remaining sides. Expressed mathematically, it is a rectangle in which the adjacent sides are in the ratio $(1 + \sqrt{5})/2$. This geometric form provides the necessary information for the Fibonacci series of numbers—the infinite sequence in which successive numbers are formed by adding the two previous numbers. The logarithmic spiral (a function of *pi*), based on the Fibonacci series, is derived when each quarter-turn of the spiral is determined by the length of the side of the square in which it is inscribed. The value of this for each succeeding square is in turn determined by the Fibonacci series.

Whether or not the *Egyptians* of the old kingdom possessed a command of advanced mathematics, someone apparently did. Without question certain elements of the Great Pyramid suggest that, at the very least, the builders had a wider knowledge of the heavens than would seem to be useful to a quasi–stone-age culture. Given that fact, Sitchin's supposition that space travelers were using Mars as a way station, begins to take on more credibility. These extraterrestrials might find such advanced astronomical knowledge not only useful but essential, particularly if it was derived from the marker of the Earth's prime meridian.

But Hoagland was looking for something more precise, a "mathematical link; a verifiable, testable link between [Cydonia] and Giza." He found it in the latitude of the two locations on their respective planets. According to Hoagland, the latitude of the D & M pyramid on Mars, is 40.9° north, the latitude of the Sphinx at Giza is 30° north. The cosine of the angle of the latter is 0.866 (*e* prime divided by *pi*), which is precisely the same as the tangent of the D & M pyramid.[10] "That," said Hoagland, "was a verifiable link, interesting but," he added, "not conclusive."

The logarithmic spiral, based on the Fibonacci sequence and drawn within a golden rectangle, when overlaid on the position of the Giza pyramids, does provide a very interesting result. According to Hoagland, the "mean spiral divides the Giza Plateau into a series of rectangles. The positioning of the Sphinx in relation to these rectangles and the pyramids turns out to be precisely, according to the critical *e/pi* ratio, 0.865 . . . [which is] again, the key constant ratio of Cydonia. The Sphinx," Hoagland asserts, "is not oriented at

---

[10] The cosine function is the horizontal component of a point on a circle between 0° and 90°, (0 and $\pi/2$ radians). A tangent is a straight line or plane that touches a curve or surface without cutting through it. On a graph, the slope of the tangent to a curve is the slope of the curve at the point of contact. The tangent function, like the cosine function, is periodic but repeats itself every 180°.

random in relation to the pyramids, but according to the key message of Cydonia itself. The implications for this precise positioning of Earth's most awesome work of art, in terms of a mathematical code now undeniably linked to another planet, are clear."[11]

Anthropologist Richard Grossinger is quoted in the book, *The Monuments of Mars*, as saying, in a discussion with Hoagland:

> So to have a humanoid, and a humanoid on the very next planet over from Earth, suggests one of two things, both of them very disturbing to progressive liberal scientific mentalities. You are suggesting either that there is an intrinsic 'humanoidizing' force in the universe (which goes against the atheistic basis of science itself), or that humanoids have come from elsewhere and been associated with the planet, this solar system. If it's the former, then you are very close to spiritualizing the universe. If it's the latter, then you are giving aid and comfort to the whole ancient-astronaut fringe which is so distasteful to modern astronomers.[12]

Distasteful or not, the message seems to be constant and getting louder. Long before the "face" on Mars was photographed, Zechariah Sitchin was telling the world there was a connection between not only Earth and Mars, but between Earth and the larger galaxy as well. If the translations of the Sumerian texts are correct, the pyramids were already there long before the first pharaoh, or perhaps even the first Egyptian, was born.

An intriguing and exotic idea, but it doesn't explain how the pyramids could be of use to travelers from another

[11] Richard Hoagland, *The Monuments of Mars* (Berkeley, CA: North Atlantic Books, 1992).
[12] Ibid.

world. As big as they are, they are not visible from outer space. For this theory to be credible the pyramids would have to radiate energy, something an ordinary pile of stones won't do. But then, as we have seen, the Great Pyramid is no ordinary pile of stones.

Author and science lecturer Roger Oakland tells us that, "The pyramids are essentially crystalline in structure, therefore highly receptive to radio-like energy waves, or even cosmic microwaves. The Great Pyramid of Giza with its five granite slabs above the King's Chamber is what the ancient Egyptians called 'spirit' stones, and they could have been a massive receiver tuned to some distant part of the Universe of which we are still ignorant."[13]

Author Greg Nielsen adds: "There's a vortex of energy emanating from the apex of the pyramid which actually expands in diameter as it rises higher and higher into the heavens. Although we don't know why or how," Nielsen insists, "the Great Pyramid seems to be an accumulator of energies."[14]

That being the case, might not the pyramids have been exactly what the ancient Sumerian texts seem to claim—a sort of cosmic lighthouse for passing space travelers? Or is all of this just another tale told by "pyramidiots?" As incredible as this may sound, the apparently otherworldly theory does seem to be the first explanation of the Great Pyramid that truly covers all the known facts of its construction, placement, and design. The same Sumerian texts, remember, refer to Earth as the "seventh" planet, as if being counted from the outside of our solar system *in* toward the sun. According to Dr. Sitchin, no one but space travelers coming to Earth past Pluto, Neptune, Uranus, Saturn, Jupiter, and Mars could have considered Earth the seventh planet.

---

[13]   Charles E. Sellier, *Mysteries of the Ancient World* (New York: Dell Books, 1995).
[14]   Ibid.

When we stop to consider that we ourselves have begun the exploration of space, even if in the most primitive of ways, is it so hard to believe that other, more advanced civilizations somewhere in the galaxy or in galaxies yet unknown might be capable of taking "giant steps" that would bring them to our very door? And in the vast expanse of space, would not Mars literally be on our doorstep?

According to Hoagland, "The fundamental mathematical relationships communicated by the structures at Cydonia are now eerily replicated in the Giza complex here on Earth, including the very placement of the Sphinx. Even the key latitude of Giza, north of the equator, is now linked directly to the D & M pyramid's latitude at Cydonia on Mars.

"So we can't tell who the builders were. There is a clue, however, and it's in the mile-long, fifteen-hundred-foot-high humanoid face [photographed on Mars]. Our thinking now, our team's thinking, is that that face is our face. Or what we once were. So in a sense, some day, not now but some day, we may discover that we, in fact, were the Martians."[15]

Perhaps, but the notion of extraterrestrial visitors constructing the pyramids of Egypt seems to be just too outrageous for many if not most people to accept. As Hoagland said in his report to the United Nations in 1992, the suggestion has modern Egyptologists "frothing." And it is true that these theories of alien pyramid builders do ignore the ancient Egyptians and any contribution they might have made in the creation of the Great Pyramid. But as we mentioned earlier, the Egyptians of the Old Kingdom seem to have ignored that contribution also.

August Tornquist, a prominent Giza pyramid researcher, reminds us that "The Great Pyramid was the greatest single undertaking in the whole history of mankind, and yet there is not one picture or drawing, not one artifact, not one inventory or tally sheet to tell of its construction. The

[15] *Hoagland's Mars, Vol II.*, B. C. Video, Inc., New York, 1992.

Egyptians left us some three thousand years of written and pictorial history covering virtually everything that happened in their culture from babies being born to plowing and harvesting, building, weaving, sacrificing, praying, embalming, but nothing about the pyramids of Giza. Why?"[16]

The question is fairly asked. Do the Egyptian records fail to mention the construction of the pyramids because they were already there when the Nile Valley culture *began* to flourish? Perhaps the only thing that *can* be proved is that the pyramids are the keepers of a mystery that we may never solve.

We did run across one other curious and thought-provoking item that bears mentioning, however, if only because of its source. In his book Hoagland recounts finding an anthology of articles edited by a man named Ian Redpath, who was formerly published in the respected *Journal of the British Interplanetary Society*. "It contained," writes Hoagland, "a provocative chapter heading: 'Signpost to Mars.'" He turned to the chapter and discovered the following:

"One of the weirdest coincidences of the whole affair is that Cairo, the site of the [two greatest] pyramids, was originally named El-Kahira, from the Arabic El-Kahir—*meaning 'Mars'* (emphasis mine).

"What were the *random* probabilities," Hoagland asks, "that there would exist two isolated worlds, both with 'pyramids' and 'sphinxes' and now that the *one* site on this planet where the most perfect, most archetypal forms still stand—Cairo—would also form the key linguistic bridge that *links* those worlds?"[17]

Perhaps it's time to take a new look at some of the other ancient messages that dot the planet. We'll do that in the next chapter.

[16] Charles E. Sellier, *Mysteries of the Ancient World* (New York: Dell Publishing, 1995), p. 174.
[17] Richard Hoagland, *The Monuments of Mars* (Berkeley, CA: North Atlantic Books, 1992).

CHAPTER 10

TECHNOLOGY— Launchpad to the Future or Door to the Past?

>> **The symbols on the idol record the state of the heavens 27,000 years ago.**

H. S. Bellamy and P. Allan, The Great Idol of Tiahuanaco

Galileo built a crude telescope and turned it toward the night sky. What he saw convinced him that everything he had been taught about the nature of the universe was wrong. He undoubtedly thought this new information would be warmly and enthusiastically received. Instead he was criticized by scholars and threatened with excommunication from the church if he did not recant his "heretical" pronouncements. But the seed had been planted. In the face of Galileo's discoveries scholars, clerics, and scientists were forced to rethink their dearly held beliefs. It took many years, but eventually supposition was supplanted by the reality of Galileo's observations.

Today our space probes have given us a picture of our solar system that is rich in detail and stunning in its diversity. The Hubble telescope can look to the edge of the galaxy and beyond, and astronomers have discovered several planets in distant star systems they believe to be capable of supporting life. We have also learned that it is possible to overcome gravity, calculate the time and distance to other worlds, and send objects into outer space and bring them back again. We have even walked on the moon, the modern equivalent of Galileo's rustic telescope. Although we have proved that intelligent beings can cross the void of space, our scholars and scientists seem reluctant to accept the notion that other intelligent beings might have done the same thing a long time ago and from much farther away. Has anything changed since Galileo's day?

That's a question worth investigating. Technology has made us more aware certainly, but can it help us to understand ourselves and the universe we inhabit? Puzzles are scattered all over the globe, from the high plains of the Andes in Peru to the fragments of an ancient map; from the huge monoliths of Stonehenge to an amazingly intricate stone relief, tucked away in a long-forgotten temple. Can technology help us understand these ancient clues? Some people believe they may actually reveal our future and our place in the universe.

Let's begin with the secrets of Tiahuanaco in Bolivia. You'll remember we told you earlier about the "Mother Goddess," Oryana, whose image adorns the Gate of the Sun. Carved from a single block of stone weighing over ten tons and still standing in splendid isolation among the ruins of Tiahuanaco, the Gate of the Sun is one of humanity's most enduring mysteries. Forty-eight square figures in three rows surround this flying goddess, who, according to tradition, came from the stars in a golden spaceship, created the city, gave birth to seventy children, and then returned to the stars.[1]

First Lieutenant Walter Haut (back row, second from right), the Roswell Army Air Field public information officer who released the official press statement that a flying disk had landed on a ranch near Roswell and was subsequently recovered by the Air Force. Also shown, left to right: (top row) Robert Shirkey (Operations Officer), Trudy Nagohara, Kevin D. Randle, Thomas Carey, Glen Dennis; (bottom row) Loretta Proctor, Frank Kaufmann, Stanton T. Friedman, Jesse A. Marcel, Jr. (Courtesy of Stanton T. Friedman)

Robert O. Dean, former Master Sergeant of Supreme Headquarters Allied Powers of Europe (SHAPE). (Courtesy of Robert Dean)

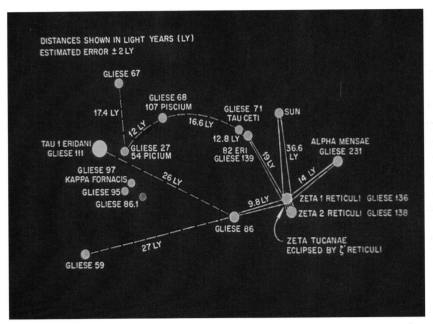

DISTANCES SHOWN IN LIGHT YEARS (LY)
ESTIMATED ERROR ± 2 LY

GLIESE 67

GLIESE 68
107 PISCIUM

17.4 LY

12 LY

16.6 LY

GLIESE 71
TAU CETI

SUN

TAU 1 ERIDANI
GLIESE 111

GLIESE 27
54 PICIUM

12.8 LY

82 ERI
GLIESE 139

36.6
LY

ALPHA MENSAE
GLIESE 231

19 LY

14 LY

GLIESE 97
KAPPA FORNACIS
GLIESE 95
GLIESE 86.1

26 LY

9.8 LY

ZETA 1 RETICULI GLIESE 136

ZETA 2 RETICULI GLIESE 138

GLIESE 86

ZETA TUCANAE
ECLIPSED BY ζ RETICULI

27 LY

GLIESE 59

The Zeta Reticuli system. Notice its similarity to Betty Hill's star map, as pointed out by Marjorie Fish. (Courtesy of Stanton T. Friedman)

The U.S. government is attempting to seize the mountains surrounding Area 51 to shield the base from observers on the ground. (Courtesy of Norio Hayakawa)

Groom Lake, the hidden base inside Area 51, where the U.S. government develops secret projects. The government continues to maintain secrecy regarding the base. (Courtesy of Norio Hayakawa)

Robert Lazar, a physicist who claims to have worked on flying saucers recovered by the U.S. government at Area 51. (Courtesy of Norio Hayakawa)

Warning signs posted at the boundaries of Area 51 to discourage visitors from entering the base include the warning "Use of Deadly Force Authorized." (Courtesy of Sean Fahey)

The Sphinx. Note its astonishing similarity to the face on Mars. (Courtesy of Sun International Pictures, Inc.)

Noted researchers believe that the intricacy of this pattern could not be a human hoax. (Courtesy of Colin Andrews, Circles Phenomenon Research International)

Not only is this pattern interesting, but the genetic structure of the wheat within the pattern has been altered. (Courtesy of Colin Andrews, Circles Phenomenon Research International)

Geometric patterns such as this one have led researchers to hypothesize that the circles are a message from another world. (Courtesy of Colin Andrews, Circles Phenomenon Research International)

On July 11, 1991, people gathered on rooftops and in the streets of Mexico City to witness the solar eclipse. They were also able to capture videotape and photographs of this cylindrical object, which hovered in the sky for twenty-five minutes. (Photograph provided by Genesis III Publishing)

The circles have evolved into shapes resembling insects and animals, like the one shown here. (Courtesy of Colin Andrews, Circles Phenomenon Research International)

Edward (Billy) Meier shot this vivid photo of a UFO in Ober-Sadelegg, Switzerland, on March 8, 1975. He reported that the ship approached, turned away, turned left, and then turned away again. (Photograph provided by Genesis III Publishing)

Modern archaeologists are quick to discount this version of the mythical tale. If that were the only thing found in the ruins of this nearly inaccessible city, we might find it easy to concur. "But," Erich Von Däniken asks, in his monumental bestseller, *Chariots of the Gods*, " . . . what if there were a calendar which gave the equinoxes, the astronomical seasons, the positions of the moon for every hour and also the movements of the moon, even taking the rotation of the earth into account?"[2]

According to Von Däniken, just such a calendar, " . . . was found in the dry mud at Tiahuanaco. It yields irrefutable facts and proves . . . that the beings who produced, devised and used the calendar had a higher culture than ours."

And there is more. What has been described as a "great idol" was found in the ruins of the Old Temple, so-called because of the primitive nature of its construction. The idol itself, however, displays quite different construction techniques. Carved from a single block of sandstone twenty-four feet tall and weighing over twenty tons, it has hundreds of symbols carved all over it. These symbols, according to H. S. Bellamy and P. Allan in their book, *The Great Idol of Tiahuanaco*, " . . . record an enormous body of astronomical knowledge and are based . . . on a round Earth. The symbols on the idol record the state of the heavens 27,000 years ago."[3]

Bellamy and Allan are quoted as saying, "Generally, the idol inscriptions give the impression . . . that it had been devised also as a record for future generations." Von Däniken himself is properly awed by " . . . the existence of such a sophisticated body of knowledge 27,000 years ago."[4]

Modern computer technology permits us to see what the heavens were like that long ago. Will this newfound ability

[1] Roy Stemman, *Visitors From Outer Space* (London: Aldous Books, Ltd., 1976).
[2] Erich Von Däniken, *Chariots of the Gods* (New York: Bantam Books, 1970).
[3] Ibid.
[4] Ibid.

help us to understand the message put there as "a record for future generations"?

Not far from Tiahuanaco as the crow (or the spaceship) flies, lies one of the most baffling archaeological enigmas on Earth. Strange messages are permanently inscribed on a landscape of rock covering some 200 square miles. This is the flat, barren landscape of southern Peru known as the plains of Nazca. Scattered across this huge wasteland are gigantic birds, spiders, monkeys and oddly enough, precise geometric designs.

The explicit symmetry of these designs, given their gigantic size, is enough to stagger the mind. What is even more astonishing is the fact that the designs of these great drawings cannot be seen unless you fly over them. What's more, the complete figures can be seen only at altitudes of over 1,000 feet. If, as modern archaeologists insist, they were drawn with pebbles by the Nazca Indians some 1,500 years ago, long before we developed the ability to fly, the inescapable question is, why would a primitive people spend generations devising patterns they would never see?

Coming upon the plain from the air, the similarity to the crisscross lines and runways of a modern jet airport is inescapable, causing some theorists to propose that this was, indeed, a landing site for extraterrestrial craft. The drawings, representing various animals and insects, may have been runway markers telling the pilots (who had lately dropped out of orbit) where they were and what heading they were on.

Like all unexplained mysteries, the plains of Nazca evoke a broad range of theories. Many of them, like the "spaceport" idea, are essentially unprovable. But what exactly has modern science been able to find out?

In the first place we know the designs were made by scraping away the surface soil to show the yellowish soil beneath. In many cases these lines were then accentuated by pebbles placed along both sides. We also know that the straight lines appear to start and end . . . nowhere. If the Nazca Indians needed roads across this desert waste it would be logical to assume that at least one of them would extend far enough to get someplace. None of them does. Interestingly enough, however, one set of lines does appear either to begin or terminate (it's not possible to say which) in the ruins of some long dead "town." The impression (again from the air since that is the only way anything at Nazca can be clearly seen) is not unlike the system of runways that converge on a modern airport terminal.

Why haven't these lines been washed away over the last fifteen centuries, since they seem to be so delicately formed? The short answer is there has been no geological or weather activity in that area that could wash them away. Nazca is located at a latitude where one would normally expect lush, tropical vegetation to grow, but no rain has fallen on these vast plains in at least 10,000 years. That's not all. In a singularly amazing coincidence, experts tell us that " . . . the erosion on the bare slopes of southern Peru is believed to be similar to that revealed by space probes on Mars. [In fact] NASA . . . has sent experts to study the area as part of their research into the possibility of life on Mars."[5]

Let's assume for the moment that the Nazca Indians (who predated the great Aztec culture by several hundred years) did give up most other activities in their culture to haul tons of small rocks over many miles of barely passable terrain (there are no stones like those used anywhere near the Nazca plain) to create these giant figures. Given the size and number of these "drawings" the Nazca people would have had to forego any other type of building project as well because everything had to be carried on their own backs. The people had no draft animals. They probably wouldn't have had time for hunting or gathering either, but let's

---

[5] *The World's Last Mysteries* (Pleasantville, NY: Readers Digest Association, Inc., 1978).

assume they did it anyway. And let's assume they devoted several generations to creating these sprawling representations. There is no mountain, no high point from which the work can be viewed, either to check the accuracy of the work or contemplate its completion. Why would they do it?

Arthur C. Clarke believes it was nothing more than the Indians' desire to leave their mark upon the land, a sort of "Kilroy was here," on a grand scale. But other researchers have theorized a more practical application. Maria Reiche, a German archaeologist and astronomer, has devoted forty years of her life to studying the drawings of Nazca. She believes, among other things, ". . . that the basic elements of units of radii could have represented numbers that were carefully hidden in the drawings—a sort of mathematical code. She further suggests that periods of time were represented by numbers. The regularity with which certain numbers appear among the figures seems to suggest they were connected with the periodicity of the movement of stars and planets."[6]

The presence of what appears to be a stylized "killer whale" and a "monkey" also puzzles investigators. Neither of these animals can be found within any reasonable distance of the plain. That the Nazca Indians were at least aware of such animals is evidenced in some of their pottery. What is not clear is where the awareness came from.

Some investigators, notably Reiche and a professor by the name of Paul Kosok, believe the drawings have an astronomical explanation. Before his death in 1959 Dr. Kosok pointed out that he had observed the sun set "almost exactly" on one of the lines on June 22, the winter solstice in the southern hemisphere. Reiche has also discovered many other astronomical alignments among the hundreds of lines; but the question still remains, was this something the Nazca

[6] *Mysteries of Mind, Space, and Time*, Volume 17 (Westport, CT: H. S. Stuttman Inc., 1992).

Indians needed to know? Is it possible there were interplanetary visitors using the plain for a more practical purpose?

A "star" in his own right, astronomer Gerald S. Hawkins applied modern computer technology to the problem and came up with a disappointing conclusion for those who had become convinced the drawings were some sort of astronomical map. "The measurements of 93 alignments and 45 stars were fed into the computer along with the key question: are there significant alignments of the Nazca lines with positions occupied by the sun, moon and stars since 5000 B.C.? The computer found no statistical evidence that the Nazca lines had been designed as a calendar."[7]

Von Däniken is not surprised. "The plain of Nazca," he states emphatically, "is a gigantic abandoned airport."[8]

But if that's true, who used to land there? Perhaps we will know if and when they decide to land there again. It will not be difficult for them to find the area when they come back. Hundreds of miles away, near the coast of Peru, a giant 300-foot trident carved into the side of a mountain, points the way to the plains of Nazca, just as it has for hundreds, perhaps thousands, of years.

In 1935 in Palenque, Mexico, a stone relief was discovered in what has come to be known as the Temple of Inscriptions. It was obviously of ancient origin, but its intricate and highly detailed carvings were totally unfathomable to those who first saw it. The sculpture is in a spot so narrow, a head-on photograph cannot be taken, but a drawing of the relief demonstrates how amazingly complex this inscription is. In the midst of a staggering array of elaborate geometric and decorative designs sits, or more appropriately, lies a human figure. The back of his head and neck is supported in a fixed position. The figure is looking intently at

---

[7] *The World's Last Mysteries* (Pleasantville, NY: Readers Digest Association, Inc., 1978).

[8] Erich Von Däniken, *Chariots of the Gods* (New York: Bantam Books, 1970).

an object directly in front of his face. Both hands appear to be grasping well-defined objects while the visible left heel seems to be resting on some sort of pedal. The clothing looks to be tight fitting with what we would describe today as elastic cuffs around the ankles and the wrists. If it was intended to give us a "cutaway" look at the interior of something, then the exterior lines hold another surprise. Conical at the front end, or top, the drawing changes as the lines swoop downward past the reclining figure to cut in sharply and form an almost square base. From this base stylistic flames sprout, completing the sculpture.[9]

Today most of us, having seen any number of spacecraft cockpits on television in which the astronauts recline in their specially built chairs and watch the screens and banks of switches in front of them, the Palenque relief is no mystery at all. What we are looking at is eerily and easily identifiable as an ancient representation of a modern-day reality. The traditional concept that this is just a native "priest" in some exotic headdress performing the tasks of some long-forgotten ritual is difficult to sustain in light of our modern awareness of the rudiments of space travel.

Depictions of even more ancient origin can be found in Australia. Some experts believe they may be the earliest messages yet discovered from prehistoric man. These drawings are treasured by the Australian aborigines and are called "Wondjinas." Wondjina is the legendary goddess of the Milky Way, who came from heaven to instruct the children of Earth. There are scores of these drawings, each of them depicting the round, space-helmet-like headdress and "goggle" eyes. Curiously, the marks on the headdress of the particular Wondjina in the photograph are hieroglyphics of the same type George Adamski claims to have received from a Venusian in the California desert in 1952. To the modern UFOlogist that is not surprising. In their view

[9] Roy Stemman, *Visitors From Outer Space* (London: Aldous Books, Ltd., 1976).

extraterrestrial visitors have been visiting Earth from time immemorial. Perhaps these oldest of all prehistoric messages confirm that view.

Also in 1935, a strange map turned up in the Topkapi Seraglio in Turkey. The map, believed to have been owned by a sixteenth-century Turkish admiral named Piri Re'is, contains astonishing details unknown to world cartographers or mariners of that period. According to Von Däniken, the map was a copy of a copy of a copy, and so on, handed down from generation to generation, until it landed in the possession of Admiral Re'is. The original, however, Von Däniken insists, could have been made only through the use of aerial photography.

Two atlases, preserved in the Berlin State Library, containing exact reproductions of the Mediterranean and the region around the Dead Sea also came from Piri Re'is. All of these maps, according to Von Däniken, were turned over to American cartographer Arlington H. Mallery. Mallery confirmed the fact that all of the geographical data was there, but it was in the wrong place. A U.S. Navy cartographer by the name of Walters was brought in to assist. Still wondering at the mapmaker's apparent knowledge of geographical characteristics but puzzled by the person's inability to put them all in the right place, the two cartographers took a different approach. They constructed a grid and transferred the map to a modern globe. The result was amazing. When the grid was placed on a sphere rather than on a flat surface, everything fell into place.

"The maps were absolutely accurate," Von Däniken said, "and not only with regard to the Mediterranean and the Dead Sea. The coasts of North and South America and even the contours of the Antarctic were also precisely delineated. The maps not only reproduced the outlines of the continents but also showed the topography of the interiors. Mountain ranges, mountain peaks, islands, rivers, and plateaus were drawn in with extreme accuracy. What's more, the mountain ranges in the Antarctic, which already figure on the Piri Re'is maps, were not discovered until 1952. These mountains have been covered in ice for untold years. Present day maps [are] drawn with the aid of echo-sounding equipment."

Comparison with modern satellite maps would seem to prove that the original data required for creating the Piri Re'is maps was obtained through high-altitude aerial photography taken by some sort of aircraft *hovering high above Cairo, Egypt.*[10]

We have already mentioned the ghostly similarity between Avebury in England and some of the structures on Mars, which along with the Great Pyramid, form a possible mathematical link between the two worlds. Just a few miles south of Avebury is one of the world's best known and least understood mysteries, the megaliths of Stonehenge.

For centuries it was assumed that Stonehenge was constructed by Druids for purposes of practicing their cultic or religious rituals. Scholars wondered how such huge pieces of diorite got to this empty Salisbury plain. Until fairly recently, however, most were willing to settle for the simple fact that they were there; whoever was around at the time must have managed it.

Today modern archaeologists believe the construction of Stonehenge was begun in 2800 B.C., and for the next thousand years or so it was under more or less constant change. Not fully excavated until the 1950s by Professor Richard J. C. Atkinson, Stonehenge is lucky to still be there. At one time, visitors could rent hammers in nearby Amesbury to chip off a piece of the stones for a keepsake.

Stonehenge owes its celebrity to Hollywood, whose producers and directors found any number of ways to use the ghostly looking structure in motion pictures, and to Dr. Gerald S. Hawkins, one-time professor of astronomy at Boston University and a research associate at the Harvard

---

[10] Ibid.

College Observatory. In 1960 professor Hawkins began a computer study of Stonehenge. The result would shake up the traditional theorists and archaeologists.

Before we get into that, however, it's important to have a comprehensive view of exactly what Stonehenge is. Modern photographs, for all their clarity, simply don't do it justice.

Stonehenge is an open structure consisting of several concentric circles with two inner circles opened and spread to form U-shaped arrangements. The innermost arrangement of stones is called the "bluestone horseshoe." Outside the arrangement of bluestones, and dwarfing them, stand the huge stones of the trilithon horseshoe. These are free-standing sets of two upright stones topped by a crosspiece, called a lintel. There are five of the trilithons, forming a U-shaped set of frames through which the sunrise, sunset, moonrise, and moonset can be viewed at the equinoxes and solstices. Surrounding the horseshoes is the bluestone circle, and immediately outside the bluestone circle is the Sarsen circle. The Sarsen circle was originally composed of thirty upright stones and thirty lintels. The inner faces of these uprights, for some unknown reason, were dressed and highly polished. The mean circumference of this remarkable circle is 316.8 feet. Then, far out beyond the Sarsen circle, lies the Aubrey circle, a circle of fifty-six small holes.

Standing approximately on line with the Aubrey circle were, at one time, four unhewn monoliths that formed the corners of a rectangle perpendicular to the summer sunrise. Only two of these stones remain today, and one of them is lying on its face. To the northeast of the Aubrey circle, standing alone and separate, is the heel stone, a vital part of the monument as it serves as a marker for sunrise at the summer solstice.[11]

The trilithon stones are the tallest stones in the monument, and the lone remaining stone of the great central

[11] Bonnie Gaunt, *Stonehenge and the Great Pyramid* (Jackson, MI: Author, 1993).

trilithon towers above them all. It weighs fifty tons. How these gigantic stones got to this lonely plain no one knows. The smaller blue stones are believed to have come from the Preseli Mountains of Wales, a trip of some 240 miles over land and water. Where the central trilithon stones were found and how they were transported is a complete mystery. No one has even the slightest clue.

Now that we know what Stonehenge is, let's get back to Dr. Hawkins' computer study and see if we can find out what it does. Basically Dr. Hawkins calculated the positions of the sun and moon over Stonehenge during its assumed period of construction. He then concluded that the monument was an observatory for studying cycles of the sun and moon. It was, he suggested, an astronomical observation post.

Interestingly, many of today's scientists, with the help of modern technology, find a direct correlation between Stonehenge and the Great Pyramid. Could these two megaliths, so different in their construction, have shared the same architect?

To begin with, Stonehenge is located at 51° 17' north latitude. At this exact latitude the solstice movements of the sun and moon form a rectangle precisely in line with the four corner or "station" stones of the monument. A few miles north or a few miles south and this would not be the case. How did the architect know of the only latitude in the Northern Hemisphere that would make this unique geometry possible? Furthermore, if you bisect this rectangle from the northwest corner through the southeast corner, you can draw a line that will take you directly to the Great Pyramid of Giza.

As noted earlier, the angle of the Great Pyramid, rounded off, is 51° 52'. The more precise angle is 51° 51' 14.3", which also happens to be the angle at Stonehenge of the summer solstice sunrise to north. As professor Hawkins so succinctly stated, "the alignment of summer-solstice sunrise is not man-maneuverable." Neither, we might add, is the direction of north. Keep in mind that this angle between sunrise and north exists at Stonehenge, not at Giza, yet the builder of the Great Pyramid used this exact angle long before Stonehenge was built.

It is also interesting to note that the complete circle of Stonehenge, including the ditch which surrounds it, fits precisely into the triangle formed by one side of the great pyramid, just scribing each of the interior sides.[12]

These and a number of other remarkable geometric similarities seem to suggest, at the very least, that the builders of the Great Pyramid and the builders of Stonehenge shared a common mathematical language. Could the same engineers who moved seventy-five-ton blocks of granite thirty stories up into the King's Chamber of the Great Pyramid have been the same engineers who moved fifty-ton blocks of iron-hard diorite onto the Salisbury plain of southern England and stood them upright?

One of the oldest traditions of Stonehenge is the story of Merlin, the mythical court magician of the King Arthur legend. According to the myth, an ancient king of the Britons wanted to build a monument in memory of some of his nobles. Merlin advised the king to go to Ireland and bring back a sacred stone structure that would be found there. An army made the journey, found the stones, and defeated the Irish; but the men were unable to move the stones. Merlin then constructed "wondrous engines" that could move the stones across the water and reconstruct the monument with ease.[13]

Could Merlin, the most powerful wizard of ancient times, have been something other than a myth. Did he simply employ the same "wondrous engines" that had been used

---

[12] Ibid.

[13] *Mysteries of the Ancient World* (Washington, DC: National Geographic Society, 1979).

in the construction of the Great Pyramid to construct Stonehenge?

But not all of the mysteries left on Earth are giant monoliths. Some, in fact, might fit in your pocket or sit on a shelf in a museum.

We all know, for example, that Count Volta invented the electric cell some 400 years ago. But in Iraq, in a museum in Baghdad, there are small clay cups dating back to a time before Christ. A copper tube found with the cups is placed inside and a rod, made of an alloy of different metals, is inserted into the tube. When filled with hydrochloric acid these cups produce an electric current.[14] Why, we are left to wonder, did the early inhabitants of Iraq want to create electricity?

In Moscow two prehistoric relics exist which cannot be explained by our present understanding of history. One is the skull of a bison, believed to have roamed the Siberian landscape nearly 40,000 years ago. It was apparently shot by . . . a bullet. A neat, round hole in the skull is unmistakable, and ballistics experts have established that it could have been put there only by a high-speed projectile. They also concluded that the beast was alive when the hole was made. A shot? Fired forty thousand years ago?[15]

The second relic is a rock painting found by Soviet scholars in Uzbekistan near the Chinese border. Amazed by what they were seeing, the Soviet scientists copied the painting carefully for further study. To grasp the significance of this prehistoric drawing one must suspend all notions of earthly isolationism, for there, in clear detail, is a creature wearing the unmistakable headgear of an astronaut. The helmet is attached to the space suit and connecting tubes and breathing apparatus are clearly visible. Farther back, in a perspec-

---

[14] Erich Von Däniken, *Chariots of the Gods.* Alan Landsburg Productions, Inc., 1970.
[15] Ibid.

tive view never before seen in prehistoric rock paintings, a small figure in a space helmet with unmistakable antennae stands beneath the representation of a "flying saucer," to all appearances a re-creation of a photograph out of yesterday's newspaper. The small, two-legged figure is reaching out in a gesture of openness. Both figures seem to be holding some circular object close to their breast.[16]

As we look at this remarkable drawing the horizon of history is pushed back even further. We are left to wonder if the future may not be simply a matter of catching up to the past.

This brief offering by no means exhausts the fantastic mysteries that surround us on every side. Every portion of the globe can offer some strange and unexplainable enigma that, in turn, may point to some supernatural event that took place in some prehistoric time. Coming to the realization that we cannot explain everything we can see and touch does not, of course, prove that extraterrestrial beings are the solution to every riddle. However, it does prove that we must keep our minds open to even the most fantastic of possibilities. As Sir Arthur Conan Doyle put it, through his famous character, Sherlock Holmes:

> When all rational explanations have been exhausted, whatever remains, no matter how improbable, must be the truth.

It might be well to keep that in mind as we move into the next chapter and examine a different kind of message. Those messages are inexplicable, indecipherable and, for most of us, enormously frustrating.

We are about to come face to face with reality as described by British physicist, Sir James Jeans: "The great architect of the Universe," he declared, "now begins to appear as a pure mathematician."

[16] Ibid.

CHAPTER 11

MESSAGES FROM THE STARS

>> Almost from the beginning crop circles
have appeared in association with
reports of aerial phenomena.

Colin Andrews, Circles Phenomenon Research

I f the language of the universe is geometry, someone is shouting at us. The message comes in the form of a perfect equilateral triangle. In its center is a circle with straight lines radiating to each point of the triangle. Another circle surrounds the first and is just large enough to scribe the interior sides of the triangle. Outside of that circle, as equidistant from the second as the second is from the first, is yet another circle. At the outer corner of two of the three points of the triangle is still another circle. Within one a stylized "X" is etched; within the second, the line from the innermost circle extends precisely to the center of this corner circle. On the third point of the triangle, a circular shape begins, but soon becomes a zig-zag line turning in a circular motion toward its center, ending in yet another small circle.

The design is so geometrically accurate that if a line were to be drawn from the center point of each of the exterior point circles, another equilateral triangle would be formed.

Even as a basic geometric design on a piece of paper this would be something to write home about. But in this case, the "message" was etched in a grain field near Stonehenge and covered several hundred square yards. The line of its axis pointed directly toward Silbury Hill. Experts believe it would have taken several people up to a week to have created the intricate design in such huge dimensions. Instead, it appeared suddenly, out of the darkness, in a single night.

Called Barbury Castle by "crop circle" researchers, this design appeared in 1991. It was neither the first nor the most complex of the hundreds of crop circles that have been investigated seriously since the late 1970s. Barbury Castle, however, did emphasize an important aspect of these messages, if that's what they are. Although crop circle formations are a worldwide phenomenon, nearly 80 percent of the global total have occurred in the United Kingdom, and 75 percent of these have been found in a small area of central southern England. This area forms an equilateral triangle between the towns of Wantage at the north apex of the triangle, Warminster at the southwestern corner, and Winchester at the southeastern corner. Within this triangle are found some of the world's greatest archaeological treasures, including Avebury, Stonehenge, and Silbury Hill.

In some respects these crop circles, or "agriglyphs" or "pictographs" as they are interchangeably referred to, are like the giant drawings on the plain of Nazca, as they can be truly appreciated only when seen from the air. Unlike the Nazca depictions, however, the creators of the agriglyphs are sharing their message with the entire world. So far crop circles have been discovered in Australia, the former USSR, Canada, the United States, Italy, Germany, Afghanistan, Turkey, Norway, and Japan. Furthermore the designs are becoming increasingly more complex and more numerous, with as many as fifteen glyphs appearing in a single night.

What does all of this mean? Have these agriglyphs (the term means "crop writing") been deciphered? Is there a message for the human family in these amazing, geometric designs? Could it be a warning, as some have suggested? If so, a warning of what and from whom?

Colin Andrews, formerly a highly paid electrical engineer working for the British government, gave up his lucrative job upon seeing his first crop circle and has devoted the last seventeen years of his life to trying to answer those questions. So far his research has produced far more questions than answers. The first question is, aside from the complexity and sheer beauty of some of the designs, what sets them apart from, say, somebody tromping around in a cornfield? According to Andrews, a great many things.

"In the beginning," Andrews tells us, "there was a simple, single circle. These [circles] continued to appear throughout the landscape of southern England until 1978 when we saw the arrival of five circles, forming a cross. This marked the beginning of a continuous evolution of development. Circles were recorded with single rings, double rings and even triple rings. Separate circles forming equilateral triangles. [Then] from a simple cross form arrived a tremendous, complex, beautiful Celtic cross."[1]

But it was the nature of the circle's construction as much as its design that excited the engineer in Andrews. He was fascinated by the precise symmetry each design displayed. In spite of the fact that they were frequently several hundred feet in length and breadth, their geometry was seldom off by more than a quarter of an inch. The sides, that is, the point at which the crop was depressed and the rest of the crop remained standing, looked as if they had been made with the precision of a cookie cutter. Stalks were lying flat while just three millimeters away other stalks stood completely unaffected. There was yet another puzzling aspect of the formations. The stalks were bent, not broken; and they would lie,

---

[1] Colin Andrews, *Undeniable Evidence.* ARK Soundwaves Productions, 1991.

frequently in a counterclockwise fashion as if "swirled" into place. Nevertheless, the crop continued to grow. If anything, studies have shown the grains to be "improved" by the experience. Even more puzzling, in some cases the crop would be "layered." One layer going clockwise, the next counterclockwise, neatly and precisely interleaved up to five layers deep. Again, the crop, aside from lying flat, was undamaged.

The nature of the construction of the designs, coupled with the sheer beauty and geometric precision of the finished glyphs, have captured the imagination of many investigators worldwide. Not least among them are UFO researchers, who see in the ever-growing number and complexity of the phenomena a message from the stars. Could it be that with the discovery of the geometric links between Mars and Earth we have finally reached a stage where extraterrestrial visitors are convinced we can begin to understand the mathematical language of the universe?

When the circles first came to public attention, Andrews was one of only three people in the world who began seriously to investigate what was happening. His background as an electrical engineer made him the ideal person to tackle the job. He brought to the task all of the care and precision he would have used in any major project. He formed an organization called Circles Phenomenon Research (appropriately, CPR) and began amassing a research database. Today that database includes over a thousand circles that he has personally visited, measured, and photographed. He has taken the research far beyond just the superficial observations. The database also includes soil and plant analyses; extensive ground, aerial, and infrared photography; precise measurements of radiation and magnetic field readings—all of it supported by his own computer resources. His conclusions from all of this study have drawn fire from the press and, as we have come to expect, the ridicule of so-called mainstream scientists.

"Almost from the beginning," Andrews says, "crop circles have appeared in association with reports of aerial phenomena. In the most extreme cases people have reported beams of light touching ground level where crop circles have been later discovered. Or indeed, in many cases, little balls of orange light dancing over the field, and on occasions, literally appearing in them. Those sightings have often been followed by discoveries of the crop circles."

But Andrews was mindful of the fact that UFOs were not the only possible explanation. There might be some natural solution to the phenomenon of which he was unaware. During the early days of his investigation, and for nearly three years, Andrews worked closely with Dr. Terence Meaden, head of a tornado and research organization in Great Britain. Dr. Meaden, also an electrical engineer, physicist, and meteorologist, ultimately concluded that there was no mystery. The solution, which he presented in three technical reports to the Thatcher government, stated flatly that the patterns were caused by stationary "whirlwinds" or "plasma vortices." The government's chief scientific adviser so informed Parliament, and so far as the British government was concerned, the problem was resolved.

Andrews thought the assertion was clearly absurd. Anyone who even glances at the photographs of these huge constructions (see photo section) can see that random wisps of wind could not possibly create such intricate designs. Quite apart from the obvious, Andrews points out that, "What they have overlooked is the fact that most of the crop circles appear at night and the thermally produced whirlwinds in southern England form only by day. Whirlwinds," he continues, "also rotate in only one direction. Half of the crop circle formations found are rotated in the wrong direction to be a stationary whirlwind effect."[2]

---

[2] Michael Norris, Those Mysterious Circles, UFO *Encounters*, 1992, p. 9.

That, however, was only the beginning of the problems CPR would face in trying to establish a provable origin for the circles. By 1988 the circles had garnered worldwide attention. Major television networks and producers, including the BBC and National Geographic, had done specials on the phenomenon, stressing the unknown origin of their construction. Apparently it was only the British government who was satisfied with the "whirlwind" solution. The idea that they might be messages of some sort from aliens from another world suddenly seemed to be gaining ground. Then in 1991 two English gentlemen by the names of Doug Bower and David Chorley entered the picture. They had, they said, personally created all of the crop circles themselves.

Here was the practical answer all of the skeptics had been seeking. It was no big mystery after all. The "Doug and Dave" solution was simplicity itself. They took a piece of board about four feet long, attached a cord or rope to either end, which allowed them to keep the board firmly against one foot, and then marched around in the grain or cornfield until the crop had been flattened in the desired design. It was all done after dark and was, they said between pints in the local pub, really quite easy to do.

They had begun the hoax in 1978, they told the press, indicating that there were no crop circles before then, and they just kind of got carried away with it. The media, happy to have the puzzle solved, trumpeted a wide variety of "see, I told you so" stories and let the matter drop. Much of the public, likewise, seemed perfectly happy with the solution.

It was now Colin Andrews' turn to play the skeptic.

Andrews pointed out that the phenomenon was hardly new and certainly began long before 1978. He produced a letter he had received from a farmer who lives in an area where the circles have appeared for many years. The farmer wrote that he had discovered crop circles as far back as the 1920s. Andrews also challenged the two men directly with regard to one of the specific circles they claimed to have created. Andrews knew that the plants in the outer ring of the formation were found lying in several directions. Andrews drew the outer ring of the layout and sketched the direction in which the plants were found to be lying. "If you constructed this," he asked, pointing to his sketch, "how did you construct that [outer ring]?"

The two men looked at each other in complete silence. After several seconds had passed they said, "We didn't make that one."

On another occasion Central Television in England asked Andrews if he would appear in a live debate with the two. Andrews quickly agreed and showed up at the studio at the appointed time. Unfortunately the network had not told Doug and Dave who they would be confronting. About twenty minutes before air time they discovered they were to participate in an exchange with Colin Andrews. Both men immediately withdrew, forcing the network to drop the show.

Andrews also points out that many of the glyphs are being created in locations that cannot easily be seen. "Who in the hell" (we're quoting here) "would want to hoax a formation one-sixth of a mile long in a location that cannot be seen or appreciated by the public? No hoaxer is going to do it. The energy required would be a total waste of effort."

It has also been suggested that if these two had indeed created all of the crop circles, they would have needed the energy and abilities of Superman, traveling all over the world to create pictographs at a rate that would task even the man in the red cape.

In a matter of months serious investigators were referring to the "Doug and Dave Scam of 1991." Even though the two men had demonstrated they could make a crop circle by the means they had developed, they had also unwittingly demonstrated their methods were incapable of producing the size, number, and complexity of the pictographs already in existence. By 1992 the "wind vortex" or "plasma vortices" theory had also been set aside, Dr. Meaden's credentials notwithstanding. But that only seemed to sharpen the focus of the skeptics. According to one report, a serious effort was launched to create such a variety of "hoax circles" that Colin Andrews and Pat Delgado (a former NASA engineer who had joined CPR) would "be sorry they ever saw a crop circle." Indeed, a great many pictographs were hoaxed with infrared cameras recording the entire affair. A competition was even held, and upwards of a dozen groups participated, virtually destroying some poor farmer's crop. In the final analysis the group of skeptics that mounted this angry effort did little more than demonstrate once again, that while it's possible to forge a hundred-dollar bill, not all hundred-dollar bills are forgeries.

Unfortunately the net result of all this has been the scattering of fake pictograms among the genuine article. They are, according to Andrews and Delgado, easily spotted, but most likely it is only CPR who would take the time and effort to make the distinction.

If "plasma vortices" can't be shown to create complex geometric patterns and the "Doug and Dave" types can only duplicate the process in the most superficial way, are we any closer to knowing how the circles are really made?

We might be, but then again, we might not. Andrews realized the only way to eliminate the word "hoax" from any sentence about crop circles was to catch one being made. With that object in mind CPR set up two surveillance operations using the most modern equipment available. Operation "Blue Hill" and operation "Chameleon" were set up on the sides of two hills overlooking each other. The two groups were about 700 yards apart and in full view of each other. One of the operations was equipped with radar that had a range of about four and a half miles and with infrared cameras. The other operation had infrared and low-light cameras, along with an intruder detection system of infrared beams. As an added precaution, dogs were also brought along. The groups were prepared to be there for several nights, but happily they didn't have to wait that long.

During the first night a fog or mist developed over the field which as dawn approached began to melt away. As the mist receded there remained a single cell of fog in the center of the field. Around 6:30 A.M. this single cell of fog lifted, leaving a basic, but undeniable pictograph in the field. "For the first time," Andrews said, "we could positively say no man or woman entered that field."[3]

They also demonstrated another fatal flaw in the "plasma vortices" theory. Because wind and fog are mutually exclusive (indeed, fog is created by the *absence* of air movement), they could also state positively that "plasma vortices" had no part whatsoever in the creation of the glyph.

Although the presence of a fog or mist is reported frequently in connection with crop circles, it is by no means the only phenomenon. Many witnesses report seeing silvery, cylindrical objects, sometimes horizontal and sometimes in a vertical position, "spinning" where a circle later appears. A strange buzzing or "sparrow" sound is also a frequent part of such reports, including an incident in 1989 in which a director for the BBC was filming Andrews and Delgado inside a crop circle. During the course of the filming an extraordinary sound was heard. They recorded the bizarre noise, but somehow the sound had mysteriously destroyed $65,000 worth of hi-tech television equipment.

"These were hard-nosed journalists," Andrews said, "one of many television crews that had arrived from around the world in southern England [to film] all that was going on there. All of them thought it was just one of those rubbish UFO type stories. They think they know it all and they've seen it all. There were few who left with that attitude."

As it has become clear that these are not human-made formations, more serious researchers and scientists have

[3] Ibid., p. 11.

taken an interest in these circles, though many of them still do not want their names associated with the phenomenon. Nevertheless they have discovered a number of interesting and baffling anomalies. For example, plants are sometimes braided, and in one case, as we noted earlier, spiraled in layers alternately clockwise and counterclockwise. Within the circle itself compass needles sometimes rotate wildly. Studies have shown that the internal crystalline structure of affected plants differs from that of unaffected plants, including a highly unusual, polyembryonic development within the grain. The bizarre aerial phenomena referred to earlier, frequently are observed around the sites of the pictographs, and there is a growing correlation between the shape and location of the formations and that of ancient megalithic structures.[4]

All of these strange observations have so far defied efforts to interpret them in any kind of cohesive, clearly understandable way, but the effort is widening. On July 22, 1991, a bizarre set of circles appeared in a wheat field near Hildesheim, Germany. The pictograph was huge, measuring 300 by 150 feet and encompassing over 45,000 square feet. The design was thought to resemble an ancient Scandinavian rock painting of a "Chariot of the Sun." Even more intriguing is the fact that the area where the circle appeared was considered sacred ground for nearly 4,000 years. A witness reported seeing orange pulsating flashing lights dancing about the area—phenomena that have become almost commonplace in reports from England. A strange noise was reported as well. But the unique aspect of this particular crop circle didn't emerge until several days after the glyph was discovered.

Following the appearance of the formation, the curious came in such numbers that the farmer decided to charge

[4] Colin Andrews, *The Crop Circle Phenomenon* (Branford, CT: Circle Phenomenon Research International, 1992).

admission to his field. We don't know how much he charged, but there was no noticeable letup in the number of visitors. One research group (EFODON) said they measured unusually high radioactive readings there in the field. But it was a peculiar, unnamed guest that made the most fantastic discovery. Prowling the area with a metal detector, he had three positive "hits." Each hit was located within one of the three circles of the formation that had half rings. Digging down a couple of feet in each spot, the man recovered three metal plates. Each plate was about twelve inches in diameter and heavily encrusted, indicating it had been buried for a considerable time. Although they were heavy, the man carried them off, telling a farmhand he was taking them to the owner of the farm. In fact he disappeared from the area. In a bizarre twist he did call the farmer five days later and even sent him a picture of one of the plates. Amazingly, the embossed design on the plate was an exact replica of the crop circle formation.

And there's more. A short time later, all three plates were shown to the local press. The man who had them (presumably the thief) and a newspaper editor took them to a jeweler for inspection. The jeweler reported that one of the plates was silver, another gold, and the third bronze. All were of extremely pure content. Even though under German law the plates rightfully belonged to the landowner, the farmer apparently made no effort to recover them. Eventually the finder of the plates was tracked down (his name was not revealed), and the silver and bronze plates were purchased for $30,000. Unfortunately the thief had sold the gold plate to a jeweler for a few hundred thousand deutschmarks. It had been melted down. The high purity of the two remaining plates, however, was verified by the German Federal Material Inspection Authority, which for all practical purposes, ruled out the possibility of a hoax.[5]

Could the creators of this particular formation have been trying to point us toward some truth about our past?

The similarity between the plates and the glyph would seem to indicate some distinct purpose for the creation of the crop circle. Perhaps the similarity between this pictograph and a Scandinavian god is a clue that can turn us in the right direction. Interestingly, Jon Erik Beckjord has been using the characteristics of an ancient and archaic Nordic language system to decode some of the pictographs found in England.

According to Beckjord it is a "pictographic" language dating back 4,000 years, (another coincidence?) called Tifinag. This language, along with one called Ogam, was used by both the ancient Vikings and Britons in their rock paintings.

The "cup and ring" characteristic of the German crop circle and plates are found in ancient rock carvings. Beckjord has translated some of the pictographs using the Tifinag system and has come up with the following "translations."

Hazely Farm, Hampshire—"This is the place of the Serpent (or Devil), an evil place."

At Barn Field, Hampshire—"This is a dangerous place to camp."

Near Avebury, Wiltshire—"Thor, god of thunder."

Same location, nearby—"Spurting out upon."

According to Beckjord, by taking the last three translations together you might have an alien-logic warning of the war in Kuwait that began a week after these crop circles appeared.[6]

All of this, of course, is pure speculation. As Dennis Stacy pointed out in a follow-up to Beckjord's article, "it [the theory] imposes 'facts' on crop circle formation that don't match the available evidence and ignores available evidence that doesn't fit the theory."[7]

[5] Update: A German Crop Circle and Three Amazing Plates, UFO *Encounters*, 1993, p. 25.

[6] Jon Erik Beckjord, Decoding the agriglyphs, UFO *26*, 6(5) (1991).

[7] Dennis Stacy, A Faulty Translation, UFO *26*, 6(5) (1991).

On the other hand, Mr. Stacy may not have seen the German pictograph and plates, which seem to add considerable weight to the "available evidence" of Tifinag language forms in at least one very puzzling crop circle. The fact that it was created on what was once considered, "sacred ground" for several millennia by some ancient civilization must also be figured into the equation.

Several governments have studied and collected information related to the UFO and crop circle phenomena. So far none of them has been able to make any public statement on any matter associated with either, except to say in somewhat guarded terms that they don't exist. With regard to the crop circles it's a little more difficult to deny them because they obviously do exist and in splendid technicolor. What they are not, according to most governments, is meaningful.

Mohammad Ramadan, president of the parapsychology group at the United Nations, took a slightly different view. It was Ramadan who sponsored Richard Hoagland's report to the United Nations on his Mars Mission investigation. He also wanted to know what was going on with the crop circles, as they were obviously a global phenomenon. In 1993, Ramadan met with Colin Andrews at the United Nations and challenged him to discover the meaning, not only of the crop circles but other ancient writings, including those referring to alleged UFO extraterrestrials. Andrews was to present his report by October of that year. He had the mammoth task of trying to piece everything together to see if there was a cohesive message. The task could not be done in so short a time, but Andrews is still working on it.

If we hearken back to Hoagland's U.N. report, however, we are reminded that his sense of cosmic physics began with the classical tetrahedron, a four-sided, pyramid-shaped object that when circumscribed in a sphere predicts certain anomalies (e.g., the giant storm on Jupiter and the erupting volcanos in Hawaii referred to earlier) on just about every planet in the solar system. Is it just another coincidence that the Barbury Castle crop circle with which we began this chapter, is a two-dimensional representation of the three-dimensional tetrahedron?

According to Peter Sorensen, in an article published in *The Cereologist*, "[The tetrahedron's] four faces, all equilateral triangles, unify the three and the four harmoniously and resolve the conflict between odd and even, (the ultimate opposites) in a most elegant way. The tetrahedron . . . is the first and foremost Platonic solid [and] is a widely revered archetype or model of God. The sphere or circle is the only geometric entity that is more fundamental—indeed these dramatically different shapes are complementary building blocks in the architecture of creation."[8]

Could the message of the crop circles be the same as the message of Mars, Giza, Stonehenge, and hundreds of other mysterious structures, drawings, and carvings all over the globe? Could it be that someone is simply trying to tell us they are here?

As we mentioned earlier, one of the recurring phenomena reported by witnesses who have been in the vicinity where crop circles have ultimately been found is the presence of orange or golden balls of light that seem to skip or dance about the area. Throughout the triangular area where most of the pictographs are found, numerous hills still carry the names they were given hundreds of years ago. One of those hills, for some reason unknown to modern scholars, is called "Golden Ball" hill.

Could it be possible that "visitors" to our planet have been trying to bring us a message since time immemorial? One observer pointed out that, "somehow they [the pictographs] all look familiar." Perhaps we are simply being given a reminder of some deeply hidden part of ourselves that *knows* we are just one of many intelligent races in the universe.

[8] Peter Sorensen, Barbury Castle, the Geometry of God, *The Cereologist*, (No. 8, Winter 1993) p. 17.

Colin Andrews, according to a MUFON article, feels that evidence continues to suggest a graphic link with ancient symbols and an intelligent source for these mysterious crop markings. His view is that, "the phenomenon is evolving toward an event of profound importance and will ultimately influence scientific understanding of the world around us at a time when all living things are moved by a parallel shift in consciousness."[9]

So far we have found allusions to extraterrestrials in scores of seemingly unsolvable mysteries. But what are the chances that alien beings are real? So far governments, which according to most reports have taken possession of any real or "hard" evidence, have managed to keep the facts, whatever they are, very well hidden.

Still UFO reports continue to pour in from around the world. Some governments seem to be softening their stance in the face of a growing public perception that there is something about this phenomenon that is definitely real. Will that changing perception bring us any closer to the truth?

We'll try to answer that question in the next chapter.

---

[9] MUFON *Symposim Proceedings* (Seguin, TX: Mutual UFO Network, 1994).

CHAPTER 12

PERSONAL PERCEPTION AND THE WORLDVIEW

>> People have asked why, if UFOS exist, don't they just come down and land beside the White House?

George Wingfield, UFO witness

O n May 9, 1996, the following item (including the e-mail, phone, and fax numbers of the president, vice-president, and first lady) moved across the Internet.

Being an insufferable rabble-rouser, I just can't resist the overwhelming urge to smash a grapefruit into Uncle Sam's face right now. I want to urge all of you who are serious about breaking the military/intelligence community's stranglehold on UFO/ET information to please write with reckless abandon to President Clinton, vice-President Gore, and First Lady Hillary Rodham Clinton (all e-mail addresses, phone/fax follow).

Let them know how you feel and that you want the

truth! Also tell 'em you want Clinton to sign a PRESI-
DENTIAL EXECUTIVE ORDER releasing certain
individuals from their national security oaths and clear-
ances in order to accomplish this. Far be it from me to tell
anyone how to vote, however I plan to let Bubba know if
he sucks it up, does the right thing and rips the lid off the
UFO/ET cover-up, I promise to vote for him in November.
That WILL get their attention.

The tone of the message is fairly typical of modern U.S.
citizens' attitudes. If you were to attend any of the dozens of
symposiums, seminars, and workshops on UFOs held around
the country each year, you would find that level of frustration expressed over and over again. It is a frustration born of
knowing just enough to be concerned but not enough to do
anything about it.

Just for the sake of supposing, imagine what would happen if you woke up tomorrow morning, poured your usual
cup of coffee, flipped on the radio, and heard:

President Clinton announced late last night that he has
instructed members of the Department of Defense, the
CIA, and the National Security Council to release all documents and photographs relating to the recovery of an
extraterrestrial spacecraft recovered in the New Mexico
desert in July 1947. The president said his aim was to get
all technical data into the hands of the broader scientific
community in order to bring out into the open secret government dealings with extraterrestrial visitors over the
past fifty years.

"I believe," the president said, "it is time the American people were told the truth about our ongoing dealings
with these beings who have been coming here primarily to
observe our species and to determine whether we had progressed far enough to be welcomed into the galactic
confederation of worlds."

The president also confirmed the existence of a group of international scientists who have been charged with the responsibility of working with the extraterrestrials and said he has instructed them to share their findings with others in the scientific community. He stopped short of naming them as several of them have been active in efforts on behalf of the government to ridicule and otherwise inhibit private investigations into the subject of UFOs.

The president also said he was convening an international conference of heads of state to try to establish mechanisms for sharing all information gathered over the past half century with all other nations. "It is my hope," he said, "the nations of the world will follow the lead of the United States and share their findings with the world at large."

In a related matter the president also confirmed the authenticity of what has been popularly referred to as the "Santilli autopsy film." "It is authentic," the president said, "I was made aware of this and many other pieces of information relating to our association with extraterrestrials upon taking the oath of office. All of this information will be made public through established media sources," the president concluded.

We have already seen what the Brookings Institute thinks would happen (a complete breakdown of all social, religious, and political order) if such an event were to take place, but what do you think would happen? Relaxed in the comfort of your own home, what do you honestly think the effect of such a pronouncement would be on you personally?

In point of fact, something very much like that happened in 1938 when radio's *Mercury Theater*, under the direction of a relative newcomer named Orson Welles, presented a fictional drama called, *The War of the Worlds*. Set in the New Jersey countryside and couched in terms of a live broadcast from the actual scene, a story of horror unfolded as spaceships from Mars were described disgorging their horde of invaders who immediately set about destroying the countryside and everyone in it.

In spite of repeated announcements by the show's producers that they were listening to a drama that was simply the weekly radio *Mercury Theater* presentation, thousands of Americans all across the country rushed into the streets in panic. Those closest to the "invasion" tried to flee, choking roads and bridges. Many were injured. Farther away men, women, and children rushed into the night, searching the skies with fear and alarm.

As a testimony to the power of the media to move people, *The War of the Worlds* has become a classic. What it says about how we see ourselves in the universal scheme of things is still not clear. Are we more sophisticated now? After all we poke fun at the whole concept of extraterrestrial life on a weekly basis. One of the most popular television shows of the 1996 season, *Third Rock from the Sun*, brings us the slapstick adventures of three extraterrestrials stranded on Earth, trying to fit into our "primitive" culture. We see films that show the citizens of Earth bravely challenging invaders from outer space, as in *Aliens* or *Predator*, always somehow finding a way to defeat even the most hideous and cruel life form. The July 1996 film offering from Hollywood, *Independence Day*, graphically depicted our greatest fear: a worldwide invasion from a fleet of super-powerful spacecraft, capable of blowing up the White House and the entire U.S. Capitol building with a single blast from some kind of destructive particle beam. It all supposedly takes place on Independence Day, July 4th. The ominous subtitle, *ID-4, The Day We Fight Back*, says something about the anticipated outcome. By the time you read this you will undoubtedly know whether or not we won.

Ours is a world replete with the terms of intergalactic space travel. Captain Kirk and Captain Jean-Luc Picard have taught us the meaning of "warp" speed, "antimatter propulsion," "gravitron," and "dilithium crystals." They have also taught us the universe is populated with strange-looking creatures, most of whom are smarter and more powerful than we are.

The reality, however, may be quite different. The reality the anonymous writer on the Internet is demanding, for example, will not come to a successful conclusion at two minutes before the hour with all of the aliens either being dispatched or accommodated. The question of UFOs is, by all accounts, an ongoing puzzle of sightings, enigmatic clues and fantastic eyewitness accounts from all over the globe. But the overriding question remains: when faced with the substance of truth, are we prepared to deal it? Thousands, perhaps hundreds of thousands of people in virtually every nation on Earth have already had to face that proposition.

Beginning July 11, 1991, and continuing to the present day (as this is being written), the longest-running wave of UFO sightings on record began in Mexico City. On that date the most extensive total solar eclipse of the century was scheduled to occur. People moved out into the streets and onto rooftops to get a better view of this spectacular event. Then, suddenly, before the eclipse began something entirely unforeseen took place. There in the largest city in the world, with hundreds of thousands of eyes looking up to the sky, a silver, cylindrical object appeared. In the over 700 videotape recordings made while it hovered in the sky, the object can be seen clearly beneath the sun. It did not just flit in and out but stayed in place for twenty-five minutes.

Jaime Maussan of Mexican Televista had stationed eight video teams along the calculated path of the eclipse from Baja, California, to the Yucatan. One of those teams filmed the flight of a silvery, disk-shaped object on broadcast-quality video during the progress of the penumbra, or shadow of the moon falling on Earth. The weekend following the eclipse, Televista broadcast an eight-hour UFO marathon, showing the film, interviewing UFO experts, and accepting calls from viewers. The show resulted in dozens of black-and-white and color photographs being sent in, all showing the object in and about the vicinity of the eclipse.

The "wave" of UFOs (some call it an invasion) has continued. Everyone is taking pictures and videotaping the phenomenon. Far from throwing the country into a panic, the citizenry seem to be enjoying the whole affair. Groups have been formed to watch the skies twenty-four hours a day, camcorders at the ready. They throw parties and wait for the UFOs to show up. A Catholic priest has seen several objects and videotaped four of them. When asked if their existence conflicted with his religious views, he replied, "Not at all. God created many worlds." He seems quite comfortable with the notion that God's creative power extends beyond just our Earth.[1] It would seem the citizens of Mexico are handling the reality of their "invasion" with a good deal of poise and self-confidence.

But what about Europeans? Would their response be different?

In July 1990 the National UFO Center (NUFOC) in Belgium reported its own "invasion" of UFOs. The sightings started in and around the area of Eupen, but soon spread to many parts of Belgium. Eupen, however, soon became the new Mecca for UFOlogists.

It all began on Wednesday, November 29, 1989. A police brigade noticed a bright light near the village of Kettenis. The light beams illuminated a large area of grassland near the road and seemed to emanate from a triangular "platform," which hung almost directly above their vehicle at an altitude of not more than 300 meters. On the bottom of the object they could clearly see three bright light beams and a flashing red light. When they first saw the object, it appeared to be hanging in the sky, then it moved off toward

---

[1] Lee and Britt Elders, The great flap over Mexico, 1991–93, Part II, *International UFO Library* (Oct./Nov. 1993), p. 60.

Eupen. The police said they barely noticed any noise, but there was a "soft humming," like the sound of an electric engine.

The police brigade followed the object to a dam near Gileppe, where it circled for forty-five minutes before flying away. About an hour later the same police patrol noticed a second and much bigger triangle suddenly appear as if being catapulted from behind the trees. It flew above the road in large circles "as if looking for something." During its flight, the policemen said, "it seemed to rotate around its [axis]."

Note that these objects did not travel at high speed nor were they very high in the air. They seemed to be completely indifferent to whether they were seen or photographed, or by whom.

On December 1, four or five different objects were reported in the Eupen area including a spectacular light show. In Battice a police-patrol saw a "red ball" come out of a triangle and fly away. In Eupen a woman reported a disk with a dome on top of it flying above her house. On December 2nd or 3rd a young man ran away in panic when he saw a gigantic, massive object coming toward him. Sometimes three or four triangles were seen together.

On December 7, in the neighborhood of Mont Rigi, a red ball covered with lights was reported. On December 11, people saw a triangle flying by at a speed of no more than fifty or sixty kilometers per hour (km/h). On December 24, a commercial pilot spotted one of the triangles and was especially impressed by the absence of any sound.

These are just a few of the hundreds of reports that flooded officials in Belgium, where, coincidentally, the Supreme Headquarters Allied Powers, Europe (SHAPE) had been relocated. In fact, some thought the mysterious triangles might be the U.S. F–117A, or Stealth fighter, but that notion was quickly rejected. "Stealth" in this instance, is a reference to the plane's invisibility to radar. While the F–117A is roughly the shape of a triangle, it is anything but "silent" nor does it have the capability to "hang in the sky" at low altitudes.

By July 1990 NUFOC was describing this rash of sightings as the "Belgian UFO Wave." Certainly what was happening was unique in Belgian UFO history. Noting the credibility of many of the eyewitnesses, in April 1990 NUFOC, together with the Belgian Air Force, set up a night watch near the village of Fraineux, west of Nandrin. Their purpose was to determine if Belgian ULM aircraft could be the source of the sightings. At about seven minutes after 11 P.M., a strange light was seen heading toward their position at a low altitude. Even with a telescope the shape of the object could not be discerned. The Air Force was notified and an aircraft equipped with infrared cameras was dispatched to the area but saw nothing.

About fifteen minutes earlier, however, a Mrs. O (Belgian reports only permit the initial of the last name to be used) and her children had seen a triangle passing by at a low altitude. It was traveling so slowly that it could be followed on a bicycle. The triangle had the usual characteristics, three white lights underneath and one red light, but the witnesses could also see a strange, yellowish circle around the object. When asked to draw what she had seen, the result looked exactly like Hoagland's tetrahedron circumscribed in a sphere.

Sightings continued. A Mr. B. spotted a strange light in the sky and followed it, finally stopping directly beneath it. He stepped out of his car and looked up. He was looking at a gigantic, triangular-shaped object about 500 meters above him. It was, "at least six tennis courts big," according to Mr. B., and, again, no sound could be heard.

Dozens of similar sightings have been recorded since the beginning of the "Belgian Wave." What makes this "wave" unique is that the Belgian government and Air Force have been very active in their investigation of the phenomenon and have cooperated fully with NUFOC. The objects have been tracked with radar and even aircraft and have shown that in addition to their hovering capability they can also achieve enormous speeds. The net result is there have been some more or less "official" observations issued.

According to the quarterly NUFOC *Journal*, Issue 2, July 1990, the Belgian Air Force has admitted they don't have a clue as to what these objects might be. However, more and more people are beginning ". . . to consider the ET hypothesis as the only possible one." There are a number of reasons for this development. For example:

- The air force has recorded radar echoes they say can't be caused by any meteorological phenomenon such as inversions.
- F–16s have been able to "lock on" to the object from time to time, but when they do the UFO drastically changes course, altitude, and speed. There is absolutely no doubt that the object is controlled by some kind of intelligence.
- The objects have been tracked at speeds far in excess of Mach 1. The F–117A can't fly that fast, proving once again that that particular plane isn't playing UFO over Belgium.
- Each time a UFO accelerated beyond Mach 1, no sonic boom was ever heard. No explanation for this has ever been suggested.
- Although while radar showed only a single blip, several lights were observed from the ground. Pilots of the F–16s registering the radar contact never reported visual contact.
- One object has registered acceleration from 1,445 km/h to 1,833 km/h in less than two seconds. It also descends from 10,000 feet to 4,000 feet in less than two seconds. No known aircraft has that capability.

These facts and observations, along with hundreds of eyewitness reports in the past five years, led one official to state publicly that ". . . it could *only* be ETs."[2]

Perhaps it is the shadow of doubt that still accompanies these reports that has prevented the mass hysteria predicted should people ever come face to face with an undeniable fact of extraterrestrials coming here to Earth. Whatever the reason, reports continue to pour in from Germany, Costa Rica, Wales, France, China, England, Italy, Bolivia, Canada, Brazil, Australia, and the former Soviet Union. All of these reports are supported by highly credible sources, most of them accompanied by film and photographs. In Brazil an eyewitness reported seeing a UFO kill four hunters with a beam issuing from the craft. The story was widely reported in the Brazilian press, but there were no reports of widespread panic. Could it be the social scientists are wrong?

In the meantime what has the ongoing UFO investigation in the United States done to alleviate fears and encourage official participation in the investigation process?

Let's go back to April 13, 1992, Washington, D.C. It was late in the afternoon. Dozens of tourists were milling around the great obelisk which is the Washington Monument. Slowly at first, but then in ever-increasing numbers people began to look toward the pinnacle of the monument. Many of them were pointing at . . . something. Some looked for a moment then turned away, as if not wanting to be bothered with what they couldn't understand. Most stood transfixed as a bright disk floated silently westward at an altitude estimated to be near 30,000 feet. Following this huge disk were seven smaller objects, also shining brightly as they moved silently above the obelisk. It was obvious that these were not airplanes. According to George Wingfield, who was there with his wife and daughter and watched the event firsthand, "the large, disk-shaped object must have

[2] Paul Van Brabant, Triangles reveal more of themselves, *NUFOC Journal* (Quarterly Issue 2, July 1990), p. 36.

subtended an angle of about one quarter the diameter of the full moon, or seven minutes of arc." A very large object indeed.

Just forty years earlier, in the summer of 1952, a "fleet of UFOs" had been photographed above the Capitol dome in Washington, D.C., flying in a neatly organized formation. The Pentagon had registered some concern at the time, but a retired Major, Colman S. Von Keviczky, had analyzed a photograph of the formation and announced it was nothing more than a reflection of a row of lamps on the buildings balcony. The event was soon forgotten.

This new sighting, however, was no reflection. As if to underscore the point another small object, much lower and ". . . flying rapidly westward, flew behind the monument, halted in flight, flew back again, reversed westward and brightened, suddenly turning orange before apparently vanishing in thin air."

The event seemed to create no great excitement among those who witnessed it. One small boy asked Wingfield what the first circular object was. Wingfield answered, "a UFO." The boy was puzzled but apparently not overly concerned.

Walking back toward the Tidal Basin where their car was parked, the Wingfields saw another object flying on a course from the Capitol toward the Pentagon. According to Wingfield, "This object seemed to drift silently across the sky changing shape as it did so. At first it looked to be shaped like a cross, then perhaps a cigar, then like an airplane viewed from above. But this was clearly not an airplane . . . the only conceivable object which it resembled would have been an enormous irregular cluster of balloons strung together and tumbling across the sky."[3] Another small object also followed this one and would occasionally emit a bright flash, perhaps due to the sun catching its reflective surface.

[3] George Wingfield, Eleven UFOs over Washington, D.C., *Flying Saucer Review* (Vol. 37 No. 2, Summer 1992), pp. 10–11.

"On countless occasions," Wingfield reminds us, "people have asked why, if UFOs exist, don't they just come down and land beside the White House? On April 13, 1992 it really looked for a time as if they would do just that."

On the other hand the folks in Washington have never given the impression they would be very hospitable to alien visitors, even though there have been some signs along the way that the U.S. government might be taking the sightings seriously. In Volume 6, No. 2 of the publication *UFO Magazine*, Vicki Cooper-Ecker enumerates some of the "official milestones," that at one time seemed to point to serious government involvement resulting in an official public policy.

- There was the top-secret *"Estimate of the Situation,"* mentioned earlier, prepared by the Air Materiel Command at Wright Field in 1948.
- A veritable blitz of UFOs over the nation's capitol in 1952 forced an official response. Surprisingly, an Air Force intelligence analysis of that event (Major Von Keviczky's photo analysis notwithstanding) concluded that UFOs were interplanetary spaceships.
- In 1955, General Douglas MacArthur stated that ". . . the next war will be an interplanetary war. The nations must someday make a common front against attack by people from other planets." Thirty some years later President Ronald Reagan would reawaken that suggestion in a speech before the United Nations.

  "In our obsession with antagonisms of the moment," he said, "we often forget how much unites all the members of humanity. Perhaps we need some outside universal threat to make us recognize this common bond. I occasionally think how quickly our differences, worldwide, would vanish if we were facing an alien threat from outside this world."

Beginning in the '60s a few political VIPs tried to give at least give some credibility to UFO beliefs.

- In 1965, Senator Barry Goldwater tried to gain access to a secret building at Wright-Patterson Air Force Base but was refused.
- In 1966, former President Gerald Ford recommended an official committee to investigate the UFO phenomenon.
- In 1976, presidential candidate Jimmy Carter promised that, upon his election, he would make public all government information on UFO sightings.[4]

No such information was ever forthcoming. Indeed, despite these small blips of hope, the U.S. government has continued to pursue a policy almost guaranteed to create an atmosphere of mistrust and cynicism.

But what about you? Having now given it careful thought, are you prepared to know, with absolute certainty, that UFOs not only exist, but are piloted by intelligent beings, in all likelihood far more intelligent than ourselves, from other worlds, even other galaxies? What would you do if one came down in your backyard? What would you expect the government to do?

There is strong evidence that something exactly like that happened not long ago in a small town in Pennsylvania. What people in the community did and what they say the government did may surprise you.

[4] Vicki Cooper-Ecker, Official Milestones, UFO *Magazine*, 6(2) (1991), p. 19.

CHAPTER 13

THE KECKSBURG MYSTERY

>> A number of local residents saw the
object go down in the woods.

Stan Gordon, UFO researcher

A t approximately 4:45 P.M. on December 9, 1965, residents of Kecksburg, Pennsylvania, saw a meteor streak across the sky and crash to Earth in a ravine just a few miles from their village. Or . . .

Late in the afternoon of December 9, 1965, residents of the village of Kecksburg, Pennsylvania, became the unwilling wards of a Soviet space probe that crashed into a wooded area just outside of town. Or . . .

An unidentified flying object came down in a ball of flame near Kecksburg, Pennsylvania, late in the afternoon of December 9, 1965. Eyewitnesses say the strange-looking craft reminded them of a huge acorn with indecipherable markings all around the base.

Each of the above scenarios has been advanced as a plausible explanation for an event that took place just over thirty years ago and has remained the subject of heated controversy ever since. Each description has its adherents, and each has been defended vocally and energetically.

The points of agreement are the date, December 9, 1965; the time, late afternoon, some witnesses have placed more precisely as between 4:30 P.M. and 4:45 P.M.; and the location, a small ravine, extending about 800 yards through a wooded section of farmland roughly one-half mile from the village of Kecksburg, Pennsylvania.

Let's take each of these possibilities and examine the arguments that have been and in some circles, are still being made.

The proponents of the meteor argument point to the fact that a brilliant ball of fire was seen, according to a story in the *Philadelphia Inquirer*, ". . . streaking across seven states and Canada, [crashing] into the woods 20 miles south of [Pittsburgh]. Flaming objects from it touched off fires in Pennsylvania and Ohio."[1] Von Del Chamberlain and David J. Krause of the Abrams Planetarium, Michigan State University, in East Lansing, Michigan, wrote an article about this ball of fire with the imposing title "The Fireball of December 9, 1965—Calculation of the Trajectory and Orbit by Photographic Triangulation of the Train."[2]

There was, in fact, a meteor seen over a wide area of Ontario and at least six states, moving in a generally northeasterly direction, that disappeared some fifteen miles southeast of Windsor, Michigan. According to the paper, "loud sonic booms were heard in the Detroit–Windsor region at intervals after the visual sighting, which a majority of observers gave a duration of 3 to 4 seconds." This would

[1] Fireball Lands Near Pittsburgh; Seen in 7 States, *Philadelphia Inquirer*, Dec. 9, 1965.

[2] Von Del Chamberlain and David J. Krause, The fireball of Dec. 9, 1965— Part 1, *R.A.S.C. Journal*, 61(4), p. 184.

mean that the meteor, as would be expected, entered the Earth's atmosphere at a very high rate of speed. Furthermore, the Geophysics Laboratory of the University of Michigan near Ypsilanti recorded a shock phenomenon on a seismograph shortly after the fireball event. The assumption that this pulse was generated when the meteor finally hit, coupled with variations of speed and altitude, pinpointed the time of the event at 4:43 P.M. [3]

Whether this particular meteor could have been the object that wound up in the woods near Kecksburg, Pennsylvania, we'll leave until later in the chapter. But for now we can be fairly certain that a meteor did blaze across the late afternoon skies of the northeastern United States and Canada on December 9, 1965.

Interestingly enough, a Soviet space vehicle known as *Cosmos 96* also fell from orbit on December 9 of that year. Designed to explore Venus, *Cosmos 96* was in parking orbit when its booster section exploded. The bell-shaped capsule plummeted back to Earth and landed . . . where?

Adding to the credibility of the theory that *Cosmos 96* was what really landed near Kecksburg is the fact that the Venus probe did have a characteristic "bell" shape that might easily be described as looking like a giant "acorn."

Which brings us to the third possibility, an unidentified flying object. Could the "fireball" that was seen by so many residents of Kecksburg actually have been a vehicle of some sort from outer space? There are a number of witnesses, some of whom were children at the time, who have provided sworn affidavits attesting to the truth of their observations. According to these witnesses the object was neither a meteor nor a Russian space probe. Yet many Kecksburg citizens claim that nothing out of the ordinary has *ever* happened there. For thirty years this small Westmoreland County village has been divided by this bizarre set of circumstances.

[3] Ibid.

What is the truth about the strange, metallic-looking object witnesses say they saw in the woods within a half mile of their town? Why did the military virtually take over the village within two hours of the first report of its location? To find the answers, we must return to that December afternoon in 1965.

According to Stan Gordon, a UFO researcher who has spent seventeen years looking into the mystery, the object impacted into the woods near Kecksburg at approximately 4:47 P.M., which coincides almost exactly with the timing of the meteor. "A number of local residents," Gordon tells us, "saw the object go down in the woods. While none of these people reported any type of sound on impact, almost [instantly] there was a column of blue smoke that rose up out of the woods."

Kecksburg residents soon rushed to the spot where they now saw smoke rising through the trees. There, they say, they discovered a metallic object partially buried at the bottom of the ravine, still smoking from its long descent through the Earth's atmosphere. The best estimates tell us it was approximately ten feet high and perhaps six to eight feet in diameter at its base. Similar, in fact, to the size of *Cosmos 96*. Unfortunately no one thought to take a camera with them, or if they did they have kept it to themselves. No photographs taken by Kecksburg residents are known to have survived the incident.

But there was something else peculiar about the object. James R. Romansky was there and according to Romansky: "Here was this large metal object in front of me. I've described it as a large acorn. The reason I say acorn is because around the bottom of this object there was a bumper that went the whole way around this thing. It was dented and it had a very distinct color; it was a bronzish, copperish steel. It's hard to even describe."

Romansky also noted some strange markings going all the way around the "bumper," markings that were unlike anything he had ever seen or anything he has been able to discover since.

"My dad is originally from Kiev," Romansky tells us, "and I went to him one time and I said, 'Dad, you can read and write Polish and Russian?' He says, 'Yeah.' I said, 'Write me something in both dialects.' He says, 'What?' I said, 'Just write me anything.' The Polish and Russian writing that I see doesn't come nowhere near it. I mean it was like circles and stars and dashes and all kinds of markings on it."[4]

Before long a fairly large group of local citizens had gathered at the crash site, but none of them would have time to inspect the object very closely. A local housewife, hearing an announcement on the radio that an airplane was believed down somewhere in the local area, had called authorities telling them she had seen a pillar of smoke just a few hundred yards from her farm. The first officials to show up at her home were a state trooper and two men in civilian clothes, one of them with what appeared to be a Geiger counter. Leaving the trooper and the woman behind, they carefully approached the woods. No one is sure who contacted the military, perhaps these two men, but within two hours armed U.S. soldiers were on the scene. Trucks and other heavy equipment soon followed.

According to Romansky and many other witnesses, "The military started coming in and we were under martial law. Jeeps and trucks were everywhere. Down through the woods came two guys," Romansky said, "trench coats, crew-cut hair, straight as ramrods. They looked around, looked at the object and in a very authoritative voice told us that this area is now quarantined; it's restricted [and] to get out."[5]

Before the witnesses were completely dispersed they reported one other curious thing. A van-type vehicle showed up and two men in full protective clothing carried a large

[4] James R. Romansky, taped interview, Salt Lake City, 1995.
[5] Ibid.

wooden box, approximately five feet square down to the crash site. It was not nearly large enough to cover the object, but it was obviously designed to contain something.

Stan Gordon believes the object only remained in the ravine for a few hours. Witnesses he has spoken to say the soldiers quickly recovered the object and took it somewhere else.

"Here comes this big, flatbed truck," Romansky says, a trace of anger in his voice, "tractor-trailer. On the back of it [were] two pieces, either a tow-motor, one of those things they lift things with, or a front loader. The back of the flatbed had a big tarp on it and it was stretched down around the object. It had the same outline, in fact I know I could see the bumper under this tarp, 'cause you could see the shape of this thing and I knew in my mind that was what they brought down off the mountain . . . the object."[6]

The military had literally taken over the town. The local firehouse was commandeered as some kind of command center, and even a farmhouse near the crash site was taken over. Lillian Hays, whose family had rented the house barely a month earlier, said in a sworn statement given to me on September 23, 1991, that "on the evening of December 9, 1965, military personnel came to our house and used our telephone . . . during the Kecksburg UFO incident [sic] that occurred in the woods nearby." They did not ask permission, they simply took over. As far as Lillian Hays and other Kecksburg residents were concerned, they had been invaded twice; once by some unidentifiable object from the sky and, even more menacingly, by the U.S. military.

The truck and flatbed trailer with the object on it departed late that evening from Kecksburg. According to Gordon, ". . . from the information we now have, the truck continued on and went to Lockport Air Force Base in Columbus, Ohio, where it stayed for a short period of time.

---

[6] Ibid.

From there it went over to Wright-Patterson Air Force Base in Dayton, Ohio. It seems very likely," Gordon adds, "that our government had tracked the object and they had notified the quick-response recovery team that is involved in this type of operation."[7]

The object, whatever it was, was gone, apparently out of their lives forever. To the Kecksburg residents the incident was over. Or was it? A number of witnesses tell us the most terrifying aspect of their encounter with a UFO had just begun.

John Murphy, at that time news director of radio station WHJB, felt the story was of great importance and launched his own investigation into the matter. Over the next several days he interviewed a number of eyewitnesses who told him, among other things, that the object appeared to be burning as it fell toward the woods. Some witnesses indicated it didn't seem to be "falling" at all, but appeared to slow down and go into the woods very smoothly. Other witnesses confirmed Romansky's assertion that there was some kind of writing on the object, and, like Romansky, none of them could identify any of the characters or letters.

Most of the people Murphy interviewed believed the object "landed," as opposed to crashed, and in one way or another they described it as a "ship" or "craft" of some sort. It soon became apparent that those who had both seen the object up close and witnessed the military takeover at the site were also very frightened. The special radio broadcast planned by Murphy never made it on the air. The people interviewed withdrew their permission to have the interviews aired and refused to let their names be used.

According to Stan Gordon, "It seems as though something must have occurred between the time of the interview with John Murphy and the time the radio special was to be

[7] UFO Diaries, The Mystery of Kecksburg. Sun International Pictures, Salt Lake City, 1995.

aired, because these people were willing to be interviewed and then suddenly they decided they didn't want their name or any information aired with this report."

Why? What happened to cause the witnesses to refuse to make their testimony public after they had been so willing, some of them only hours before?

Romansky believes he knows what happened. "I think these people knew that something had come down," he said, "and the military presence was so strong that night that a lot of people who they, the military, knew had seen something or lived real close to it [were] either told to be quiet or were bought out, or something."[8]

That view would seem to be consistent with other incidents where the military was involved—Roswell, New Mexico, for example. Does that imply there is a policy of some sort to deal with the general public when these incidents occur?

Kevin Randle, author of *A History of ufo Crashes*, is convinced there indeed is such a policy. "The government," he says, "does have an official policy on UFOs. They are not vehicles from any other planet. But they do know that some UFO sightings actually are piloted by alien life-forms. So one likely explanation for the behavior of the military at Kecksburg is that they knew they were dealing with a spaceship."[9]

As confused as that sounds it is not out of character with other "policies" we have encountered when it comes to the attitude of the government toward UFOs. In fact the only "policy" that seems to be consistent *is* confusion. That being the case, how do we go about trying to learn the real truth of the matter? Perhaps we can come closer to discovering what actually landed near Kecksburg by first determining what did not land.

---

[8] James R. Romansky, taped interview, Salt Lake City, 1995.
[9] *ufo Diaries, The Mystery of Kecksburg*. Sun International Pictures, Salt Lake City, 1995.

To begin with let's look at the meteorite theory. Jim Romansky has maintained for thirty years that this story was given to Kecksburg residents by the military. Romansky and another man were just emerging from the ravine, having been ordered out by whoever it was that had taken charge. Both men had actually seen the object up close. Then, Romansky says, "Someone said, 'Hey, what the hell was that up there anyhow?' And the guy [in charge] hollered back, 'Oh, it was just a meteorite.' And I looked at the guy [next to me] and we both bust out laughin' 'cause we knew it was no meteorite."[10]

But the fact that a meteor did cross the northeastern skies at approximately 4:45 P.M. on December 9 is indisputable. It was seen in several states and its train (sometimes called a "tail") was photographed and analyzed. Could this, in spite of witnesses to the contrary, have been the object that landed in Kecksburg?

Stan Gordon doesn't think so. His investigation indicates the Kecksburg object was tracked coming down from the tip of Ontario, passing down in a northwest to southeast trajectory. The object appears to have made about a twenty-five degree turn toward the east near Cleveland, Ohio, and come in on a straight path over the Pittsburgh area. According to Gordon, in an interview aired on *Unsolved Mysteries*, ". . . the new data suggests the object made a turn towards the south then the object made another turn toward the village of Kecksburg, proceeding into there towards the northeast. The interesting thing is that within several miles of the crash site, multiple witnesses tell us that this object was coming in at a very, very slow speed of descent. Meteors do not make controlled turns, do not come in at a slow speed like this and they do not, in fact, glide in as this thing apparently did."

[10] Ibid.

The meteorite theory raises other questions. For example, meteorites, even small ones, are known to leave extensive craters where they strike the Earth and are frequently accompanied by the unmistakable sound of an explosion. Even though the object at Kecksburg came down within half a mile of the town, no one reported any loud or unusual noise, only a column of smoke. The impact did not leave a crater, but more of a "rut" where the object appeared to have skidded to a stop. Furthermore, in spite of the fact that most witnesses reported it as a "flaming" ball and in spite of the fact that it landed in a wooded area, there was no fire.

Taking all these observations together, it seems unlikely that the object at Kecksburg landed with enough impact to be read on a seismograph machine in Ypsilanti, Michigan. It also seems unlikely that Michigan residents photographed a train from an object that turned east at Cleveland on the other side of Lake Erie when they reportedly saw the meteor disappear at a point over land southeast of Detroit. Although a meteor was undoubtedly tracked at approximately the same time as the object that landed near Kecksburg, it would appear they were two separate and distinct events.

But what of the second theory that has been advanced? The Soviet space capsule that supposedly could have been the object recovered at Kecksburg? Certainly this theory makes more sense in terms of direct government involvement in the retrieval process. And it would explain, in large measure, the requirement for secrecy, since under international law nations are bound to return intact to the country of origin any such recovered space debris. But *Cosmos 96*, supposedly containing the latest Soviet missile warhead technology, would have been too juicy a prize to give up. James Oberg, a Houston space scientist and writer, suggested in the September 1993 issue of OMNI magazine that the government actually fostered the UFO idea in order to fool the Russians and give themselves time to examine the failed probe at their leisure. "UFO buffs," he writes, "could be counted on to maintain the phony cover story, protecting the real truth."[11]

A delicious morsel of speculation but, alas, the facts dispute the supposition. According to Air Force spokesmen, the Soviet spacecraft came down twelve hours earlier in Canada. In an article published in UFO *Magazine* in 1991, Stan Gordon references a report written by David Templeton, a reporter for the *Pittsburgh Press*,[12] who conducted an independent follow-up on the Air Force claim. According to the data in Templeton's article the Soviet probe came down at 3:18 A.M. somewhere in Canada. Templeton even quoted a known UFO skeptic as saying, "*Cosmos 96* is not guilty." That skeptic? James Oberg, the same space scientist who believes the Air Force is not above fostering a belief in UFOs to further their own aims.

Cosmos 96, it seems has been eliminated as a plausible answer to the mystery of Kecksburg. Which brings us back to where we started. If it wasn't a meteor and it wasn't the Soviet space probe, these amazing coincidences notwithstanding, what was it? And why would our government take such an immediate and forceful position with regard to . . . what? Could it have been just a hoax?

Stan Gordon doesn't think so. "I think first of all," he said, "we can rule out that the incident in Kecksburg is a hoax. Something did occur there that night that created a lot of activity. That the military responded the way they did indicates the fact that this was something that was important to our government and the military. The bright fireball object was reported first in Canada, then over a number of states including Michigan, Indiana, Ohio, and Pennsylvania. So a lot of people did indeed see something."

[11] James Oberg, Antimatter: UFO Update, *OMNI* (September 1993), p. 75.
[12] David Templeton, The Uninvited, *The Pittsburgh Press* (May 19, 1991), pp. 10–11.

According to the eyewitness accounts, we are dealing with an object that was moving very, very slowly almost gliding in, a flaming object that made a controlled landing. It had a metallic surface without joints or seams and strange markings unlike any writing on Earth. Then there is the rapid military deployment. If all of this is based on actual fact then, indeed, it would seem we are trying to describe a craft of some sort that is very likely from another world.

"There are numerous documents," Gordon says, "that indicate the United States government has had in place, for many years, a system for handling the recovery of space objects that safely reenter the Earth's atmosphere. It is very likely that the specialized recovery teams would only have responded to something of great importance to the military. This most likely would have been, one: Some type of foreign space device that had landed in our territory that they would like to have studied; or two: something more unusual, such as the possibility of an extraterrestrial spacecraft."

Does the U.S. military have an official answer to all of this? What do they say the object recovered at Kecksburg actually is? Could it be some top secret spy satellite that accidentally dropped out of orbit? Or will they admit to the possibility that they have recovered something that is not of this Earth?

Gordon went to the files of the Air Force 662nd Radar Squadron to try and get answers to those and other questions. He tells us that, "There are indeed records that indicate that there are specially trained intelligence teams of military personnel that are on call to quickly respond to crashes of space objects that survive the reentry of the Earth's atmosphere. The 662nd Radar Squadron was assigned as a Norad surveillance site, and Air Force documents verify the fact that at least a few personnel from that squadron were directly involved in the investigation at Kecksburg that night. However, when we look at the historical records for December [1965] there is no entry whatsoever of any activity for that squadron on that day.

That leaves us to believe that this mission was classified and the paperwork went up the ladder. The question is, why after so many years, is our government still not telling us all the facts it knows about the Kecksburg incident? What is so secret about what they found at that location, that even today they refuse to comment about the incident?"

At the time we might have suspected there were some national security concerns, given the status of the Cold War and the intractability of the Soviet Union. But if that was the reason for such a deep level of secrecy the reason vanished with the demise of the Soviet Union. They simply no longer exist as a threat, either militarily or as a space competitor. We can't help wondering . . . why the continuing silence?

Without the object itself, of course, there can be no final proof, but it is possible the object might still be held in some military storage facility. Investigators believe they have tracked it to Wright-Patterson Air Force Base near Dayton, Ohio, a relatively short trip from Kecksburg. But as we have learned, not even a United States senator can get through some of the doors at Wright-Patterson. So far all attempts to get further information on the object's whereabouts have come to a dead end. The Russian embassy has indicated, however, that they have no knowledge that *Cosmos 96* or any other Soviet device ever crashed in Pennsylvania on December 9, 1965. Meanwhile information obtained from the United States government indicates that there was no re-entry of any U.S. space debris or any type of weapons system that could account for the Kecksburg incident on that day.

Gordon was able to obtain the official document regarding the Kecksburg incident from Project Blue Book (the Air Force UFO investigation arm—we'll be devoting an entire chapter to this program), and according to Gordon they stated, ". . . that the object which was involved with the Kecksburg incident was a meteor that had been observed over a large area."

Robert Blystone, a Kecksburg resident and witness to the event states bluntly: "All I can say about that is, the people that are saying this are lying." Blystone adds, without flinching, "I think it was a UFO."

Is that, in fact, the most plausible solution? Something large enough to require the use of a truck and flatbed trailer was hauled out of there. The impact area, trajectory, and rate of descent appear to eliminate the "meteorite" contention, even though Project Blue Book was willing to accept that notion. And both the Russians and the U.S. Air Force have ruled out the possibility of some sort of international space junk being the cause of the mystery. That being the case there would seem to be no reason for the continued secrecy. Yet if anything, there is even less willingness, in official circles, to discuss the Kecksburg incident than there has been in the past.

Perhaps Gordon has it right. "If we can eliminate those possibilities," he says, "then we have to deal with the fact that we might be dealing with an actual, extraterrestrial spacecraft. Something did indeed fall from the sky that day in December of 1965 into the Kecksburg woods. The military responded very quickly, located the object, recovered it, and took it away from the site. Investigation into the incident continues, and until we have more information this is the only [viable] speculation as to what the object might really be."

If unidentified flying objects are crashing and being recovered by our government, as appears to be the case with both Roswell and Kecksburg, isn't it possible that at least some of the thousands of sightings reported by people all over the world are true? Even if we concede that many such reports are explainable by perfectly natural causes, what of those that can't be explained? And if UFOs are a reality, is it not also conceivable that they could be picking up an occasional "earthling" for a little closer study?

We'll be taking an in-depth look at that possibility in the next chapter.

CHAPTER 14

ABDUCTIONS

>> **Probably the majority of abductees have some sort of an implant in them.**

Dr. David Jacobs, Temple University

L iterally the day before yesterday, as this is being written, while attending an artists' conference I made the acquaintance of a woman from Florida who was hoping to gather a few new ideas for a musical she was writing. We shared a few moments at lunch, and the conversation turned to what we were doing artistically and what we hoped to do. I mentioned I was working on the final chapters of a book about UFOs. In an instant her demeanor changed from casual to very serious.

"What are your conclusions," she asked.

"I'm not sure I've come to any," I replied.

She set the taco salad she was working on aside and looked me straight in the eye. "I know they're real," she whispered.

"How do you know that?" I said, trying to bring the conversation back to a more cheerful tone.

"I have seen them."

It was suddenly very clear to me that this was not going to be just another of those lighthearted, slightly embarrassed, "haven't you got anything better to do . . ." kind of discussions I have come to expect every time I mention the project I've been working on. This woman wanted to share something that was both frightening and important to her. "Ummm," I said, pushing my own lunch aside to let her know I would be a willing listener, "tell me about it."

"We lived in Ohio when I was a teenager," she glanced over her shoulder as if looking to see if anyone else was listening, "and I had to drive several miles from school to our home. It wasn't an interstate or anything, just a regular two-lane road that cut through the cornfields in an almost straight line. One night when I was driving home the car suddenly filled with light. I turned around expecting to see a truck or something behind me with its brights on, but there was nothing there. Then I looked up. And I saw it." She stopped and looked at me, trying to determine, I'm sure, if I was buying any of this.

"You saw what?" I asked, as matter-of-factly as I could.

"The ship, or aircraft, or whatever it was. I've tried to give it a name for years now but I don't know what it was. I pulled over to the side of the road, stopped and rolled down the window to get a better look. I remember thinking I should be trying to get away from there as fast as I can. I even remembered telling myself that if I ever saw anything like a UFO I'd run like crazy. But I didn't. I just stopped there and watched it as it hung there in the sky. The feeling I had was that it was huge, but I can't be sure. It was certainly bigger than my car by several times, and it just sort of stayed above me, lighting up the whole countryside. Then it moved off over the cornfields. I wanted to follow it . . . to chase after it, but I couldn't. The thing never turned its lights off and I can't remember that it made any sound at all."

"That must have shook you up a bit," I said, retrieving my sandwich. It was not a particularly unusual story, and I thought that was probably the end of it.

"There's more," she added quickly. "A few nights later I decided I wanted to sleep out on a hillside near our home. It surprised me, because I'm not into that kind of thing. I mean, I like a nice comfortable bed and a bathroom close by, but for some reason I had to sleep outside on that hill. My brother was six years old at the time, and for some reason I insisted that he come with me."

She paused, took a deep breath, and began fidgeting with her rings. "Sometime during the night I remember waking up, or maybe I wasn't awake, but I have this memory of seeing that ship again just a little ways away from the hill where we were sleeping, only this time my brother was going inside. I remember feeling terrified, but I couldn't move. The next morning when I woke up I looked over and his sleeping bag was empty. My heart jumped inside of me, and I ran into the house. But he was sitting at the table eating a bowl of cornflakes. He didn't even look up when I came in."

"Did you ever ask him about it?" I asked.

"No, no, I didn't," she said, "I just thought it was a dream, probably from my seeing the thing before and I never mentioned it to anyone. But. . ." she turned and looked around again before continuing, "years later, when he was grown up he came to me at a family gathering and asked, 'Do you know anything about me and a UFO?' I told him, yes, I did, and I told him about that night."

"What did he say?"

"He said, 'I thought so. They keep coming back to get me.'"

I would have liked to have asked her what her brother told her about his experiences, if he was still being visited, or where I could get in touch with him, but she had said everything she was going to say. My newfound friend glanced at her watch, smiled, and left. I sensed a feeling of guilt, that she somehow felt her brother's experience was all her fault and the less she knew about it or talked about it the better. We didn't speak again, but our brief conversation did leave me with at least one conclusion. Regardless of the attitudes generally that guide the various media and others in their handling of UFOs and more particularly, abductions, the inescapable fact is that there are thousands of people all around the world who deeply believe that something inexplicable, except in terms of extraterrestrial involvement, has happened to them. Few of them seek celebrity. Of those who find it thrust upon them, most try to escape the limelight as quickly as possible. Rooted in their belief is a confused mixture of fear, guilt, anxiety, and isolation. Yet in spite of public attitudes they cannot avoid the private consequences of remaining silent, and through some sense of concern or responsibility, they seem to feel obligated to tell their story. More and more that obligation to communicate appears to be shared between those who have experienced these events and a public increasingly willing to listen with a more open mind.

That the thousands of abductees truly believe they have been taken against their will by some force or entity over which they have no control is not at issue. Whether any of these reports could actually be true, however, is at the heart of a thirty-five-year-old controversy that might, at last, be subject to actual verification.

Prior to 1961 the public was blissfully unaware of anything like "alien abductions." Then one night in September of that year, a young couple named Betty and Barney Hill were returning from a vacation in Canada. They were driving through the rural New Hampshire countryside when, according to Betty, ". . . all of a sudden, without any rhyme or reason or anything, Barney stopped suddenly and made this sharp turn off the highway."

Barney was a postal worker, as steady in his personal habits as he was on the job. That he would do something so completely unexpected, surprised and even frightened Betty.

Barney stopped the car and stared out through the windshield. Betty followed his gaze and saw a light in the distance that seemed to be coming right toward them. They got out of the car and Barney took out his binoculars to get a better look. As the strange looking "star" got closer, he was able to distinguish red, amber, and green flashing lights. The couple panicked, jumped back in the car, and began speeding down the road.

Up to this point the experience of Betty and Barney Hill was just another routine UFO sighting. It wasn't until they arrived home that they realized that somehow, and in spite of the rush they were in after spotting the UFO, the trip had taken two hours longer than it should have.

Betty was a social worker with a heavy caseload and didn't have time to worry about the lost two hours, but within a week to ten days following the incident she began having strange dreams. She saw herself and Barney being taken aboard a ship or aircraft of some kind where both were required to undergo some kind of weird and painful examination. The dreams were, in every sense, colossal nightmares.

Whatever had happened out there on Route 3 in the isolated White Mountains, was taking its toll on Barney as well. They sought the help of Dr. Benjamin Simon, a well-known Boston psychiatrist. It was Dr. Simon who unwittingly and probably unintentionally opened the door to what has become the favorite method of abduction investigation. Dr. Simon put both Betty and Barney Hill into a hypnotic trance to try and extract any repressed information they might have about the missing two hours.

An actual transcript of the hypnosis session was aired on an A & E special in May 1996. The tape recording gives a very real sense of the fear Barney felt. He talked about trying to be brave for Betty's sake, spoke of getting his gun to protect them, but at one point he confessed, " . . . oh God, I'm scared." Later, fully conscious, he would draw sketches to illustrate his story. For his part, Barney seemed to recall what he saw from his position on the road as the craft approached, stopped, and "tilted" toward them.

Betty, on the other hand, gave Dr. Simon a very detailed description of what happened when they were taken inside the UFO. "The examiner," she said, "has a long needle in his hand, and I see the needle and it's bigger than any needle I've ever seen. And I ask him what he's going to do with it, and he says just a simple test that won't hurt me . . . and he sticks the needle into my navel, and I'm crying and I tell him it's hurting . . . take it out. And then their leader, he comes over and he puts his hand in front of my eyes, and he says I'll be all right . . . I won't feel it . . . and all the pain goes away."

Betty would also tell of having their eyes checked as well as their ears, nose, and throat. Samples were taken of hair and scrapings from their skin, and then they were released. From all indications they were simply returned to their car. They consciously remembered jumping in and racing for home. But the entire time between getting out of the car to look at the object with binoculars to getting back in the car and speeding away had been a complete blank until the hypnosis session.

Dr. Simon, by the way, maintained a proper professional skepticism of the Hill's story, even though he had elicited it from them.

But Betty Hill also remembered something else, something that turned out to be quite remarkable. Apparently while on board the ship she was conscious enough to look around and ask questions. She saw what appeared to be a star map on the wall inside the ship, and she asked the entity she took to be their leader what it represented. She was told it represented their sector of the universe. Apparently the image was imprinted on her subconscious, and later she was able to reproduce what she had seen in a sketch. At the time it appeared to be quite meaningless, just dots and lines.

But Marjorie Fish, you'll remember, had taken a keen interest in Betty Hill's star map and had created a number of star clusters within a thirty-five-light-year radius of Earth. When the *1969 Catalogue of Nearby Stars* was published, she discovered that Betty's map corresponded very closely to a group of stars near the Zeta Reticuli system. Several astonomers confirmed the accuracy of Fish's findings, but even more interesting was that a number of these stars were unknown prior to the publication of the 1969 catalogue.[1] Betty Hill was either telling the truth, or through the most bizarre coincidence in history, she had drawn a representation of a star system that was still to be discovered. For many people the latter possibility was just too fantastic to be believed. Over time, however, except for a cover story in *LOOK Magazine*[2] five years later and a book, *The Interrupted Journey*, that received little attention outside UFO circles, the Betty and Barney Hill abduction case was all but forgotten.

But not by everyone. Robert O. Dean (the SHAPE "Assessment") has done considerable research on his own into the Betty and Barney Hill story. He's convinced their experience was real. "Betty and Barney didn't make it up," Dean says, "because over the years since that's [just] a tiny part of a vast amount of evidence that these are real events. The emotional involvement, the impact of this experience on both of them, indicate to me that this was . . . real."

The Betty and Barney Hill abduction was the first to be reported in the United States, but it was far from the last. In 1973, newspapers and TV stations from coast to coast exploded with an even more fantastic story. Two ordinary guys, just out on a fishing trip, had been abducted. Charlie Hickson and Calvin Parker, according to UFO researcher

---

[1] *A Time of Close Encounters: The UFO Phenomenon* (Alexandria, VA: Time-Life Books, 1987), p. 84.

[2] John G. Fuller, Aboard a Flying Saucer, *LOOK Magazine* (October 4, 1966) pp. 45–56.

Kevin Randle, ". . . were in Pascagoula, Mississippi, on October 11, 1973. They heard a noise [and] described a hazy blue light that quickly became visible as a dish-shaped object. They said three beings that appeared to be robots floated out of the craft toward them."

Both Hickson and Parker later claimed they had been taken inside the UFO. And both told terrifying stories of medical samples of various kinds being drawn, cut, or scraped from various parts of their bodies. Then, like the Hills, they were abruptly released.

The Charlie Hickson/Calvin Parker abduction got worldwide attention and reminded researchers of the story the Hills had told a decade earlier. A serious search for real proof got under way and has been going on ever since. But does real proof exist? Is there such a thing as "hard" evidence?

These are fair questions—ones not easy to answer. The truth is we probably would have left the entire matter of abductions out of the book if the only clues were just the words of the abductees themselves. But other elements of these events are difficult to dismiss, and there are other witnesses, sometimes several of them, who seem to have no other involvement than that they happened to be at the scene or nearby. In fact the most astounding tale of an alien abduction ever reported took place in New York City at night, bathed in lights, and in full view of a number of stunned onlookers.

Budd Hopkins, formerly a professional artist and illustrator, has devoted his entire adult life to investigating UFO abductions and working with the post-abduction trauma that almost all of the victims experience. Hopkins was called in to help with this particular abductee, whom we'll call "Linda," and discovered much more than he had bargained for.

"In this particular case," Hopkins told us, "the woman who had been abducted consciously remembered being paralyzed . . . seeing a figure at the foot of the bed, and so on. When we did hypnotic regression on it she remembered having been floated out the window."

Remember, the abduction took place on the twelfth floor of an apartment building in New York City. It would not have been an easy matter to "fake" any of the events being described.

Linda's memories, both conscious and hypnotically induced, are quite straightforward. She remembers light filling the room and a "being" standing at the foot of the bed and slowly coming toward her. It reached out and touched her face, which made her feel as though there was a white veil over her features. Then her body went numb and she was immersed in lights. The next thing she remembered she was in a ship of some kind, which she described as "huge."

You can hide a lot of things in a city like New York, but a "huge" spaceship hovering near a large apartment building is not one of them. Hopkins began hearing from witnesses who saw the whole episode from their vantage point on the street below where their cars had stalled.

"They saw this craft above the building that she lived in," Hopkins told us. "They saw the blue light being applied. They were transfixed looking at it. And they saw four figures [which they described as] being rolled up in a kind of a fetal position, like moles, come flying out the window, twelve stories off the ground."

The witnesses then reported seeing the figures "unroll." One of the aliens first, followed by Linda, still in her nightgown, and then two more aliens. They were all lifted up into the craft and then the craft zoomed away.

"This is extraordinarily important," Hopkins insists, "because one car of witnesses was located at one place, another car was located on the Brooklyn Bridge. I have three other witnesses at other locations in New York City, some very close, [and all of them] saw aspects of this. There is absolutely no doubt that this took place."

In fact, Hopkins says, "one of the witnesses who saw this was an extremely important political figure. It was as if they were showing him, this is what we can do. It would seem that this is an attempt on the part of the UFO phenomenon to have a role, in effect, or to, let's say, affect world politics."

Reports such as these, with several uninvolved witnesses that come forward after the fact, continue to fuel the search for definitive answers to the UFO phenomenon. Serious investigators know that while it may be possible to disbelieve or even discredit a witness, you cannot, in good conscience, ignore them.

There's more than just uninvolved witnesses that continues to peak our interest—a certain amount of physical evidence also exists. Since the Hickson/Parker abduction over twenty-five years ago, literally thousands of people have reported strange and painful incidents. They tell of being taken aboard alien vessels and subjected to various kinds of "tests." The trauma is evident and dramatic. In spite of Dr. Simon's skepticism about the validity of Betty and Barney Hill's hypnotic regression, most researchers today believe this method is the surest way to get at memories that are often painful, terrifying, and difficult to retrieve in a conscious state.

Hopkins is an expert hypnotist and believes there is ample "hard" evidence to support the stories told by the abductees. "I've worked with over 500 people in the past twenty years," he told us, "and of that 500 (most of those I've looked into are multiple abductions), there are many physical marks that turn up after an abduction experience. A person can describe a physical process taking place or something being done to their thigh and you check the place and there's a 'scoop' mark or a long straight cut."

Dr. David Jacobs, a professor at Temple University and the author of several books on UFO abductions, is probably the second most-quoted researcher in this field. He agrees with Hopkins and adds, ". . . this includes actual scars, that

is to say, scar tissue that is formed, which of course, is phys-
iologically not possible in just a few hour period. But that is
what we do see." Dr. Jacobs has also discovered something
else that would seem to support the validity of the abduction
claims. "I would say," Dr. Jacobs told us, "[that] probably the
majority of abductees have some sort of an implant in them.
They describe an instrument that's placed high up their nose
. . . they can hear a kind of crunching sound . . . *feel* a
crunching sound as this instrument goes up through the car-
tilage and . . . deposits a little sort of ball-like thing way up
by their optic nerve or their pituitary glands. This happens
in their ears as well. People wake up in the morning [and]
there's blood all over the pillow from their nose or from
their ear."

Hopkins told us of a similar event that he investigated.
Apparently the entire family was having these abduction
experiences. Then one morning, ". . . [the] little girl woke
up, a nine year old. She was visiting a friend [and] she woke
up in the morning with a memory of a strange face looking
at her and there was a huge, long gash down her cheek and
around underneath [her chin]. The emergency room people
put eighteen stitches in it. The doctor said it was a scalpel
cut. It was of uniform depth and extremely deep. She has
no memory of it. It didn't wake her up. This is something
that happened during the night, together with the other
memories.

"There is," Hopkins insists, "physical evidence all over
the place."

"Not only that," Jacobs adds, "but people are physically
missing from their normal environment. That is to say,
they're not there when they're in an abduction event. Their
parents are looking for them, if they're kids, or their husband or wife was, you know, doesn't know where they are.
They're actually missing."

Dr. Karla Turner is another abduction researcher and
investigator who has a very different insight into the entire

matter. Her book, *Into the Fringe and Taken*, tells of her own abduction experience. "I had no intention of becoming a UFO researcher," she says, "but the issue was forced on me by the beings who invaded my life, my home, my family, everything. There can be no doubt that something really, deeply traumatic has happened to these people. [Our] whole concept of reality has been shattered by bizarre and inexplicable events. We certainly can no longer laugh at the idea of flying saucers and people from outer space the way other people can."

Which brings us to another aspect of these abduction reports that is perhaps the most terrifying of all. One of Budd Hopkins' clients, a young woman named Kathy Davis, believes she lost her unborn child. Dr. Turner is convinced something similar happened to her.

"I met Kathy Davis in 1983," Hopkins tells us, "when she wrote to me about these marks that turned up on the ground after an odd experience." She complained of not being able to sleep and assumed the problem, whatever it was, could only mean that something was wrong with her mentally.

Kathy apparently lived a normal life in an ordinary neighborhood. She had a comfortable home, a dog, and a garden she loved to work in, and she was expecting her first child. Everything seemed to be perfect in her life, and then one day she began to notice that something was different; just little things at first but then her whole life suddenly, inexplicably changed. Under hypnosis, however, Kathy Davis told Hopkins the following story:

"There were too many things happening that didn't make sense. The tool shed door was open and I know I closed it. But I couldn't see anything in there when I looked. And then, weeding my garden, I was outside and there was a burn on my lawn that was a perfect circle. I couldn't explain it. Rusty, my poor dog Rusty, was so scared he hid under the car. He never does that. [Then] as I was standing on my porch looking around, there was a light. A light over me. And they came . . . they came down and they got me. Somebody got me. And I was there! I was on the table! They hurt me. They hurt me bad! My baby's gone. Did they take my baby? Where is he?"

Kathy was certain she was pregnant when the event took place. Afterwards she went to her doctor and had all of the tests done. The results were negative. She was definitely not pregnant, but she is sure she had been prior to this event. Could she have been mistaken? Was her abduction experience simply a vivid dream?

Dr. Turner doesn't think so. "There is no doubt," she says, "that the aliens are profoundly interested in human reproduction. The missing fetus aspect of the UFO abduction phenomenon is far more widespread than people would like to believe. Kathy Davis' encounter is not that rare." And she adds, a trace of sadness in her voice, "apparently this happened to me too."

Dr. Turner's discovery came at a family get-together several years after the actual event took place. "When we finally got up enough information," she told us, "we felt comfortable to talk with other family members and it was several hours of talking about the whole [abduction] thing. My former husband glanced over at his wife and said: 'I guess maybe that's what happened when we [Karla] lost the baby.' And I said, 'I never lost a baby.' And he said, 'No, you've got to remember this.'"

Apparently in 1970 when Dr. Turner was on birth control pills, she became pregnant. A couple of months later, according to her ex-husband, she had a very painful miscarriage. She was hysterical but wouldn't let him take her to the doctor.

"Even after he told me," Dr. Turner added, "I have no conscious memory of this occurring."

Dr. Jacobs doesn't find that surprising. Loss of memory, he says, is quite common. In many cases it's a matter of remembering *which* event is being discussed. "The problem with the abduction phenomenon," he says, "is that it begins in infancy and goes through old age. And it does not stop, from what we can tell. So everybody who's had abduction experiences often times can look forward to having them again and that's [one of the] really unfortunate aspects of this."

Still the skeptics remain skeptical. Perhaps rightly so. All of the eyewitness reports notwithstanding, the cuts and scars and bruises and missing time all taken into consideration, isn't it possible there could be some other explanation?

At Laurentian University in Sudbury, Ontario, Canada, a neuroscientist, Dr. Michael Persinger, believes he may have found an answer. It is his belief that these experiences are simply created in the brain. In an A & E special dealing with UFOs, he said, "From a neuropsychological point of view and a neuroscience point of view, the abduction experience is another variation on the sense of presence. And it is tied," Dr. Persinger says, "fundamentally to the way the human brain is organized."[3]

According to Dr. Persinger, the temporal lobes of the brain are highly charged electrically and are responsible for, among other things, dreams and "meaningfulness." It is in this part of the brain that fantasies are generated that are so real we label them "alien abductions." But the theory goes deeper than that. It begins, not with neuroscience, but with geology and the demonstrable fact that when rock is broken energy is released. The energy can be recorded on film as flashes of light. This occurs in nature, according to the theory, when the earth's rocky crust shifts. The energy released can cause a "startling, luminous display." Dr. Persinger suggests that, "these lights, perhaps occurring over a city, might also emit electromagnetic waves that cause temporal lobe hallucinations, later recalled as an abduction experience."[4]

[3] *Where Are All the UFOs?* A & E, May 1996.

Dr. Persinger has gone so far as to conduct experiments in a chamber where controlled electrical fields are introduced into the brain. A subject with no related UFO experiences was chosen and fitted with a helmet having solenoids capable of delivering weak magnetic fields to the brain. Following the experiment, the subject was interviewed without Dr. Persinger present. He did indeed, report feeling, "light for awhile, just drifting." He then reported a feeling of complete weightlessness and patterns of light and, ". . . all of a sudden, in an instant, I feel as though there's another presence there, uuuh, someone there. I can feel it. I'm almost sure that if I turn my head I'm going to see something there."

The young man who underwent the experiment also reported seeing "distorted images of people he knew . . . and then I felt this sort of, tremendous rush of fear . . . if I could have ripped off the electrodes and gotten out of the room, I would have." But perhaps most significantly he reported seeing white lights, "and then, I saw the people . . . they were grayish, a grayish color . . . they seemed to not really shine . . . it's like wax . . . grayish, elongated, wax people."[5]

UFO investigators might point out that the young man did not report anything like a complete abduction experience, nor were there any of the many physical abnormalities involved that seem to accompany so many abduction experiences. Nor did the young man offer to draw a star map that astronomers might find useful at some future date. Nevertheless Dr. Persinger is pressing his study. He is attempting to correlate UFO abduction reports with earthquake activity around the globe.

Meanwhile there are other serious scientific efforts being made to contact extraterrestrial intelligence. Dr. Paul Horowitz, a physicist at Harvard University, heads up the

[4] Ibid.
[5] Ibid.

BETA project. BETA is an acronym for Billion-channel Extra Terrestrial Assay. "We're looking, first and foremost," says Dr. Horowitz, "for a signal generated by an intelligent species somewhere else." As part of the Search for Extra Terrestrial Intelligence, or SETI, this effort has to rank up there with the most expansive. According to Dr. Horowitz they have the capability to monitor 250 million channels, *simultaneously*, easily the largest radio spectrometer on Earth.

Is it all just a kind of intergalactic "snipe" hunt? Or is it possible there is someone else out there?

"That there's other life in the universe, guaranteed," says Dr. Horowitz. "That there's other life in the galaxy, guaranteed. That there's advanced life somewhere in the universe, guaranteed. Somewhere else in the galaxy, so extremely probable that I would give you at least hundred to one odds that interstellar communications could well be taking place."[6]

So it isn't so much a question of "is anybody out there?" but more a matter of "is anybody coming down here?" According to Budd Hopkins, Kevin Randle, Dr. Karla Turner, Dr. David Jacobs, and many other reliable UFO researchers, there is a vast amount of evidence to suggest that, indeed, someone or something is coming down here, evidently to find out more about us. There are eyewitness accounts from credible individuals, even cases where multiple witnesses see the same event. In fact as we recounted, one of the most astounding tales of an alien abduction was seen by many people in the heart of New York City. But there is still no documented proof. In a world full of cameras and camcorders there are no pictures of an abduction. Or to be more precise, there haven't been any . . . until now.

Recently the producers of a UPN network television show called *Paranormal Borderline*, received an anonymous letter

---

[6] Ibid.

telling the story of a worker who had been abducted by aliens.[7] Along with the letter was a videotape, ostensibly taken from one of the surveillance cameras where this person worked. The tape shows a typical, four-quadrant, black-and-white, surveillance-type picture. In the upper right-hand quadrant the worker can be seen leaving the work compound. At the bottom right of the screen the time is clearly shown. As the worker walks through the gate the image is obliterated by a brilliant flash of light, and the worker is gone. The surveillance cameras appear to continue to be working without interruption, but the picture is a series of moving gray frames. Then suddenly all four pictures lock up again in exactly the same position, except the timer clearly indicates nearly two hours have elapsed.

There is a second flash of light and the victim reappears, but now he is on his hands and knees. He seems to be shaken; in fact, he can clearly be seen throwing up on the ground while still doubled over. Seconds later he stands up and staggers out of the frame.

The letter accompanying the tape said the employee quit soon after this event and left the area. The letter writer wanted $1,500, *minimum*, for the tape. The program producers have turned the video over to experts to be analyzed, one of whom, Dr. William H. Schneid, holds a Ph.D. in criminology and psychology and is an expert in creating and cracking security systems. Dr. Schneid believes the tape is authentic though he is unwilling to vouch for the content. He believes the person submitting the tape took advantage of some electrical disturbances, ". . . or other disturbances we have yet to discover that surrounded this day . . . but it does appear to be an authentic video."

Yvonne Smith, another prominent UFO researcher and regression hypnotist, sees it as perhaps the one piece of evidence the world has been waiting for. This is ". . . something

---

[7] *Paranormal Borderline*, UPN, May 1996.

we can get our hands on," Smith says. "We have the time here, the flashes of light, the power surge, everything went out, then the guy comes back and it's two hours later. We have cases upon cases like this, but here we have it on tape."

"Both experts agree on one thing," according to show host William Frakes, ". . . if there is no explanation for the flashes and the missing time, this tape may be a major breakthrough in abduction research."[8]

Could this accidental bit of surveillance video validate the thousands of UFO abduction stories? A search is on for the man on the tape, and given the tenacity of most UFO investigators, it's a good bet he will be found . . . perhaps by the time you read this book.

And what about you? Would you believe an abduction event if you saw it happen with your own eyes? Even setting aside the abductions, how do you now regard the whole idea of extraterrestrials on earth?

Hopefully you now have more than just a passing acquaintance with the subject of UFOs, so this might be a good time to examine the *official* government response to the subject. Not just to individual events, but to the whole idea of visitors from another planet. What did the government do after the "Estimate of the Situation" was prepared? Was there any follow-up to Project Sign? Who was in charge of the "asylum," so to speak?

We think you'll find the answers to those questions fascinating and perhaps a little bit less confusing as we move on to the *official* government response.

[8] Ibid.

CHAPTER 15

PROJECT BLUE BOOK

>> The citizen who tried to examine Blue
Book files was given a polite run-around
or an outright refusal on various grounds.

Dr. J. Allen Hynek, astronomer

It was a lazy fall afternoon. I was on a back road leading to a farm occupied by a retired Air Force colonel who had spent a good portion of his active service working with Project Blue Book. For twenty-one years this group, under the direction of the Air Force, had been the official investigative arm of the United States government, looking into reports of UFOs at every level.

The project had been unceremoniously shut over a quarter century before I made this trip, but my own investigations had revealed that many of the Blue Book reports and analyses still rankled UFO researchers. It seemed like a good idea, in the context of the work we were doing for this book, to talk to someone who had, "been there and done that," as the saying currently goes.

I had come across the colonel quite by accident. A mutual friend happened to mention that her husband (now deceased) knew this man, and in fact had served with him in the Air Force. The colonel, she assured me, was honest and forthright. If he was willing to talk about his work, he would be an important source of information. I called, introduced myself and the project we were working on, and asked if he might be willing to tell me a little bit about Project Blue Book.

"Yes, a little bit," he replied. I discovered later that that was typical of his candor.

I missed the lane he had told me to look for and had to turn around and go back, which meant I was late arriving for our appointment. Military officers being what they are, I didn't know how that would sit with him. When I finally pulled up next to the house, however, he and his wife were sitting comfortably on the porch, a veritable Norman Rockwell picture of retirement. He smiled and greeted me warmly. "It's a long drive for so little," he said, indicating the chair his wife had been sitting in. "Mother isn't interested in war stories."

"Thank you," I said, and added, "Sorry I'm late. I missed the lane."

"Nearly everyone does." He smiled. "That's one of the reasons we like it here."

My friend had described him perfectly. Even though the colonel had been retired for several years, he was still every inch the career military man. He was extremely bright with a quick wit and a no-nonsense approach to the subject. Yes, he had been with Project Blue Book for nearly half of its active life, and yes, he did participate directly in probably hundreds of investigations, but there would be no betraying of trust and no discussion of still classified material. He also requested I not use his name. He did not want to get drawn into the loop of UFO investigators. Besides, he was contemplating writing a book of his own. I agreed to honor his request.

It's tempting to simply recount some of the more outrageous and ridiculous reports that were investigated by Project Blue Book and what many consider the equally outrageous and ridiculous conclusions arrived at by the Air Force. That, however, was not my purpose in driving 300 miles to talk to this man, nor would that be reason enough to devote a full chapter to this subject.

Some of you may be wondering why, since Project Blue Book began so early in UFO history, I didn't put this information up front. That's a good question, and one with which our research team struggled. We were optimistic that many people would read the book who, up to this point at least, were unfamiliar with the UFO phenomenon in any historical sense. As a result, we felt that it was important to establish first an understanding of what has kept the investigation of UFOs alive. Project Blue Book did, after all, give up and go away more than twenty-five years ago. A comparison, however, between the *official* government investigators and the independent investigators who are *still* seeking answers is inevitable. Now that we have provided some insight into what keeps the investigations and the controversy energized, we hope the comparison will be more meaningful.

The first point we established in my conversation with the colonel was that Project Blue Book was not a book. It is a compilation of some 140,000 pages of information relating to various UFO sightings that were called or mailed in to Project Blue Book headquarters.

You'll remember in Chapter 2 we discussed the beginning of the U.S. government's involvement with UFOs. To recap briefly, it began with a letter from Lt. General Nathan F. Twining to the office of the commanding general of the Army Air Corps that really ignited official interest in the phenomenon. The letter was in the form of a report on the unusual assignment he had been given in the wake of all the UFO sightings that had come to the attention of the Army Air Corps over the summer of 1947. In the letter Twining said, "The phenomenon reported is something real and not visionary or fictitious." Twining described these "flying disks" as metallic in appearance, disk-shaped, soundless in all but a few cases, and remarkably maneuverable. "It is recommended," Twining wrote, "that . . . Headquarters, Army Air Forces issue a directive assigning a priority, security classification and Code Name for a detailed study of this matter." The Air Force had been saddled with the responsibility ever since, first as Project Sign, then Project Grudge, and finally as Project Blue Book.

The project officially began with the code name "Blue Book" in 1948. In 1969, largely on the basis of an independent study commissioned by the government known as the Condon Report (more about that later), the effort was closed down. In just over twenty years Project Blue Book investigated some 12,000 sightings.

According to Dr. J. Allen Hynek, an astronomer and for many years a sort of "scientific liaison" to the project, there were no tears shed by the Air Force when the decision to shut the effort down was made. "It was no secret," he wrote in his book,[1] ". . . that the Air Force had been seeking, for several years, an honorable way out of processing UFO reports. Project Blue Book had become more and more of a public relations burden to the Air Force and as long as its attitudes and methodology remained unchanged this burden was likely to increase."

It was partly curiosity about what those attitudes and methodologies actually were that had brought me to my discussion with the colonel. In all fairness it must be pointed out that of the thousands of reports that came in to Project Blue Book, most of them were pure nonsense. The colonel told me his all-time record, from the time he received the phone call reporting a UFO to identification of the object in question, was twenty minutes. "At least 95 percent of all the reports we

---

[1] J. Allen Hynek, *The Hynek UFO Report* (New York: Dell Publishing, 1977), p. 279.

TOP SECRET / MAJIC
NATIONAL SECURITY INFORMATION
EYES ONLY

```
• • • • • • • • • • • • •
•  TOP SECRET  •
• • • • • • • • • • • • •
```

EYES ONLY   COPY ONE OF ONE.

BRIEFING DOCUMENT: OPERATION MAJESTIC 12

PREPARED FOR PRESIDENT-ELECT DWIGHT D. EISENHOWER: (EYES ONLY)

18 NOVEMBER, 1952

WARNING: This is a TOP SECRET - EYES ONLY document containing
compartmentalized information essential to the national security
of the United States. EYES ONLY ACCESS to the material herein
is strictly limited to those possessing Majestic-12 clearance
level. Reproduction in any form or the taking of written or
mechanically transcribed notes is strictly forbidden.

```
• • • • • • • • • • • • •
•  TOP SECRET  •
```

TOP SECRET / MAJIC
EYES ONLY   T52-EXEMPT (E)

EYES ONLY   001

* TOP SECRET *
****

EYES ONLY   COPY <u>ONE</u> OF <u>ONE</u>.

SUBJECT: OPERATION MAJESTIC-12 PRELIMINARY BRIEFING FOR
  PRESIDENT-ELECT EISENHOWER.

DOCUMENT PREPARED 18 NOVEMBER, 1952.

BRIEFING OFFICER: ADM. ROSCOE H. HILLENKOETTER (MJ-1)

NOTE: This document has been prepared as a preliminary briefing
only. It should be regarded as introductory to a full operations
briefing intended to follow.

* * * * * *

OPERATION MAJESTIC-12 is a TOP SECRET Research and Development/
Intelligence operation responsible directly and only to the
President of the United States. Operations of the project are
carried out under control of the Majestic-12 (Majic-12) Group
which was established by special classified executive order of
President Truman on 24 September, 1947, upon recommendation by
Dr. Vannevar Bush and Secretary James Forrestal. (See Attachment
"A".) Members of the Majestic-12 Group were designated as follows:

            Adm. Roscoe H. Hillenkoetter
            Dr. Vannevar Bush
            Secy. James V. Forrestal*
            Gen. Nathan F. Twining
            Gen. Hoyt S. Vandenberg
            Dr. Detlev Bronk
            Dr. Jerome Hunsaker
            Mr. Sidney W. Souers
            Mr. Gordon Gray
            Dr. Donald Menzel
            Gen. Robert M. Montague
            Dr. Lloyd V. Berkner

The death of Secretary Forrestal on 22 May, 1949, created
a vacancy which remained unfilled until 01 August, 1950, upon
which date Gen. Walter B. Smith was designated as permanent
replacement.

****
* TOP SECRET *

TOP SECRET / MAJIC
EYES ONLY

EYES ONLY   T52-EXEMPT (E)

002

* TOP SECRET *
* * * * * * * * * * * * * *

On 24 June, 1947, a civilian pilot flying over the Cascade
Mountains in the State of Washington observed nine flying
disc-shaped aircraft traveling in formation at a high rate
of speed. Although this was not the first known sighting
of such objects, it was the first to gain widespread attention
in the public media. Hundreds of reports of sightings of
similar objects followed. Many of these came from highly
credible military and civilian sources. These reports resulted in independent efforts by several different elements
of the military to ascertain the nature and purpose of these
objects in the interests of national defense. A number of
witnesses were interviewed and there were several unsuccessful
attempts to utilize aircraft in efforts to pursue reported
discs in flight. Public reaction bordered on near hysteria
at times.

In spite of these efforts, little of substance was learned
about the objects until a local rancher reported that one
had crashed in a remote region of New Mexico located approximately seventy-five miles northwest of Roswell Army Air
Base (now Walker Field).

On 07 July, 1947, a secret operation was begun to assure
recovery of the wreckage of this object for scientific study.
During the course of this operation, aerial reconnaissance
discovered that four small human-like beings had apparently
ejected from the craft at some point before it exploded.
These had fallen to earth about two miles east of the wreckage
site. All four were dead and badly decomposed due to action
by predators and exposure to the elements during the approximately one week time period which had elapsed before their
discovery. A special scientific team took charge of removing
these bodies for study. (See Attachment "C".) The wreckage
of the craft was also removed to several different locations.
(See Attachment "B".) Civilian and military witnesses in
the area were debriefed, and news reporters were given the
effective cover story that the object had been a misguided
weather research balloon.

* * * * * * * * * * * * * *
* TOP SECRET *
* * * * * * * * * * * * * *

A covert analytical effort organized by Gen. Twining and
Dr. Bush acting on the direct orders of the President, resulted in a preliminary concensus (19 September, 1947) that
the disc was most likely a short range reconnaissance craft.
This conclusion was based for the most part on the craft's
size and the apparent lack of any identifiable provisioning.
(See Attachment "D".) A similar analysis of the four dead
occupants was arranged by Dr. Bronk. It was the tentative
conclusion of this group (30 November, 1947) that although
these creatures are human-like in appearance, the biological
and evolutionary processes responsible for their development
has apparently been quite different from those observed or
postulated in homo-sapiens. Dr. Bronk's team has suggested
the term "Extra-terrestrial Biological Entities", or "EBEs",
be adopted as the standard term of reference for these
creatures until such time as a more definitive designation
can be agreed upon.

Since it is virtually certain that these craft do not originate in any country on earth, considerable speculation has
centered around what their point of origin might be and how
they get here. Mars was and remains a possibility, although
some scientists, most notably Dr. Menzel, consider it more
likely that we are dealing with beings from another solar
system entirely.

Numerous examples of what appear to be a form of writing
were found in the wreckage. Efforts to decipher these have
remained largely unsuccessful. (See Attachment "E".)
Equally unsuccessful have been efforts to determine the
method of propulsion or the nature or method of transmission
of the power source involved. Research along these lines
has been complicated by the complete absence of identifiable
wings, propellers, jets, or other conventional methods of
propulsion and guidance, as well as a total lack of metallic
wiring, vacuum tubes, or similar recognizable electronic
components. (See Attachment "F".) It is assumed that the
propulsion unit was completely destroyed by the explosion
which caused the crash.

EYES ONLY

COPY ONE OF ONE.

A need for as much additional information as possible about
these craft, their performance characteristics and their
purpose led to the undertaking known as U.S. Air Force Project
SIGN in December, 1947. In order to preserve security, liason
between SIGN and Majestic-12 was limited to two individuals
within the Intelligence Division of Air Materiel Command whose
role was to pass along certain types of information through
channels. SIGN evolved into Project GRUDGE in December, 1948.
The operation is currently being conducted under the code name
BLUE BOOK, with liason maintained through the Air Force officer
who is head of the project.

On 06 December, 1950, a second object, probably of similar
origin, impacted the earth at high speed in the El Indio -
Guerrero area of the Texas - Mexican boder after following
a long trajectory through the atmosphere. By the time a
search team arrived, what remained of the object had been almost
totally incinerated. Such material as could be recovered was
transported to the A.E.C. facility at Sandia, New Mexico, for
study.

Implications for the National Security are of continuing importance in that the motives and ultimate intentions of these
visitors remain completely unknown. In addition, a significant
upsurge in the surveillance activity of these craft beginning
in May and continuing through the autumn of this year has caused
considerable concern that new developments may be imminent.
It is for these reasons, as well as the obvious international
and technological considerations and the ultimate need to
avoid a public panic at all costs, that the Majestic-12 Group
remains of the unanimous opinion that imposition of the
strictest security precautions should continue without interruption into the new administration. At the same time, contingency plan MJ-1949-04P/78 (Top Secret - Eyes Only) should
be held in continued readiness should the need to make a
public announcement present itself. (See Attachment "G".)

. . . .
* TOP SECRET *
. . . .

EYES ONLY

COPY ONE OF ONE.

ENUMERATION OF ATTACHMENTS:

*ATTACHMENT "A".......Special Classified Executive
Order #092447. (TS/EO)

*ATTACHMENT "B".......Operation Majestic-12 Status
Report #1, Part A. 30 NOV '47.
(TS-MAJIC/EO)

*ATTACHMENT "C".......Operation Majestic-12 Status
Report #1, Part B. 30 NOV '47.
(TS-MAJIC/EO)

*ATTACHMENT "D".......Operation Majestic-12 Preliminary
Analytical Report. 19 SEP '47.
(TS-MAJIC/EO)

*ATTACHMENT "E".......Operation Majestic-12 Blue Team
Report #5. 30 JUN '52.
(TS-MAJIC/EO)

*ATTACHMENT "F".......Operation Majestic-12 Status
Report #2. 31 JAN '48.
(TS-MAJIC/EO)

*ATTACHMENT "G".......Operation Majestic-12 Contingency
Plan MJ-1949-04P/78: 31 JAN '49.
(TS-MAJIC/EO)

*ATTACHMENT "H".......Operation Majestic-12, Maps and
Photographs Folio (Extractions).
(TS-MAJIC/EO)

. . . .
* TOP SECRET *
. . . .
TOP SECRET / MAJIC
EYES ONLY
EYES ONLY

T52-EXEMPT (E)

September 24, 1947.

MEMORANDUM FOR THE SECRETARY OF DEFENSE

Dear Secretary Forrestal:

     As per our recent conversation on this matter, you are hereby authorized to proceed with all due speed and caution upon your undertaking. Hereafter this matter shall be referred to only as Operation Majestic Twelve.

     It continues to be my feeling that any future considerations relative to the ultimate disposition of this matter should rest solely with the Office of the President following appropriate discussions with yourself, Dr. Bush and the Director of Central Intelligence.

July 14, 1954

MEMORANDUM FOR GENERAL TWINING

SUBJECT: NSC/MJ-12 Special Studies Project

The President has decided that the MJ-12 SSP briefing should take place during the already scheduled White House meeting of July 16, rather than following it as previously intended. More precise arrangements will be explained to you upon arrival. Please alter your plans accordingly.

Your concurrence in the above change of arrangements is assumed.

ROBERT CUTLER
Special Assistant
to the President

were asked to investigate," he said, "were easily identifiable
as either natural phenomenon or somebody playing games."
But then he became more serious. "The other 5 percent," he
said, "we didn't have the foggiest idea what they were. As far
as I know, we still don't." He paused for a moment and
added, "That 5 percent represents hundreds of events."

Suddenly the whole subject took on a new perspective. I
was curious as to how these reports were handled. Who
besides the officers of Project Blue Book had that information? What, if anything, was their mandate from the top
echelons of command?

"I had two telephones on my desk," the colonel told me.
"When the white one rang we were prepared with the usual
'swamp gas' or 'weather balloon' scenario. When the other
phone rang, we were expected to be factual and brief."

"Who was on the other end of that line?"

"I never knew," he replied, "but someone was getting the
straight story and on a regular basis."

Back in my office I began to wonder where the reports
that Project Blue Book couldn't identify may have come
from. And why, since from its very inception it was supposed
to be open to the public, none of these events were part of
the record?

Dr. Hynek supplied the answer. "Project Blue Book," he
wrote, "was always regarded officially as 'unclassified,' but
this amounted to a standing joke to those who knew better.
Not only were many of the reports labeled 'Confidential' or
'Secret' but the citizen who tried to examine Blue Book files
was given a polite run-around or an outright refusal on various grounds."[2]

It might be well here to let Dr. Hynek tell us a bit about
himself as he has been quoted extensively on both sides of
this issue. In the opening statement of his book, ahead even
of the title page, Dr. Hynek writes:

[2] Ibid., p. 7.

I had started out as an outright "debunker," taking great joy in cracking what seemed at first to be puzzling cases. I was the arch enemy of those "flying saucer groups and enthusiasts" who very dearly wanted UFOs to be interplanetary.

My transformation was gradual but by the late sixties it was complete. Today I would not spend one further moment on the subject of UFOs if I didn't seriously feel that the UFO phenomenon is real and that efforts to investigate and understand it, and eventually to solve it, could have profound effect—perhaps even be the springboard to a revolution in mankind's outlook on the universe.[3]

Dr. Hynek, by the way, was the man who created the ET encounter classification structure popularized in the movie by Steven Spielberg. It was Hynek who decided that when earthlings actually meet extraterrestrials, those events should be called, "close encounters of the third kind."

Unfortunately (for the public) Hynek's transformation was not duplicated among the officers and men who were running the project. Or if it was, the staff kept it well hidden. According to Hynek the Air Force had only two concerns about UFOs; were they a threat to the security of the United States and were they extraterrestrial? Very early on the Air Force determined, at least at the *official* level, that UFOs did not pose a threat nor were they extraterrestrial. Most of the project group's job, therefore, was done before the first report was ever filed. Now all the group had to do was to find explanations that would support their conclusions.

It would be impossible to include in a single chapter what has already filled several books, but some representative examples of reports and their Blue Book conclusions would seem to be in order.

The UFO encounter that probably resulted in the establishment of the various investigative projects and also

[3] Ibid.

resulted in the first public expressions of skepticism toward Air Force methods occurred on January 7, 1948. Flight Commander Thomas Mantell was ordered by ground control to investigate a UFO flying over Godman Field in Kentucky. After Mantell climbed to 23,000 feet, ground control lost sight of the captain and the alleged alien craft, but still maintained radio contact with the pilot. Mantell reported that he was closing in on what he described as "a tremendous metallic object."

As far as we know those were Captain Mantell's last words. At 5:00 P.M. that night, the wreckage of Mantell's P–51 fighter plane was found with his body still in the cockpit. The Air Technical Intelligence Center at Wright-Patterson Field in Dayton, Ohio, went into action. Every piece of wreckage from his plane was vacuumed up, hauled away, and classified. Eventually, under great pressure from the public and the press, the investigators issued their report. What Captain Mantell had really been chasing, they said, was ". . . the planet Venus."

The suggestion that an experienced command pilot with many years experience could have chased the planet Venus until he ran out of oxygen and passed out, especially in broad daylight, did not sit well with the press and the public. A month later, in February 1948 (many believe in direct response to the sense of public outrage occasioned by Captain Mantell's death and the subsequent report of the Air Force investigators), Project Sign was born.

Nevertheless, the furor soon died down, and eventually Project Blue Book inherited the policies and procedures of its two predecessors, Project Sign and Project Grudge. UFO sightings continued to be reported, and the project investigators continued to find "natural" causes for virtually all of them. For example:

In July 1952 the radar at Washington National Airport and Andrews Air Force Base, both within spitting distance of Washington, D.C., picked up a group of UFOs. The report pushed the Democratic National Convention off the front page. Inquiries poured in to Project Blue Book from as far away as London, Ottawa, and Mexico City. Despite the credibility of the sources, Captain E. J. Ruppelt (the *first* and the *third* head of Blue Book) refused to give reporters any information. In his book, *Report on Unidentified Flying Objects*, Ruppelt said:

> Besides being the most highly publicized UFO sightings in the Air Force annals, they were also the most monumentally fouled-up messes that repose in the files.

The official explanation? "Effects of inversion." Actually a check of the weather records on that evening showed only a trivial inversion of one and a half degrees.[4]

The investigators did not, however, discriminate. The most innocuous reports got the same treatment as their more famous counterparts. In March 1959 an amateur astronomer in Denville, New Jersey, was taking photographs of the moon through his telescope. One of the prints revealed a string of thirty-four bright objects arching in a line away from the moon. He had his camera checked for light leaks and studied the print and negative under magnification. Finding no mechanical reason for the objects, he sent the photograph to Project Blue Book.

Photographic experts examined the photograph and ruled out many explanations, including static electricity. But as there was no other logical cause to pin it on, the Blue Book report read: "Static electric discharge was arrived at as the cause by the photo analysis section."[5]

The history of Project Blue Book is filled with these kinds of flights of fancy. My personal favorite was one that appeared in the Condon Report, to wit:

---

[4] Ibid., p. 21.
[5] *The UFO Phenomenon* (Alexandria, VA: Time-Life Books, 1992), p. 92.

This unusual sighting should therefore be assigned to the category of some almost certainly natural phenomenon which is so rare that it apparently has never been reported before or since.

But why would intelligent men and women vested with a responsibility of truly global proportions lend themselves to such obviously dubious "explanations" and put them in writing?

The answer may be twofold. In the first instance the scientists of the day had said such things were simply impossible. The Air Force, which is primarily obligated to the defense of the nation and not really equipped to do objective, scientific research, developed a theorem based on that "scientific" premise. According to Hynek, Project Blue Book took the position that: "*It can't be, therefore it isn't.*" It was a position as untenable as it was *un*scientific, and it would come back to haunt the project on many occasions.

The second reason has to do with a blue-ribbon panel assembled at the request of the CIA and put under the direction of Dr. H. P. Robertson, a physicist of considerable reputation and an expert on relativity. This panel was assembled officially to "enlist the services of selected scientists to review and appraise the available evidence in the light of pertinent scientific theories." The real purpose, according to Hynek, was to ". . . defuse a potentially explosive situation from the standpoint of national security. In short, the CIA was fearful, not of UFOs but of UFO *reports* [emphasis mine]."[6]

The "selected scientists" were to meet for five days and present their recommendations. Hynek sat in on three of the five day-long meetings. Dropping in for only the last two days of the meetings was Dr. Lloyd Berkner, whom, you'll recall, was already an alleged member of the Majestic 12 committee.

[6] J. Allen Hynek, *The Hynek UFO Report* (New York: Dell Publishing, 1977), p. 20.

The report championed the, *"It can't be, therefore it isn't,"* theorem and concluded with the recommendation that "National Security Agencies take immediate steps to strip the unidentified flying objects of the special status they have been given and the aura of mystery they have unfortunately acquired." This, in effect, put Blue Book under orders to debunk UFO sightings at all costs.[7] Or as Ruppelt quoted one of his officers as saying: "The powers that be are anti-flying saucer and to stay in favor, it behooves one to follow suit."

Given this situation, the nature of the group's findings becomes less and less surprising. It also explains in large measure why the Air Force was willing, even eager, to get rid of Project Blue Book and end their twenty years of embarrassment and frustration.

It would be a mistake, however, to conclude that because the Air Force was willing to dump the project that the *government* was getting out of the business of investigating UFOs. On the contrary, as we noted in the Kecksburg chapter, quick-response teams were maintained at a number of installations around the country (under the direction of MJ–12?). Nor should we assume that all of the officers and men of Project Blue Book shared the "it can't be, therefore it isn't" hypothesis. In point of fact, many of them (like the colonel) did not. But when it comes to the military, one quickly learns that the old saying, "You can lead a horse to water but you can't make him drink," has no validity. Those in charge can, in fact, make people drink.

The Air Force "powers that be" had decided it was time to close down the project. The Robertson committee had provided the impetus, now the only issue was to find a way to legitimize the decision.

In this regard, the Condon Report and particularly its author, for whom the report is named, were made to order.

---

[7] Ibid., p. 22.

The Condon committee, under the sole direction of Dr. Edward U. Condon, a member of the physics department at the University of Colorado, was the outgrowth of a suggestion made by Dr. Hynek. The astronomer wanted several universities to be invited to participate in a program that would "provide opportunity for scientific investigation of selected sightings in more detail and depth than has been possible to date." The recommendation, in typical bureaucratic fashion, was pared down to one university and to the singular direction of one man. The Condon committee was in operation from October 1966 to November 1968, at which time it issued a lengthy report. Dr. Condon himself wrote the summary that gave the Air Force all the ammunition it needed to shoot down Project Blue Book.

In a nutshell Dr. Condon stated that further studies of UFOs "probably cannot be justified in the expectation that science will be advanced thereby. Nothing," he said, "of scientific value will come of further studies."

On December 17, 1969, after nearly a year of reflection, Air Force Secretary Robert Seaman terminated project Blue Book, based on the recommendation of Dr. Condon. It should be noted that the decision was made not on the basis of the Condon committee nor on the report itself, which, once past Dr. Condon's summary chapter, in many respects supported the notion that the UFO phenomenon was real. In large measure the Condon committee had looked at that 5 percent of reported sightings Project Blue Book couldn't identify (even though some official pronouncement of a natural cause was invariably given the public), and a summary of their findings was included in their report. Dr. Condon was apparently unfazed by what other members of the committee had to say.

"It seems incredible," Dr. Hynek wrote, "that Dr. Condon could have overlooked statements such as the following:"

This must be one of the most puzzling radar cases on record and no conclusion is possible at this time. It seems inconceivable that an anomalous propagation (AP) echo would behave in the manner described even if AP had been likely at the time. In view of meteorological situation, it would seem that AP was rather unlikely. Besides, what is the probability that an AP return would appear only once and that time appear to execute a perfect instrument landing system approach?

There was an incident that took place in McMinnville, Oregon, in 1950 that gained some national attention. The Condon committee looked into it, but apparently Dr. Condon failed to read what his group had to say about it. It was listed as case #46, p. CR 407. The conclusion of the committee was:

This is one of the few UFO reports in which all factors investigated, geometric, psychological and physical, appear to be consistent with the assertion that an extraordinary flying object, silvery, metallic, disk-shaped, tens of meters in diameter and evidently artificial, flew within the sight of two witnesses. It cannot be said that the evidence positively rules out fabrication, although there are some factors such as the accuracy of certain photometric measures on the original negatives which argue against such an assertion.

A detailed analysis of the original negatives provided strong evidence that the object photographed was at least a mile away from the camera, effectively ruling out a hoax. Dr. Condon apparently did not find this remarkable.

Another of the incidents that received national notoriety occurred near Great Falls, Montana, in August 1950. The Condon Report concluded:

The case remains unexplained. Analysis indicates that the images on the film are difficult to reconcile with aircraft or other known phenomena, although aircraft cannot entirely be ruled out.[8]

The Air Force, apparently, was not interested in what the report had to say. After all they had nearly a year to study it before making a decision. In the final analysis it was only Dr. Condon's summary chapter that was given any weight.

With the demise of Project Blue Book the Air Force was out of the investigation business, at least officially. But the 140,000 pages of sightings, investigations, reports, and summary conclusions that were the residue of its twenty years of operation, still remain. So far as their mission to "debunk" the whole idea of UFOs is concerned, they appear to have been successful. From the standpoint of providing the public with vital and useful information, however, a host of independent UFO investigators are convinced that the project was a dismal failure.

But there was something else, something that was brought home to me with some impact as I reviewed the notes of my discussion with the colonel. There are still those 600-plus pesky UFO sightings investigated by Project Blue Book that have never been explained. At least one of these involved the Air Force itself and the colonel while he was still on duty. To the best of my knowledge this incident was never publicly reported.

According to the colonel it all took place one evening at the air base in Sitka, Alaska. An object having the appearance of a bright light dropped down in front of the main gate and hovered there for forty-five minutes. Something in the neighborhood of 240 officers and airmen had it in full

[8] Ibid.

view. They launched weather balloons while the object was still there to see if one of them might drift by and give the same effect, but nothing even remotely like the object in front of them developed. Then as if to say, "Okay, we have everything we need," it left. One minute it was in front of the gate, the next it was on the other side of the bay and gone.

"Did you ever find out what it was?" I asked.

"No," he said, "we never did."

That, it seems to me, is a fitting epitaph for what was supposed to have been the official effort on behalf of the American public to discover the truth about unidentified flying objects.

CHAPTER 16

WHAT IN
THE WORLD?

>> Someone has the key that can open all of
these doors—that key is the truth.

From time to time throughout this book we have used the first-person personal pronoun to describe an event, certain experiences, or the description of interviews. In each of those cases such usage is appropriate. It does, however, leave the impression that this book has been an individual effort when indeed it was a team effort. Several people worked on different aspects of gathering, collating, and verifying the information and photographs contained in this work. Over the course of the four years it took to pull all of the information together, we made thousands of phone calls, interviewed dozens of experts and investigators, attended various UFO conferences in different parts of the country, read dozens of books, and watched nearly a hundred videos. After all this effort our research team was able to agree on only one thing:

No definitive conclusion about UFOs is possible based on currently available information.

This is not to say we have concluded nothing is really going on where UFOs are concerned. Quite the opposite. Unidentified flying objects are, we are convinced, very real. But an object that flies or appears to be flying, that cannot be identified within the framework of our normal, everyday perceptions could have many sources. For instance, there is ample evidence that something was seen at S–4 near Area 51 that fits the general description of a flying saucer. But did it necessarily originate from somewhere in outer space? Captain Thomas Mantell, remember, was ordered by ground control to intercept something they described as a UFO. Are we to assume some whacked-out flight controller sent him chasing after the planet Venus? Captain Mantell described what he was trying to intercept as large, metallic, and round. But does that mean it could have originated only on some distant planet? On the other hand, why would the Air Force concoct such an absurd justification for the loss of one of its most experienced and competent pilots?

Clearly the government is and has been hiding something for at least fifty years and probably longer. Consider again for a moment the Roswell incident and the testimony of Brig. General DuBose, Colonel Blanchard, Major Marcel, and First Lieutenant Haut. All the way down (or up) the chain of command, the men who were there, who participated officially in the events at Roswell admitted before they died (Lieutenant Haut is still living in Roswell) that the "weather balloon" story was a cover-up, pure and simple.

In the face of abundant testimony by still-living witnesses that military officials threatened them with the loss of their businesses or even their very lives, the government maintains a stoic silence. The communications and air traffic in and out of Roswell, Wright Field, and Carswell during this time is a matter of record. Yet according to a senator, a congressman, and the General Accounting Office, there is no information *whatsoever* in the Air Force files about the events at Roswell in July 1947. This was an incident that garnered worldwide attention over a period of several days. It resulted in hundreds if not thousands of news stories, photographs, and broadcasts. Top military brass from the Pentagon on down were directly associated by name with these activities. Yet we are to believe that (a) it was all over a weather balloon and (b) not so much as a memo has been kept in official Air Force files. The inescapable question is, why?

Nor is Roswell the only event that suggests a massive and well-planned cover-up. Why did the Air Force, as late as 1993, execute a huge land grab in the mountains surrounding an ancient dry lake bed in the desert wastes of Nevada, unofficially referred to as Area 51? Why did the government, as late as 1995, refuse a request by the EPA and the Justice Department to give this "operating location" a name? If Russian reconnaissance satellites can fly over it and take photographs at will, why are U.S. citizens threatened with "use of deadly force" if they even come close to the boundaries of Area 51? What in the world is going on here that the government doesn't want us to know?

Many other questions have been raised by the government's action, or in some cases, inaction. What was under the tarp on the flatbed truck that hastily departed Kecksburg, Pennsylvania? Certainly the military is not going to take over a town in order to retrieve a meteorite. Of course if it had been a meteorite of that size, most geologists would agree the town of Kecksburg and probably a good portion of the surrounding countryside would be just a memory. The government might have gone to such lengths to make off with a Soviet space probe, but if that's what it was, then what was recovered twelve hours earlier in Canada? As a matter of fact, the Russians have stated unequivocally that no Russian/Soviet satellite of any kind has ever landed anywhere in the

United States. Because today neither country would have anything to gain by hiding either the landing or the recovery, it seems reasonable to accept their word. So if it wasn't a meteorite and it wasn't *Cosmos 96*, there is obviously far more going on here than can be covered up with a canvas tarp.

Clearly the government of the United States, and other governments as well, know a great deal more about the UFO phenomenon than they are willing to admit. NASA, in the face of competent and highly skilled scientific analysis of certain physical anomalies photographed by their own instruments on the planet Mars, steadfastly refuses to even *look* at the evidence produced by independent investigators. A less scientific approach to interplanetary discovery could hardly be imagined. Did the *Mars Observer* really die? Is NASA now photographing the surface of Mars in complete secrecy? How can anyone outside of the official "loop" ever know?

No one, so far as we have been able to discern, has denied the existence of the SHAPE "Assessment" document. Neither has anyone stepped forward to join Robert Dean in his exposure of this multinational study of UFOs, that is still, so far as we know, squirreled away in the vault at SHAPE headquarters near Brussels. But if the events described in this remarkable document, as well as the earlier "Estimate of the Situation" prepared by United States Army Air Corps and documents currently emerging from the former Soviet Union have any validity at all, there is an enormous pool of information in the hands of someone. Some group of experts or scientists, or perhaps even some group of governments, already has in their hands the answer to most of the questions raised by the UFO phenomenon.

If, for example, SUE, (Santilli's-*u*nidentified-*e*ntity) is real and the autopsy film is genuine, that means the government has known all about aliens for a very long time. It means they know something of their genetic makeup, perhaps even of their origins. It means they very likely have had some kind of communication with them and might even know something of the physics of space travel. They know that Bob Lazar has been telling the truth all along; that living aliens have been and might still be among us. In short, the implications of the authenticity of those small rolls of film (approximately three minutes each) are enormous. But in light of the findings of the Brookings Institute, we might seriously ask are we prepared to know the truth?

If the government does have a fund of real information and if they are hiding it from the public, it would seem to indicate someone (or some group) at the very highest policy levels has decided that we, you and I, are not prepared to deal with the truth. More than that, it means that every administration since Truman, regardless of party or political consequence, liberal or conservative, has come to that same conclusion.

This is no small matter. Certain concepts of constitutional government are called into question, and every president and presumably vice president and at least some cabinet officers would have had to accept the notion that the secrecy, the cover-up, if you will, is more important than such things as congressional oversight and accountability, the people's right to know through a free and unfettered press, truthfulness in dealing with the electorate, protection against military takeover of civilian authority, protection against unreasonable search and seizure, and the right of citizens to speak out. (Under the provisions of the First Amendment, can a radio station be shut down for broadcasting an official military press release?) The list goes on and on. As we have seen, not even our elected representatives can break the barrier of secrecy.

The reality is that once any constitutional safeguard is abridged, all constitutional rights become vulnerable. Everyone, including the government, stands to lose far more than can ever be gained through secrecy and deceit.

Yet the evidence seems clear. For some reason every administration since the end of World War II appears to have participated in a focused effort to keep the public from having access to any official information about UFOs. If President Eisenhower was briefed on the official status of the government's (MJ–12) UFO investigations when he took office (over ten years of intensive research has failed to demonstrate the Eisenhower briefing papers to be anything other than genuine), then it is logical to believe that all incoming presidents have received the same briefing. Former President Jimmy Carter claimed to have personally seen a UFO. Prior to his election he promised full disclosure of all government activity in this area. Once elected the subject was never raised again. Why? What is it that convinces officials of every political stripe that secrecy is better than the truth? Given the tenacity of the U.S. press corps and the public attitude toward official cover-ups, that attitude would seem to involve considerable political risk.

Perhaps extraterrestrial activities is not the only explanation. Perhaps there is something of a more down-to-earth nature that accounts for all of this strange activity. If there is some other interpretation of all these events, UFOs might just be a convenient way of hiding something that would have an even greater negative impact on the public. Think about it. UFOs, to this point, at least, remain essentially unprovable and easily ridiculed, yet the very idea creates an ongoing public focus that has obscured almost all other inquiries.

You'll recall that in our chapter on Area 51, Norio Hayakawa suggested that while all the events and incidents reported might very well be real, that did not mean they were necessarily "extraterrestrial." He put forth the idea that some extragovernmental group of international proportions (but with the approval of the various governments), might be creating and using UFO incidents for their own purposes.

It is an intriguing concept, but does such a notion have the necessary criteria? In order for it to make sense as a plausible theory, we will have to discover a logical genesis for the program, a reason to maintain absolute secrecy at all costs. In the end our theory must demonstrate an ability to solve all the problems raised by the UFO encounters.

Up to this point we have left speculation to others. But in order to examine theories that might persuade governments to perpetuate a cover-up of such long-standing and universal proportions, we are required to do a little speculating of our own. It is, we hope, informed speculation, but speculation none the less.

Today in Long Beach harbor there is a floating crane capable of lifting 500 deadweight tons. It has been there since the end of World War II, a product of German engineering that we have never been able to duplicate. The Germans had three of them. The British took one and tried to float it across the English channel, but it sank. The Russians disassembled theirs and shipped it to Russia, but they were never able to successfully reassemble it. United States engineers were more careful and brought the German engineers back with the machinery. In no time this particular "spoil" of war was up and functioning over here. It is still a truly remarkable feat of mechanical engineering.

We mention this only because it is illustrative of several rather interesting technological advancements that were made immediately following World War II as a direct result of German engineering. We are all familiar with the U.S. gains in rocketry that began when Werner Von Braun and a number of other German rocket engineers "offered" their services to the United States at the end of the war. What is less known is that many other German engineers and scientists also came to this country along with train-car loads of documents and hardware. Shortly after the end of the war, for example, the United States had a functional jet fighter plane. U.S. computer science, even atomic science took a giant leap forward between 1945 and 1950.

But the Germans were doing other, more sinister experiments under Hitler's maniacal direction. We know, for example, certain of their medical scientists were using the death camps to perform horrendous experiments on human beings. Josef Mengele's experiments upon twins were widely publicized. Other experiments with "cloning" in an effort to produce the perfect Aryan race are less well known. In just the past few years it has also become known that the Germans were working on a circular type of aircraft under the direction of a group calling themselves the "Black Sun Society." Drawings and plans were recovered that look suspiciously like the UFO George Adamski claimed to have photographed over New Jersey in 1952.

Is it likely that the Allies, scooping up all of the German science and technology they could get their hands on after the war, would leave this kind of information behind? Yet even the hint several years ago, that U.S. doctors might be using some of the information gathered by Hitler's monsters brought a huge outcry from the public.

Suppose that U.S. scientists started with information that could only have been gathered from the experiments conducted in the Nazi death camps. Suppose as well that they worked along with U.S. aeronautic engineers, who had unlimited and undisclosed funds and had managed to create some kind of circular aircraft they could test fly with "artificial" humanoids—biological robots of some sort that had been created as a result of the death camp experiments. Such "alien" technology would have created something no U.S. political figure would dare to expose.

But does this theory meet the other criteria? Certainly it addresses the need for secrecy, and it might explain the origins of the craft that have been seen. Space and aeronautical engineers capable of sending *Voyager* out of the galaxy and flying the Stealth fighter for a decade before it was known to the public, might, in fifty years or so, create a flying machine capable of at least some of the things witnesses have reported seeing UFOs do. This theory might even solve the problem of the alien autopsy film. There was, after all, nothing in the being's internal structure in that film that modern forensic pathologists could identify. The markings on the craft might well be a special code decipherable only by those who work on the craft. And they could be being built and tested at Area 51.

But how does the theory explain the face on Mars, the 6,000-year-old designation of Earth as the seventh planet, the crash at Roswell (which occurred much too soon after the end of the war to have been produced through the use of German technology), or the strange markings on the plains of Nazca, just to mention a few of the questions that remain unanswered. This theory, in fact, raises more questions than it answers.

All right, let's examine the theory of the ultimate skeptics, of which there are many. This theory holds that there is nothing to the entire UFO concept. It is non-science therefore, it is nonsense, or to quote the Air Force theorem, "It can't be, therefore it isn't."

To accept this notion we must set aside all reports, photographs, and film, whether explainable or not, and conclude that the witnesses to UFO incidents are at best delusional and at worst dishonest. We must assume that Dr. J. Allen Hynek had no basis for changing his mind, even after years of intense investigation; that Robert O. Dean never read the SHAPE "Assessment" document; that Dr. Stanton Friedman is incapable of valid research; that Lt. General Nathan Twining didn't really believe what he said in his memo; and that all the officers, enlisted men, and civilians who say they saw, touched, and hefted unexplainable debris from the crash at Roswell are simply lying. We must accept the idea that, as George Knapp put it, "two barflies" from a pub in England are traveling all over the world creating intricate, beautiful, and highly geometric designs in standing crops. And they were somehow able to stumble onto a design in Germany that perfectly duplicated the design on three metal plates found buried under that very crop circle. We must discount radar contacts, reports from qualified pilots, and even sightings by astronauts. We must set aside the complex scientific and mathematical evidence now being examined in even greater detail on the Giza Plateau and overlook the uncanny chain of "coincidences" that keeps pointing toward some startling event that might have taken place between 11,000 and 10,000 B.C.

The inescapable conclusion must then be that Dr. Condon, in spite of his committee report; Dr. Menzel, in spite of his association with MJ–12; and Phil Klass, in spite of all the evidence, are really the only ones who have it right.

But if that's true, what in the world are we arguing about? Why is the government going to such great lengths to keep information not only from the public, but even from public servants. (Barry Goldwater, then a reserve Air Force general and United States senator, was barred from certain areas at Wright-Patterson Air Force Base.) Why use threats, coercion, and force against average citizens whose only "crime" was being in the wrong place at the wrong time? Why, in response to freedom of information requests, send out documents that are completely blacked out except for the salutation and the date? In short, why lie?

The theory that there is nothing at all to any of this seems to us to fail on the face of it. Clearly there is something going on. That being the case, there is a major dilemma. If the notion of terrestrial origin doesn't hold up, and the idea that it's all smoke and mirrors isn't feasible, we are left right back where we started.

But what if John Lear is right? What if there are some things the people do not have a right to know? One has only to recall the genuine fear and panic brought on by Orson Welles and his Mercury Theater presentation of *The War of the Worlds*. Even though the program was presented in the context of a weekly drama series and in spite of frequent announcements that the program was only a dramatization, thousands of people still fled in panic. In light of that fact the Brookings Institute conclusion that an extraterrestrial encroachment on Earth would spell the end of all our political, social, and religious infrastructure takes on new significance.

On the other hand, in 1996 a motion picture was produced that touched our deepest fears regarding UFOs. *Independence Day (ID-4, The Day We Fight Back)*, according to its promotion previews, is the chilling tale of the final Armageddon. Giant spaceships hover over Washington, D.C., and explode the White House and Capitol Building with a single beam of light. The Empire State Building in New York is likewise destroyed, sending cars and busses hurling in all directions, killing thousands. Small alien fighters are dispatched from the "mother ship" to eliminate any survivors. Ah, but "Independence Day is the day we fight back."

Will this Hollywood "forecast" of things to come engender the same kind of fear and panic in today's audiences? It doesn't seem likely. A young man interviewed on MTV about the movie preview said, "Man, I can't wait till we get up there and kick old ET's ass." Perhaps we have outgrown the fears postulated by the Brookings Institute. Maybe it's time to tell the truth . . . whatever that truth is.

One cannot help but be moved by Frankie Rowe's emotional confession of the terror that filled her heart when, as a teenager in Roswell, New Mexico, she was told her body would be dumped in the desert if she ever told the truth about what she had seen. Our sense of fair play is assaulted when the wives of a half dozen workers who died, allegedly as a result of their assignments while on the job at Area 51, are denied even a hearing because the government refuses to tell the truth. Several years ago, a number of families who ran sheep ranches near the Toole Army Depot in Utah's western desert were forced into bankruptcy when their sheep suddenly and mysteriously died. Deadly agents escaping from the Army's stockpile of biological weapons was suspected, but there was no recourse for the families because the government refused to tell the truth.

Each of these cases demonstrates that the power of government unchecked by any requirement of honesty is ultimately destructive. History is replete with "government knows best" policies that have destroyed entire nations. In a society that holds itself to be free, permitting the government to get away with threats, lies, and a general disregard for public opinion can lead only to disaster. A government "of the people" demands that the people be heard, that their wishes be considered, even if officials believe the public to be dead wrong.

We can't escape the belief that it is the public's desire for truth that should govern public policy, not the recommendations of the Brookings (or any other) Institute. After all, those policies will have a profound effect on each of us and on our families. Our freedom, as well as the Constitution's guarantees, depends on the public's ability to make informed choices. We cannot have it any other way and still have a nation that is self-governed.

We don't know whether the "small grays" seen by many people actually come from another planet. We don't know if there are captured flying saucers at Area 51. We can still only guess as to the authenticity of the alien autopsy film. There is only one thing that is absolutely clear and indisputable and that is we *do not know* the truth about any of this. Someone does. Someone knows what is behind those doors they wouldn't permit Senator Goldwater to enter. Someone knows what crashed at Roswell. Someone knows what is going on at Area 51, and we suspect, what is really on the surface of Mars. Someone has the key that can open all of these doors—that key is the truth.

There is another built-in difficulty when it comes to keeping the truth hidden; it leaves us vulnerable to wild and even unscrupulous speculation that, since it is out in the open, might be mistaken for the truth. Isn't it time we put an end to the speculation? Isn't it time to demand that the government open all the doors? If it turns out there's nothing there, so much the better. But wouldn't it be a shame if we were losing our constitutional guarantees over nothing?

If you've never called or written your federal or state representative or senator, now would be a good time to do it and this would be an excellent subject to take up with them. The truth—the whole truth—about UFOs will not *be* an issue until the public *makes* it an issue.

Wouldn't we all like to know, at long last, *What in the World Is Going on Here?*

INDEX